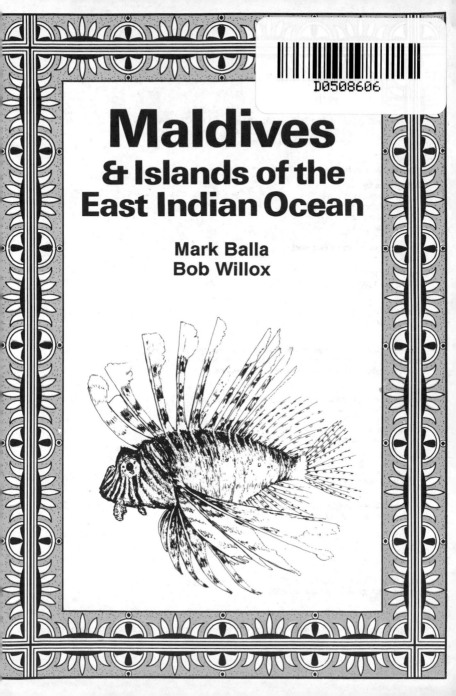

Maldives
& Islands of the East Indian Ocean

Mark Balla
Bob Willox

Maldives & Islands of the Indian Ocean – a travel survival kit

2nd edition

Published by
Lonely Planet Publications
Head Office: PO Box 617, Hawthorn, Vic 3122, Australia
Branches: 155 Filbert St, Suite 251, Oakland, CA 94607, USA
    10 Barley Mow Passage, Chiswick, London W4 4PH, UK
    71 bis rue du Cardinal Lemoine, 75005 Paris, France

Printed by
Colorcraft Ltd, Hong Kong

Photographs by
Mark Balla (MB)
Tim Godfrey (TG)
Paolo Manganaro (PM)
Paul Steel (PS)

Front cover photo by Paul Steel

First Published
January 1990

This Edition
July 1993

National Library of Australia Cataloguing in Publication Data

Willox, Robert.
    Maldives & Islands of the East Indian Ocean, a travel survival kit.

    2nd ed.
    Includes index.
    ISBN 0 86442 187 7.

    1. Maldives – Guidebooks. 2. Islands of the Indian Ocean - Guidebooks. I. Balla, Mark. II. Title.
    (Series : Lonely Planet travel survival kit).

915.49504

text & maps © Lonely Planet 1993
photos © photographers as indicated 1993

Mark Balla

Mark Balla came to Lonely Planet in 1987 as the phrasebook editor. A chronic traveller and learner of languages from way back, it was not long before the call of the road and the vocal chords took him away from the office, and afterwards, into the field to write for Lonely Planet.

Prior to covering the Maldives, Mark was based in Europe, where he wrote the Spain chapters of *Western Europe on a Shoestring* and *Mediterranean Europe on a Shoestring*. He also contributed to the Germany chapter of *Western Europe on a Shoestring*, and to the latest edition of *Mexico – a travel survival kit*.

Robert Willox

Robert Willox is a Scottish Highlander by birth and by nature, although he gets on reasonably well with the English. In fact, Australia is now his home.

A journalist since leaving school, Bob has worked for newspapers in England, Scotland, Northern Ireland and, most recently, in Australia for the *Sydney Morning Herald*.

Bob had not written much about his extensive travels until he crossed paths with Lonely Planet. Although his main connection with the Indian Ocean is City Beach in Perth, Western Australia, he is also the author of two other LP travel survival kits: *Mauritius, Réunion & Seychelles* and *Madagascar & Comoros*.

From the Author

Mark Balla Thanks to Abdullah Rasheed (Director General, Department of Information & Broadcasting), Ibrahim Mohammed and others at the Ministry of Tourism, Ministry of Home Affairs & Sport, Hummingbird Helicopters, Atoll Adventures, Paradise Travel & Tours, Sunrise Lodge, Phoenix Hotels & Resorts, Rasja Travel, Sun Travel & Tours, Mohamed Hameed and Ibrahim Noordeen of MATI (Maldives Association of Tourism Industry) and the resort management and staff at Tari Village, Farukolufushi, Maafushivaru, Angaga, Thundufushi, Athuruga, Fesdu, Halaveli, Moofushi, Nika Hotel, Kurumba, Little Hura, Rihiveli, Olhuveli, Cocoa Island, Emboodhu Finolhu, Embudu Village, Bi Ya Doo, Villi Varu, Dhigufinolhu, Veligandu Hura, Bandos, Vabinfaru, Ihuru, Thulhaagiri, Nakatchafushi, Vaadoo, Kandooma, Velidu and the Ocean Reef Club in Gan. Also to Brandy of Eurodivers for getting me hooked on diving, and to Mike and Petra of the Emboodhu Finolhu Dive School for convincing me that not all sharks want to eat me.

I would also like to express my gratitude to a number of individuals who went out of their way to help ensure that my time in the Maldives was a success. Eva, Michelle, Jo and others at Hummingbird Helicopters, Tim Booth, Tim Godfrey, captains Mike and Mark, Giacomo (Jack) Ferretti, Naseer, Mahinda, Mohamed (Juha) Zuhair, Amin, Ibrahim Shameem, Sarah Bonner-Morgan, Gerard Krzych and countless others including the many dhoni captains who helped make the impossible possible.

This book is dedicated to Tony, Zulfa, Ashley and Mishál Hussain. I hope I can return the favours some day.

From the Publisher
The first edition of *Maldives & Islands of the East Indian Ocean – a travel survival kit* was researched and written by Robert Willox who prepared the way for Mark Balla.

This book, the second edition, was edited by Frith Pike, and Greg Herriman was responsible for design, title pages, illustrations and maps. Margaret Jung and Valerie Tellinni designed the cover.

Thanks to Kristin Odijk for proofreading and production; Sue Mitra for editorial suggestions; and Sharon Wertheim for help with the index.

Thanks also to the following travellers who wrote in with their comments:

Bart Andriessens (B), Will Boverhof (NL), Anthony Chan (HK), Eleanor S Cozens, Susan Gwynne (USA), Nils Munch-Petersen (DK), Herman Verwimp (B), Kate Wall (NZ), P Woods (UK)

B – Belgium, DK – Denmark, HK – Hong Kong, NL – The Netherlands, NZ – New Zealand, UK – United Kingdom, USA – United States of America

Warning & Request
Things change – prices go up, schedules change, good places go bad and bad places go bankrupt – nothing stays the same. So if you find things better or worse, recently opened or long since closed, please write and tell us and help make the next edition better.

Your letters will be used to help update future editions and, where possible, important changes will also be included in a Stop Press section in reprints.

We greatly appreciate all information that is sent to us by travellers. Back at Lonely Planet we employ a hard-working readers' letters team to sort through the many letters we receive. The best ones will be rewarded with a free copy of the next edition or another Lonely Planet guide if you prefer. We give away lots of books, but, unfortunately, not every letter/postcard receives one.

Contents

ISLANDS OF THE EAST INDIAN OCEAN

Map Legend

BOUNDARIES

— · — · — · — ....International Boundary
— · · — · · — ....Internal Boundary
+–+–+–+–+–+ .... National Park or Reserve
– – – – – – – – .... The Equator
· · · · · · · · · · · · · · · .... The Tropics

SYMBOLS

◉ NATIONAL ....National Capital
● PROVINCIAL........Provincial or State Capital
● Major ....Major Town
● Minor ....Minor Town
■ ....Places to Stay
▼ ....Places to Eat
✉ ....Post Office
✈ ....Airport
i ....Tourist Information
◒ .... Bus Station or Terminal
66 ....Highway Route Number
☾ ✝ 🕌 ✝ ...... Mosque, Church, Cathedral
∴ ....Temple or Ruin
✚ ....Hospital
❋ ....Lookout
▲ ....Camping Area
⊓ ....Picnic Area
⌂ ....Hut or Chalet
▲ ....Mountain or Hill
⊢■⊣ ....Railway Station
≡ .... Road Bridge
⊢+⊣ ....Railway Bridge
⇒ ⇐ ....Road Tunnel
→) (← ....Railway Tunnel
〰 ....Escarpment or Cliff
⌣ ....Pass
ᴖᴖᴖ ....Ancient or Historic Wall

ROUTES

———————— ......Major Road or Highway
– – – – – – – – .... Unsealed Major Road
———————— ....Sealed Road
– · – · – · – · ..... Unsealed Road or Track
═══════ .... City Street
+–+–+–+–+–+ ....Railway
●—◉—● .... Subway
· · · · · · · · · · · · ....Walking Track
– – – – – – – ....Ferry Route
+I+I+I+I+I+ .... Cable Car or Chair Lift

HYDROGRAPHIC FEATURES

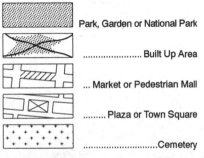

.... River or Creek
...............Intermittent Stream
........Lake, Intermittent Lake
.... Coast Line
...................................Spring
.... Waterfall
.... Swamp

.... Salt Lake or Reef

................................Glacier

OTHER FEATURES

Park, Garden or National Park

.... Built Up Area

... Market or Pedestrian Mall

.... Plaza or Town Square

.............................Cemetery

Note: not all symbols displayed above appear in this book

Introduction

Palm-fringed, sun-drenched, squeaky-white sandy beaches surrounded by shallow lagoons and vibrantly coloured coral reefs teeming with fish and other underwater life await visitors to the Maldives and the islands of the Indian Ocean. Sounds like paradise? Indeed, such images lead most visitors to this remote corner of the earth.

The Maldives and the other islands described in this book offer holiday-makers an opportunity to really get away from it all, to relax and forget about the harsh reality of living on a bigger piece of land with its pollution, violence and the nine-to-five rat-race. If just thinking about it increases your blood pressure, then all and any of these islands could be your nirvana too.

There are, not surprisingly, many similarities between the islands, however, there are still enough differences to appeal to a variety of interests. For a start, the islands are shared by five nations and even more cultures, ranging from the primitive to the most technologically advanced.

Well over half of the islands and atolls covered by this title, and the main tourist destination in the region, make up the independent Republic of Maldives, about one hour's flight to the south-west of Sri Lanka. The Maldives is a nation of 1192 minuscule islands running from north to south for over 750 km, straddling the equator. This makes for a strange and fascinating country, although much of it is overlooked by most package visitors who are confined to one of the 68 island resorts, often without ever meeting a Maldivian.

Government restrictions make contact

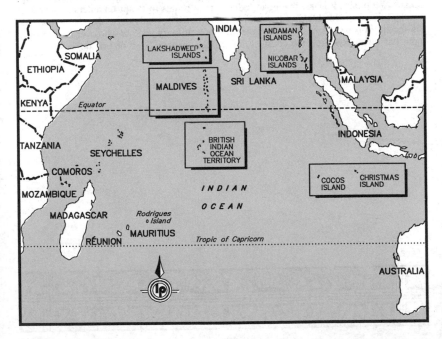

with the local people extremely difficult, so if you are fortunate enough to find yourself in one of the more remote, untouristed atolls, you will be treated to some of the most sincere and unpresuming hospitality anywhere in the world.

While terrestrial wildlife is limited, the underwater world is indescribably beautiful. Over three-quarters of the world's reef fish can be found in the Maldives, often within snorkelling distance of your island. For scuba divers the Maldives are simply heaven. Aside from the myriad of fish and corals, there is the thrill of diving with turtles, moray eels, manta rays, sharks or, occasionally, whales or whale sharks. Just by the airport is the *Maldive Victory*, a wreck said by many enthusiasts to be one of the most breath taking anywhere. Other watersports enthusiasts are also bound to have a tear in their eye as they board the plane to return home.

North of the Maldives run the score of Lakshadweep Islands. They belong to India which, following the Maldivian example, has recently opened them up to foreigners. India has also opened up the considerably larger group of Andaman and Nicobar islands in the Bay of Bengal, although thankfully not to the extent of permitting contact with some of the world's most isolated and primitive tribes.

The Andaman and Nicobar islands are actually a geographical progression of rainforested Sumatra, but if we skip the Indonesian islands (leaving them to another Lonely Planet guide), we come to the remote Christmas and Cocos islands, run by Australia and populated largely by people of Chinese-Malay descent. Christmas Island is high, volcanic and forested; Cocos is a flat, coral atoll, which has started to acquire a reputation as a fine diving destination, and also attracts intrepid surfers in search of the perfect wave.

Across 1500 km of empty ocean to the west are the Chagos Islands, owned by the UK and leased to the USA as a naval base. Contact with this 'tribe' is also forbidden, and there are no commercial flights or shipping routes to tempt travellers in search of somewhere really out of the way, so the only non-military visitors who ever pass through these waters, do so on private yachts.

Facts for the Visitor

VISAS

See the relevant island chapters for information on the visas you might need in this region. Note that with very few exceptions, tourists to the Maldives are issued with a 30-day visa at the airport. Apart from Australians, Australian residents and New Zealanders, all visitors to Cocos and Christmas islands will need an Australian visa. Special permits or packaged tours are required for visiting the Indian-administered islands Lakshadweep, Andaman and Nicobar.

MONEY

Travellers' cheques are best taken in US dollars for all countries, although the UK pound, German mark and French franc are also OK. Except for when visiting Cocos and Christmas islands, Australian dollars cannot be recommended for this region, though you shouldn't have too much trouble changing them in the Maldives. Other major currencies are also acceptable in the heavily touristed areas. Credit cards are accepted in the Maldives and on the Australian islands.

COSTS

You can survive on a low budget on the Indian islands, but not in the Maldives, unless you stay on the capital island Malé where you can survive on US$25 a day (with *survive* being the operative word).

Staying at resorts is expensive on a day-to-day basis and generally cheaper as a package holiday, although there may be some daily bargains in the low season from May to October.

Accommodation and meals for visitors on the Australian islands, Cocos and Christmas, are provided by the island authorities starting at around A$69 a day. The only alternative is a package holiday to Cocos from Perth, Western Australia, although both Cocos and Christmas are working to increase their tourism revenues, and it is highly likely that a tourist resort will open up on both islands in 1993. The plan in the Cocos Islands is to set up a resort similar to those in the Maldives, while on Christmas Island, the plans are more ambitious, with a casino expected to attract high-flying South-East Asian visitors.

WHAT TO BRING

Keep clothing light and wear cotton whenever possible. This particularly applies to your socks if you intend to do lots of walking.

Anything as formal as a suit is unnecessary, but it's good to have a smart set of clothes and shoes for dinners out. Such an outfit can also help at customs and immigration, when entering or leaving a country. If nothing else, it makes you look more respectable, and therefore respected, than you would in shorts, T-shirt and thongs.

Make sure you have adequate protection from the sun. Bring a hat, sunglasses and an appropriate-strength sun block. At the other extreme, a light raincoat will stop a downpour from ruining the odd day or week. It's a must during the wet season.

It does actually cool down a bit at night but not enough to need woolly blankets and thick jumpers.

Basic Kit

If you're going to be roughing it away from the resort accommodation and living with islanders or in guesthouses, you should bring a torch with spare batteries, toilet paper, a small mirror (shiny metal is best), a Swiss-army knife or the like, a first aid kit (see the Health section), a sewing kit with safety pins and a small padlock for locking rooms or luggage.

Also, remember to take precautions to keep your camera equipment and personal gear dry. Pack everything in plastic bags before you leave home.

All this doesn't add up to much extra

weight. If you're looking to lighten your load, keep your towels thin.

INFORMATION

For tourist and general information see the relevant island chapters.

BOOKS

If you intend to do a lot of reading, just bring a few paperbacks with you as you'll probably be able to swap them later with other travellers. In preparation for shoestring travelling, as opposed to package tripping, read *The Tropical Traveller* by John Hatt (Pan, 1982).

If you're after detailed information on the multicoloured wonders of the deep, refer directly to either *Reef Fishes of the Indian Ocean* by Dr Gerald R Allen & Roger C Steene (TFH Publications, New Jersey, 1987), or *A Guide to Common Reef Fish of the Western Indian Ocean* by K R Bock (Macmillan, London, 1987).

See also the Maldives Facts for the Visitor chapter for a more extensive list of books on the underwater world, which while specific to the Maldives, are still useful and interesting for visitors to the other island groups covered in this book.

If you're planning a more extensive exploration of the Indian Ocean, Lonely Planet has three other guidebooks to the region: *Madagascar & the Comoros, Mauritius, Réunion & the Seychelles* and *Sri Lanka*.

FILM & PHOTOGRAPHY

Buying film in this region will be much more expensive than buying it duty-free before you leave home, so stock up. Remember also to take spare batteries for cameras and flash units. If you are interested in underwater photography see the Film & Photography section of the Maldives Facts for the Visitor chapter.

If you are a reasonably knowledgeable photographer, I need only remind you about the heat, humidity, very fine sand, tropical sunlight, equatorial shadows and the great opportunities for underwater photography. If you are not, then this may be a case of the blind leading the blind. There are heaps of books on photography, but one of the best all-rounder books is *The New 35mm Photographer's Handbook* by Julian Calder & John Garrett (Pan).

Use Kodachrome 25 or 64 transparency (slide) film, rather than Ektachrome. The cost of the film usually includes processing and you can mail the rolls back to the labs in the envelopes provided. Rewrap the package to disguise it and send it registered if you don't trust the post. Kodacolor 100 film is the most popular print film and is fine for most general photography in the tropics.

Don't leave your camera in direct sunlight, keep it protected from water, dust and sand, and don't store used film for long in humid conditions as it will fade.

The best times to take photographs on sunny days are the first two hours after sunrise and the last two before sunset. This brings out the best colours. At other times, the harsh sunlight and glare washes everything out, though you can use filters to counter the glare.

Photographing people, particularly dark-skinned people, requires more skill than snapping landscapes. Make sure you take the light reading from the subject's face, not the background. It also requires more patience and politeness. Many islanders, particularly the older Muslims and Hindus, are offended or frightened by snap-happy intruders. You should always ask first before taking a photo, 'ingratiate' yourself, or snap discreetly from a distance.

Don't take photographs of airports or anything that looks like either police or military equipment or property.

Finally, if you are worried about X-ray security machines at airports ruining your film, despite assurances that they won't, simply remove your camera and film stock from your luggage and take them through separately for inspection.

HEALTH

Travel health depends on your predeparture preparations, your day-to-day health care while travelling and how you handle any medical problem or emergency that does develop. While the list of potential dangers can seem quite frightening, with a little luck, some basic precautions and adequate information, few travellers experience more than upset stomachs.

In this part of the world the sun is the greatest general threat to your wellbeing. Bring a good sun block with you as the cost of sun lotions is high and the choice limited. You can tan easily and well within a week to 10 days, using a high-protection cream.

Don't underestimate the effects of the sun, even if you think you know your tolerance level. Take it easy to begin with when you go about exposing yourself to the fiery elements. It's very easy to get badly burnt even when it's overcast. It's a good idea to wear a hat of some kind and sunglasses.

Drink plenty of liquids and keep salt intake up to replace what is lost through perspiration.

Travel Health Guides

There are a number of books on travel health:

Staying Healthy in Asia, Africa & Latin America (Moon Publications) Probably the best all-round guide to carry, as it's compact but very detailed and well organised.

Travellers' Health, Dr Richard Dawood (Oxford University Press) Comprehensive, easy to read, authoritative and also highly recommended, although it's rather large to lug around.

Where There is No Doctor, David Werner (Hesperian Foundation) A very detailed guide intended for someone, like a Peace Corps worker, going to work in an undeveloped country, rather than for the average traveller.

Travel with Children, Maureen Wheeler (Lonely Planet Publications) Includes basic advice on travel health for younger children.

Health Insurance

A travel insurance policy to cover theft, loss and medical problems is a wise idea. There is a wide variety of policies and your travel agent will have recommendations. The international student travel policies handled by STA or other student travel organisations are usually good value. Some policies offer lower and higher medical expenses options

but the higher one is mainly for countries like the USA which have extremely high medical costs. Check the small print:

• Some policies specifically exclude 'dangerous activities' which can include scuba diving, motorcycling, even trekking. If such activities are on your agenda you don't want that sort of policy. You should certainly be covered for diving in the Maldives unless you are absolutely certain that you will not dive. Keep in mind that many nondivers get caught up in a wave of enthusiasm every afternoon in the Maldives when the dive groups return to the resorts.

• You may prefer a policy which pays doctors or hospitals direct rather than you having to pay on the spot and claim later. If you have to claim later make sure you keep all documentation. Some policies ask you to call back (reverse charges) to a centre in your home country where an immediate assessment of your problem is made

• Check if the policy covers ambulances, helicopter rescue or an emergency flight home. If you have to stretch out you will need two seats and somebody has to pay for them. Keep in mind that if you need to be evacuated after a diving accident you may well need to be flown at low altitude as far as Singapore.

Medical Kit

A small, straightforward medical kit is a wise thing to carry. A possible kit list includes:

• Aspirin or Panadol – for pain or fever
• Antihistamine – useful as a decongestant for colds, allergies, to ease the itch from insect bites or stings, or to help prevent motion sickness
• Antibiotics – useful if you're travelling well off the beaten track, but they must be prescribed and you should carry the prescription with you
• Kaolin preparation (Pepto-Bismol), Imodium or Lomotil – for stomach upsets
• Rehydration mixture – for treatment of severe diarrhoea, this is particularly important if travelling with children
• Antiseptic, Mercurochrome and antibiotic powder or similar 'dry' spray – for cuts and grazes
• Calamine lotion – to ease irritation from bites or stings
• Bandages and Band-aids – for minor injuries
• Scissors, tweezers and a thermometer (note that mercury thermometers are prohibited by airlines)
• Insect repellent, sun block, suntan lotion, chap stick and water purification tablets

Ideally antibiotics should be administered only under medical supervision and should never be taken indiscriminately. Overuse of antibiotics can weaken your body's ability to deal with infections naturally and can reduce the drug's efficacy on a future occasion. Take only the recommended dose at the prescribed intervals and continue using the antibiotic for the prescribed period, even if the illness seems to be cured earlier. Antibiotics are quite specific to the infections they can treat, stop immediately if there are any serious reactions and don't use it at all if you are unsure you have the correct one.

In many countries if a medicine is available at all it will generally be available over the counter and the price will be much cheaper than in the West. However, be careful of buying drugs in developing countries, particularly where the expiry date may have passed or correct storage conditions may not have been followed. It's possible that drugs which are no longer recommended, or have even been banned, in the West are still be being dispensed in many Third World countries.

Health Preparations

Make sure you're healthy before you start travelling. If you are embarking on a long trip make sure your teeth are OK; there are lots of places where a visit to the dentist would be the last thing you'd want to do. If you are going to be diving it may be a good idea to have your teeth X-rayed. If any air pockets have developed under your fillings you risk suffering a tooth squeeze, an extremely painful affliction caused by an increase in the pressure of the gases under your filling as you ascend from your dive. While this is not a common problem, there have been extreme cases where a tooth has popped a filling or worse still, exploded.

If you wear glasses or contact lenses take a spare pair and your prescription. Losing or breaking your glasses could be a real problem.

If you require a particular medication take an adequate supply as well as the prescription, with the generic rather than the brand name, as it will make getting replacements easier. It's a wise idea to have the prescrip-

tion with you to show that you legally use the medication – it's surprising how often over-the-counter drugs from one place are illegal without a prescription, or even banned in another.

Diving Health

If you intend taking a diving course while in the Maldives or any of the other island groups covered in this book, you should have a full diving medical checkup. Ideally you should do this at home, as it is not always easy to organise once you are at your resort. Theoretically you will not be allowed to partake in a dive course without the necessary medical certificate, so contact a sports medicine clinic or a dive school at home for more information. If you are an asthmatic, have any other chronic breathing difficulties, or serious inner-ear problems, you will not pass the test and should not, under any circumstances, do any scuba diving.

Decompression Sickness

Decompression sickness is a very serious condition usually, though not always, associated with diver error. The most common symptoms are unusual fatigue or weakness, skin itch, pain in the arms, legs (joints or mid-limb) or torso, dizziness and vertigo, local numbness, tingling or paralysis and shortness of breath. Signs may also include a blotchy skin rash, a tendency to favour an arm or a leg, staggering, coughing spasms, collapse or unconsciousness. These symptoms and signs can occur individually, or a number of them can appear at one time.

The most common causes of decompression sickness (or 'the bends' as it is commonly known) are diving too deep, staying at depth for too long, or ascending too quickly. This results in nitrogen coming out of solution in the blood and forming bubbles, most commonly in the bones, and particularly in the joints or weak spots such as healed fracture sites.

There are other factors which have been shown to have a casual effect in decompression sickness. Excess body fat; heavy exertion prior to, during and after diving;

injuries and illness; dehydration; alcohol; cold water, hot showers or baths after diving; carbon dioxide increase (eg through smoking); and age are worth considering. Flying or even driving to altitudes over 300 metres shortly after diving is dangerous and should be avoided, as it causes nitrogen to come out of the blood even faster than it would at sea level.

Even if you take all the necessary precautions, there is no guarantee that you will not be hit by the bends. This is not cause for paranoia, however, it imposes a responsibility on all divers to notice anything unusual about their own condition and that of their diving buddy after diving.

The only treatment for decompression sickness is to put the patient into a recompression chamber. There are around half a dozen of these in the Maldives. Depending on the case, a patient may have to spend hours or even days in the chamber. Basically, a chamber provides an artificial means of putting a person back under pressure similar to or often greater than that of the depth at which they were diving. If you think that you or anyone else you are diving with is suffering from the bends, it is important to get to a recompression chamber as soon as possible.

Immunisations

Vaccinations provide protection against diseases you might meet along the way. For some countries no immunisations are necessary, but the further off the beaten track you go the more necessary it is to take precautions. These days vaccination as an entry requirement is usually only enforced when you are coming from an infected area – yellow fever and cholera are the two most likely requirements. Nevertheless, all vaccinations should be recorded on an International Health Certificate, which is available from your physician or government health department.

Plan ahead for getting your vaccinations: some of them require an initial shot followed by a booster, while some vaccinations should not be given together. Most travellers from Western countries will have been immunised against various diseases during childhood but your doctor may still recommend booster shots against measles or polio, diseases still prevalent in many developing countries. The period of protection offered by vaccinations differs widely and some vaccinations are contraindicated if you are pregnant.

In some countries immunisations are available from airport or government health centres. Travel agents or airline offices will tell you where. The possible list of vaccinations includes:

Smallpox
Smallpox has now been wiped out worldwide, so immunisation is no longer necessary.

Cholera
Some countries may require cholera vaccination if you are coming from an infected area, but protection is not very effective, only lasts six months and is contraindicated for pregnancy.

Tetanus & Diptheria
Boosters are necessary every 10 years and protection is highly recommended.

Typhoid
Protection lasts for three years and is useful if you are travelling for long periods in rural, tropical areas. You may get some side effects such as pain at the injection site, fever, headache and a general unwell feeling.

Infectious Hepatitis
Gamma globulin is not a vaccination but a ready-made antibody which has proven very successful in reducing the chances of hepatitis infection. Because it may interfere with the development of immunity, it should not be given until at least 10 days after administration of the last vaccine needed. It should also be given as close as possible to departure because of its relatively short-lived protection period of six months.

Yellow Fever
Protection lasts 10 years and is recommended where the disease is endemic, chiefly in Africa and South America. You usually have to go to a special yellow fever vaccination centre. Vaccination is contraindicated during pregnancy, but if you must travel to a high-risk area it is probably advisable.

Basic Rules

Care in what you eat and drink is the most important health rule; stomach upsets are the most likely travel health problem but the majority of these upsets will be relatively minor. Don't become paranoid, trying the local food is part of the experience of travel after all.

Water The main rule for staying healthy is not consuming the local water including ice: if you don't know for certain that the water is safe always assume the worst. Reputable brands of bottled water or soft drinks are generally fine, although in some places bottles refilled with tap water are not unknown. Take care with fruit juice, particularly if water may have been added. Milk should be treated with suspicion, as it is often unpasteurised. Boiled milk is fine if it is kept hygienically and yoghurt is always good. Tea or coffee should also be OK, since the water should have been boiled. In most guest houses in Malé there is a rainwater tank and the water is drinkable. In general, resorts and guesthouses supply guests with a cold flask of drinking water in the rooms.

Water Purification In the unlikely event that you do need to purify water in the Maldives, the simplest way is to boil it for around 10 minutes.

Simple filtering will not remove all dangerous organisms, so if you cannot boil water it should be treated chemically. Chlorine tablets (Puritabs, Steritabs or other brand names) will kill many but not all pathogens. Iodine is very effective in purifying water and is available in tablet form (such as Potable Aqua), but follow the directions carefully and remember that too much iodine can be harmful.

If you can't find tablets, tincture of iodine (2%) or iodine crystals can be used. Two drops of tincture of iodine per litre or quart of clear water is the recommended dosage; the treated water should be left to stand for 30 minutes before drinking. Iodine crystals can also be used to purify water but this is a more complicated process, as you have to first prepare a saturated iodine solution. Iodine loses its effectiveness if exposed to air or damp so keep it in a tightly sealed container. Flavoured powder will disguise the taste of treated water and is a good idea if you are travelling with children.

Food Salads and fruit should be washed with purified water or peeled where possible. Ice cream is usually OK if it is a reputable brand name, though beware of street vendors' ice cream that has melted and been refrozen. Thoroughly cooked food is safest, but not if it has been left to cool or if it has been reheated. Take great care with shellfish or fish and avoid undercooked meat. If a place looks clean and well run, and if the vendor also looks clean and healthy, then the food is probably safe. In general, places that are packed with travellers or locals will be fine, while empty restaurants are questionable. Visitors to the capital and to the outer, non-touristed atolls often take time to adjust to the Maldivian diet, which is heavily dependent on fish and is generally pretty spicy, however, the food is usually safe.

Nutrition If your food is poor or limited in availability, if you're travelling hard and fast and therefore missing meals, or if you simply lose your appetite, you can soon start to lose weight and place your health at risk.

Make sure your diet is well balanced. Eggs, tofu, beans, lentils (dhal in India) and nuts are all safe ways to get protein. Fruit you can peel (bananas, oranges or mandarins for example) is always safe and a good source of vitamins. Try to eat plenty of grains (rice) and bread. Remember that although food is generally safer if it is cooked well, over-cooked food loses much of its nutritional value. If your diet isn't well balanced or if your food intake is insufficient, it's a good idea to take vitamin and iron pills.

In hot climates make sure you drink enough – don't rely on feeling thirsty to indicate when you should drink. Not needing to urinate or very dark yellow urine is a danger sign. Always carry a water bottle with you on long trips. Excessive sweating can lead to loss of salt and therefore muscle cramping. Salt tablets are not a good idea as a preventative, but in places where salt is not used much, adding salt to food can help.

Everyday Health A normal body temperature is 98.6°F or 37°C; more than 2°C higher is a 'high' fever. A normal adult pulse rate is 60 to 80 beats per minute (children 80 to 100, babies 100 to 140). You should know how to take a temperature and a pulse rate. As a general rule the pulse increases about 20 beats per minute for each °C rise in fever.

Respiration rate is also an indicator of illness. Count the number of breaths per minute: between 12 and 20 is normal for adults and older children (up to 30 for younger children, 40 for babies). People with a high fever or serious respiratory illness (like pneumonia) breathe more quickly than normal. More than 40 shallow breaths a minute usually means pneumonia.

Many health problems can be avoided by taking care of yourself. Wash your hands frequently – it's quite easy to contaminate your own food. Clean your teeth with purified water rather than that taken straight from the tap. Avoid climatic extremes: keep out of the sun when it's hot, dress warmly when it's cold. Avoid potential diseases by dressing sensibly. You can get worm infections through walking barefoot or dangerous coral cuts by walking over coral without shoes. You can avoid insect bites by covering bare skin when insects are around, by screening windows or beds, or by using insect repellents or mosquito coils.

Medical Treatment
Potential medical problems can be broken down into several areas. First there are the climatic and geographical considerations – problems caused by extremes of temperature, altitude or motion. Then there are diseases and illnesses caused by insanitation, insect bites or stings, and animal or human contact. Simple cuts, bites or scratches can also cause problems.

Self-diagnosis and treatment can be risky, so wherever possible seek qualified help. Although we do give treatment dosages in this section, they are for emergency use only. Medical advice should be sought before administering any drugs.

An embassy or consulate can usually recommend a good place to go for such advice. For more information on health services see the Maldives Facts for the Visitor section. In some places standards of medical attention are so low that for some ailments the best advice is to get on a plane and go somewhere else.

Climatic & Geographical Considerations
Sunburn In the tropics, the desert or at high altitude you can get sunburnt surprisingly quickly, even through cloud. Use a sunblock and take extra care to cover areas which don't normally see sun – for example, your feet. A hat provides added protection, and you should also use zinc cream or some other barrier cream for your nose and lips. Calamine lotion is good for easing mild sunburn.

Prickly Heat Prickly heat is an itchy rash caused by excessive perspiration trapped under the skin. It usually strikes people who have just arrived in a hot climate and whose pores have not yet opened sufficiently to cope with greater sweating. Keeping cool but bathing often, and using a mild talcum powder or even resorting to air-conditioning may help until you acclimatise.

Heat Exhaustion Dehydration or salt deficiency can cause heat exhaustion. Take time to acclimatise to high temperatures and make sure you get sufficient liquids. Salt deficiency is characterised by fatigue, lethargy, headaches, giddiness and muscle cramps and in this case salt tablets may help. Vomiting or diarrhoea can deplete your liquid and salt levels. Anhydrotic heat exhaustion, caused by an inability to sweat, is quite rare. Unlike the other forms of heat exhaustion, it is likely to strike people who have been in a hot climate for a period of time, rather than newcomers.

Heat Stroke This serious, sometimes fatal, condition can occur if the body's heat-regulating mechanism breaks down and the body temperature rises to dangerous levels. Long, continuous periods of exposure to high temperatures can leave you vulnerable to heat stroke. You should avoid excessive alcohol or strenuous activity when you first arrive in a hot climate.

The symptoms are feeling unwell, not sweating very much or at all and a high body temperature (39°C to 41°C). Where sweating has ceased the skin becomes flushed and red. Severe, throbbing headaches and lack of coordination will also occur, and the sufferer may be confused or aggressive. Eventually the victim will become delirious or convulse. Hospitalisation is essential, but meanwhile get patients out of the sun, remove their clothing, cover them with a wet sheet or towel and then fan them continually.

Fungal Infections Hot weather fungal infections are most likely to occur on the scalp, between the toes or fingers (athlete's foot), in the groin (jock itch or crotch rot) and on the body (ringworm). You get ringworm (which is a fungal infection, not a worm) from infected animals or by walking on damp areas, like shower floors.

To prevent fungal infections wear loose, comfortable clothes, avoid artificial fibres, wash frequently and dry carefully. If you do get an infection, wash the infected area daily with a disinfectant or medicated soap and water, and rinse and dry well. Apply an antifungal powder like the widely available Tinaderm. Try to expose the infected area to air or sunlight as much as possible and wash all towels and underwear in hot water as well as changing them often.

Motion Sickness Eating lightly before and during a trip will reduce the chances of motion sickness. If you are prone to motion sickness try to find a place that minimises disturbance – near the wing on aircraft, close to midships on boats, near the centre on buses. Fresh air usually helps, reading or cigarette smoke doesn't. Commercial anti-motion-sickness preparations, which can cause drowsiness, have to be taken before the trip commences; when you're feeling sick it's too late. Ginger is a natural preventative and is available in capsule form.

Diseases of Insanitation
Diarrhoea A change of water, food or climate can all cause the runs; diarrhoea caused by contaminated food or water is more serious. Despite all your precautions you may still have a bout of mild travellers' diarrhoea but a few rushed toilet trips with no other symptoms is not indicative of a serious problem. Moderate diarrhoea, involving half-a-dozen loose movements in a day, is more of a nuisance. Dehydration is the main danger with any diarrhoea, particularly for children, so fluid replenishment is the main treatment. Drinking weak black tea with a little sugar, soda water, or soft drinks allowed to go flat and diluted 50% with water are all good. With severe diarrhoea a rehydrating solution is necessary to replace minerals and salts. You should stick to a bland diet as you recover.

Lomotil or Imodium can be used to bring relief from the symptoms, although they do not actually cure the problem. Only use these drugs if absolutely necessary – for example, if you *must* travel. For children Imodium is preferable, but do not use these drugs if the patient has a high fever or is severely dehydrated.

Antibiotics can be very useful in treating severe diarrhoea especially if it is accompanied by nausea, vomiting, stomach cramps or mild fever. Ampicillin, a broad spectrum penicillin, is usually recommended. Two capsules of 250 mg each taken four times a day is the recommended dose for an adult. Children aged between eight and 12 years should have half the adult dose; younger children should have half a capsule four times a day. Note that if the patient is allergic to penicillin, ampicillin should not be administered.

Three days of treatment should be sufficient and an improvement should occur within 24 hours.

Giardia *Giardia lamblia*, an intestinal parasite which causes giardiasis commonly known as giardia or 'beaver fever,' is present in contaminated water. The symptoms are stomach cramps, nausea, a bloated stomach, watery, foul-smelling diarrhoea and frequent gas. Giardia can appear several weeks after you have been exposed to the parasite. The symptoms may disappear for a few days and then return; this can go on for several weeks. Metronidazole known as Flagyl is the recommended drug, but it should only be taken under medical supervision. Antibiotics are of no use.

Dysentery This serious illness is caused by contaminated food or water and is characterised by severe diarrhoea, often with blood or mucus in the stool. There are two kinds of dysentery. Bacillary dysentery is characterised by a high fever and rapid development; headache, vomiting and stomach pains are also symptoms. It generally does not last longer than a week, but it is highly contagious.

Amoebic dysentery is more gradual in developing, has no fever or vomiting but is a more serious illness. It is not a self-limiting disease: it will persist until treated and can recur and cause long-term damage.

A stool test is necessary to diagnose which kind of dysentery you have, so you should seek medical help urgently. In case of an emergency, note that tetracycline is the prescribed treatment for bacillary dysentery, metronidazole for amoebic dysentery.

With tetracycline, the recommended adult dosage is one 250 mg capsule four times a day. Children aged between eight and 12 years should have half the adult dose; the dosage for younger children is a third of the adult dose. It's important to remember that tetracycline should be given to young children only if it's absolutely necessary and only for a short period; pregnant women should not take it after the 4th month of pregnancy.

With metronidazole, the recommended adult dosage is one 750 mg to 800 mg capsule three times daily for five days. Children aged between eight and 12 years should have half the adult dose; the dosage for younger children is a third of the adult dose.

Cholera Cholera vaccination is not very effective. However, outbreaks of cholera are generally widely reported, so you can avoid such problem areas. The disease is characterised by a sudden onset of acute diarrhoea with 'rice water' stools, vomiting, muscular cramps, and extreme weakness. You need medical help – but treat for dehydration which can be extreme and, if there is an appreciable delay in getting to hospital then begin taking tetracycline. See the Dysentery section for dosages and warnings.

Viral Gastroenteritis This is caused not by bacteria but, as the name suggests, by a virus. It is characterised by stomach cramps, diarrhoea, and sometimes by vomiting and/or a slight fever. All you can do is rest and drink lots of fluids.

Hepatitis Hepatitis A is the more common form of this disease and is spread by contaminated food or water. The first symptoms are fever, chills, headache, fatigue, feelings of weakness and aches and pains. This is followed by loss of appetite, nausea, vomiting, abdominal pain, dark urine, light-coloured faeces and jaundiced skin; the whites of the eyes may also turn yellow. In some cases there may just be a feeling of being unwell or tired, accompanied by loss of appetite, aches and pains and the jaundiced effect. You should seek medical advice, but in general there is not much you can do apart from resting, drinking lots of fluids, eating lightly and avoiding fatty foods. People who have had hepatitis must forego alcohol for six months after the illness, as hepatitis attacks the liver and it needs that amount of time to recover.

Hepatitis B, which used to be called serum hepatitis, is spread through sexual contact or through skin penetration – it could be transmitted via dirty needles or blood transfusions, for instance. Avoid having your ears pierced, tattoos done or injections, where you have doubts about the sanitary conditions. The symptoms and treatment of type B are much the same as for type A, but gamma globulin as a prophylactic is effective against type A only.

Typhoid Typhoid fever is another gut infection that travels the faecal-oral route – ie contaminated water and food are responsible. Vaccination against typhoid is not totally effective and it is one of the most dangerous infections, so medical help must be sought.

In its early stages typhoid resembles many other illnesses: sufferers may feel like they have a bad cold or flu on the way, as early symptoms are a headache, a sore throat, and a fever which rises a little each day until it reaches around 40°C or more. The victim's pulse is often slow relative to the degree of fever present and gets slower as the fever rises – unlike a normal fever where the pulse increases. There may also be vomiting, diarrhoea or constipation.

In the second week the high fever and slow pulse continue and a few pink spots may appear on the body; trembling, delirium, weakness, weight loss and dehydration are other symptoms. If there are no further complications, the fever and other symptoms will slowly go during the third week. However you must get medical help before this because pneumonia (acute infection of the lungs) or peritonitis (burst appendix) are common complications, and because typhoid is very infectious.

The fever should be treated by keeping the victim cool and dehydration should also be watched for. Chloramphenicol is the recommended antibiotic but there are fewer side affects with ampicillin. The adult dosage is two 250 mg capsules, four times a day. Children aged between eight and 12 years should have half the adult dose; younger children should have a third of the adult dose.

Patients who are allergic to penicillin should not be given ampicillin.

Worms These parasites are most common in rural, tropical areas and having a stool test when you return home is not a bad idea. Worms can be present on unwashed vegetables or in undercooked meat and you can pick them up through your skin by walking in bare feet. Infestations may not show up for some time, and although they are generally not serious, if left untreated they can cause severe health problems. A stool test is necessary to pinpoint the problem and medication is often available over the counter.

Diseases Spread by People & Animals

Tetanus This potentially fatal disease is found in undeveloped tropical areas. It is difficult to treat but is preventable with immunisation. Tetanus occurs when a wound becomes infected by a germ which lives in the faeces of animals or humans, so clean all cuts, punctures or animal bites. Tetanus is known as lockjaw, and the first symptom may be discomfort in swallowing, or stiffening of the jaw and neck; this is followed by painful convulsions of the jaw and whole body.

Tuberculosis (TB) Although this disease is widespread in many developing countries, it is not a serious risk to travellers to this region. Young children are more susceptible than adults and vaccination is a sensible precaution for children under 12 years travelling in endemic areas. TB is commonly spread by coughing or by unpasteurised dairy products from infected cows. Milk that has been boiled is safe to drink; the souring of milk to make yoghurt or cheese also kills the bacilli.

Sexually Transmitted Diseases (STDs)

Sexual contact with an infected sexual partner spreads these diseases. While abstinence is the only 100% preventative, using condoms is also effective. Gonorrhoea and syphilis are the most common sexually transmitted diseases: sores, blisters or rashes around the genitals, discharges or pain when urinating are common symptoms. Symptoms may be less marked or not observed at all in women. Syphilis symptoms eventually disappear completely but the disease continues and can cause severe problems in later years. The treatment of gonorrhoea and syphilis is by antibiotics.

There are numerous other sexually transmitted diseases. For most of them effective treatment is available. However, there is no cure for herpes.

HIV/AIDS HIV (the human immunodeficiency virus) may develop into AIDS (acquired immune deficiency syndrome). Always practising safe sex by using condoms is the most effective preventative; it is impossible to detect the seropositivity (HIV positive status) of an otherwise healthy-looking person.

HIV/AIDS can also be spread through infected blood transfusions; most developing countries cannot afford to screen blood used for transfusions. It can also be spread by dirty needles – vaccinations, acupuncture, ear or nose piercing and tattooing can potentially be as dangerous as intravenous drug use if the equipment is not clean. If you do need an injection it may be a good idea to buy a new syringe from a pharmacy and ask the doctor to use it.

Insect-Borne Diseases

Malaria Malaria has 'officially' been wiped out in the Maldives. According to the World Health Organisation, the last reported case was in 1981. However, considering the close proximity of Sri Lanka where malaria is rife, it is still worth at least considering taking a course of malaria tablets – just in case. If you are undecided, contact a tropical medicine specialist or a travellers' clinic for advice. Malaria is still prevalent in the Lakshadweep, Andaman and Nicobar islands. In the Chagos Islands, the British Indian Ocean Territories, Cocos Islands and Christmas Island, there is said to be no malaria.

In those islands in the Indian Ocean and other parts of the world where malaria is found, this serious disease is spread by mosquito bites. If you are travelling in endemic areas it is extremely important to take malarial prophylactics. Symptoms include headaches, fever, chills and sweating which may subside and recur. Without treatment malaria can develop more serious, potentially fatal effects.

Antimalarial drugs do not actually prevent the disease but suppress its symptoms. Chloroquine is the usual malarial prophylactic; a tablet is taken once a week for two weeks prior to arrival in the infected area and six weeks after you leave it. Unfortunately there is now a strain of malaria which is resistant to chloroquine and if you are travelling in an area infected with this strain an alternative drug is necessary. East and Central Africa, Papua New Guinea, Irian Jaya, the Solomons and Vanuatu are the most dangerous areas, but note that other places are not necessarily 100% safe: only in Central America, the Middle East and West Africa is chloroquine completely effective. Where resistance is reported you should continue to take chloroquine but supplement it with a weekly dose of maloprim or a daily dose of Proguanil.

Chloroquine is quite safe for general use, side effects are minimal and it can be taken by pregnant women. Maloprim can have rare but serious side effects if the weekly dose is exceeded, and some doctors recommend a checkup after six months' continuous use.

Fansidar, once used as a chloroquine alternative, is no longer recommended as a prophylactic, as it can have dangerous side effects, but it may still be recommended as a treatment for malaria. Chloroquine is also used for malaria treatment but in larger doses than for prophylaxis. Doxycycline is another antimalarial for use where chloroquine resistance is reported; it causes hypersensitivity to sunlight, so sunburn can be a problem.

Mosquitoes appear after dusk. Avoiding bites by covering bare skin and using an insect repellent will further reduce the risk of catching malaria. Insect screens on windows and mosquito nets on beds offer protection, as does burning a mosquito coil. Mosquitoes may be attracted by perfume, aftershave or certain colours. The risk of infection is higher in rural areas and during the wet season.

Cuts, Bites & Stings

Cuts & Scratches Skin punctures can easily become infected in hot climates and may be difficult to heal. Treat any cut with an antiseptic solution and Mercurochrome. Where possible avoid bandages and Band-aids, which can keep wounds wet. Coral cuts are notoriously slow to heal, as the coral injects a weak venom into the wound. Avoid coral cuts by wearing shoes when walking on reefs, and clean any cut thoroughly. For more information see Marine Dangers.

Bites & Stings Bee and wasp stings are usually painful rather than dangerous. Calamine lotion will give relief and ice packs will reduce the pain and swelling. There are some spiders with dangerous bites but antivenenes are usually available.

Certain fish and other sea creatures can sting or bite dangerously and can be dangerous to eat. To seek local advice is the best suggestion.

Bedbugs & Lice Bedbugs live in various places, but particularly in dirty mattresses and bedding. Spots of blood on bedclothes or on the wall around the bed can be read as a suggestion to find another hotel. Bedbugs leave itchy bites in neat rows. Calamine lotion may help.

All lice cause itching and discomfort. They make themselves at home in your hair (head lice), your clothing (body lice) or in your pubic hair (crabs). You catch lice through direct contact with infected people or by sharing combs, clothing and the like. Powder or shampoo treatment will kill the lice and infested clothing should then be washed in very hot water.

Marine Dangers

For some people coral reefs conjure visions of hungry sharks, fierce moray eels, stinging jellyfish and other aquatic menaces. In actual fact the dangers are slight and in most cases it's simply a matter of avoiding touching or picking up things which are best left alone. The basic rules of reef safety are:

Don't walk on reefs or in the shallow water between reefs without wearing shoes with strong soles.
Don't eat fish you don't know about.
Don't swim in murky water, try to swim when there's bright sunlight.

Sharks Hungry sharks are the usual idea of an aquatic nasty, but in the Maldives there is no shortage of meals which are far tastier and more conveniently bite-sized than humans. Hammerhead sharks are found in the Maldives, but generally on drop-offs from the outer reef. Sharks are a negligible danger if they are not provoked. That said, several diving schools offer divers the opportunity to feed sharks by hand or, for the truly foolhardy, mouth-to-mouth. These practices are discouraged by the government. It is also pretty unlikely that your travel insurance would cover you for a hand lost to a shark that you were feeding at the time.

Butterfly Cod & Stonefish These two fish are closely related and have a series of poisonous spines down their back. The butterfly cod, also known as the lionfish or firefish, is an incredibly beautiful and slow moving creature – it knows it's deadly and doesn't worry about possible enemies. Even brushing against the spines can be painful but a stab from one could be fatal. Fortunately it's hard to miss a butterfly cod so, unless you stepped on one or deliberately hit one, the danger is remote.

Stonefish are the ugly siblings of the beautiful butterfly cod. They lie on the sea bottom, where they merge into the background. When stepped on, their 13 sharp dorsal spines pop up and inject a venom that causes intense pain and can cause death. Stonefish are usually found in shallow, muddy water, but they can also be found on rocky and coral bottoms.

Wearing shoes with strong soles is the best protection, but if you are unlucky, bathing the wound in very hot water reduces the pain and the effects of the venom. An antivenene is available and medical attention should be sought as the after effects can be very long lasting.

Fish Poisoning Man-bites-fish can be just as dangerous as fish-bites-man. Ciguatera poison is a poison which seems to accumulate in certain types of fish due to the consumption of certain types of algae by grazing fish. The poison seems to concentrate the further up the food chain it goes so it isn't the original algae-eating fish which poses the danger, it's the fish which eats the fish which eats the algae-eating fish. The danger is remote but erratic and recovery, although usually complete, is very slow. Chinaman-fish, red bass, large rock cod and moray eels have all been implicated.

Stingrays Stepping on stingrays is also not a good idea. They lie on sandy bottoms and if you step on one its barbed tail can whip up into your leg and cause a nasty poisoned wound. Furthermore sand tends to drift over stingrays so they can become all but invisible while basking on the bottom. Fortunately, although they may be invisible to you, you are certainly not invisible to them and stingrays will usually wake up and zoom away as you approach. If you're out walking on the sort of shallow sandy surface which rays like, it's wise to shuffle along and make some noise. If you're stung, bathing the affected area in hot water is the best treatment and medical attention should be sought to ensure the wound is properly cleaned.

Things that Sting & Bite Don't step on spiny sea urchins as the spines are long and sharp, break off easily and once embedded in your flesh are very difficult to remove. All coral is poisonous and brushing against fire coral or the feathery stinging hydroid can give you a surprisingly painful sting and an itchy rash which takes a long time to heal. Anemones are also poisonous and putting your arm into one can give you a painful sting. Leave them to the clown fish.

If you go out of your way looking for trouble it's certainly possible to find it, and lots of fish will bite if you put your fingers in their mouths. Many scuba divers find this out when they're hand-feeding fish but fortunately a bite from most small fish is nothing more than a playful nip. A bite from a moray eel is said to be a much more serious affair, but eventually every scuba diver seems to get the opportunity to tickle a friendly moray eel under the chin and they never seem to bite anybody.

Coral Cuts The most likely marine injury is the simple coral cut. Coral is nasty sharp stuff

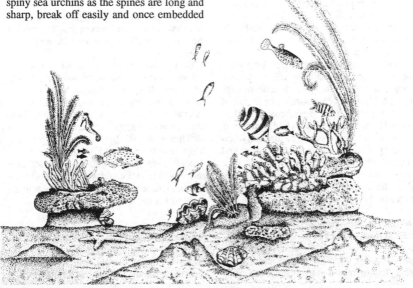

and brushing up against it is likely to cause a cut or abrasion. Since coral kills its prey with poison you're likely to get some of that poison in the wound and tiny grains of broken coral are also likely to lodge there. The result is that a small cut can take a long, long time to heal and be very painful in the process. The answer is to wash any coral cuts very thoroughly with fresh water and then treat them liberally with Mercurochrome or some other antiseptic.

An even better solution is not to get cut by coral in the first place. Wear shoes to protect your feet if you're walking over coral. If you're diving remember that wet suits don't just keep scuba divers warm, they also protect them if they brush up against coral. A coral cut is also a two-way thing, in cutting yourself you've probably damaged the coral. If you're swimming through a coral garden try not to blunder along, bumping into things and breaking off fragile branching coral.

Women's Health

Gynaecological Problems Poor diet, lowered resistance due to the use of antibiotics for stomach upsets, and even the contraceptive pill can lead to vaginal infections when travelling in hot climates. Good hygiene and wearing skirts or loose-fitting trousers and cotton underwear will help to prevent infections.

Yeast infections, characterised by a rash, itch and discharge, can be treated with a vinegar or even lemon-juice douche, or with yoghurt. Nystatin suppositories are the usual medical prescription for thrush. Trichomonas is a more serious infection; symptoms are a discharge and a burning sensation when urinating. Flagyl is the prescribed drug and medical attention should be sought if a vinegar-water douche is not effective. With all of these infections male sexual partners must also be treated.

Pregnancy Most miscarriages occur during the first three months of pregnancy, so this is the most risky time to travel if you're pregnant. The last three months should also be spent within reasonable distance of good medical care, as quite serious problems can develop at this time. Pregnant women should avoid all unnecessary medication, but vaccinations and malarial prophylactics should still be taken whenever possible, consult your doctor for advice. Additional care should be taken to prevent illness, and particular attention should be paid to diet and nutrition.

DANGERS & ANNOYANCES

Crime is not rife on any of the island groups covered in this book, however, this does not mean that you should be off your guard.

Unless you know about marine life, don't touch the coral, shells or fish – some of them sting, cut, and occasionally kill. Don't swim or let yourself drift too far away from the boat or shore in case you get caught in a strong current. Don't try body surfing unless you know where you are and what you're doing – the surf breaks over coral reefs and you could be badly grazed or lacerated. Sharks are not a problem.

Security

A waterproof money belt or kidney pouch for your passport, flight tickets and travellers' cheques is worth considering. Use a daypack to carry the bits and pieces you'll need for the day, as well as your camera and valuables.

Don't leave vital documents, money or valuables in your room or in your suitcase while travelling. Don't sleep with an open window which is accessible from the outside, or with the door open or unlocked. One traveller says he was robbed on a Maldivian island by a bedroom prowler. Most resorts in the Maldives have safety deposit boxes, or at least a safe place in a room which is locked when staff are not around, where you can leave valuables overnight or for the duration of your stay.

WORK

Work permits are difficult to get in all the island groups covered by this book. However, if you have a skill which can be directly applied to the tourism industry you may have a chance. Diving and other water-sport instructors are always in demand in the Maldives, for example. See the Maldives chapter for more information. There may be opportunities on Christmas Island late in 1993 for people who have worked in casinos, but without an Australian work permit you can forget it.

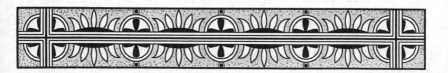

Getting There & Away

AIR

To/From the USA

The *New York Times*, the *LA Times*, the *Chicago Tribune* and the *San Francisco Examiner* all produce weekly travel sections in which you'll find any number of travel agents' ads. Council Travel and STA have offices in major cities nationwide.

The magazine *Travel Unlimited* (PO Box 1058, Allston, MA 02134) publishes details of the cheapest air fares and courier possibilities for destinations all over the world from the USA.

To/From Canada

Travel CUTS has offices in all major cities. The *Toronto Globe & Mail* and the *Vancouver Sun* carry travel agents' ads. The magazine *Great Expeditions* (PO Box 8000-411, Abbotsford BC V2S 6H1) is useful.

To/From the UK

Trailfinders in west London produce a lavishly illustrated brochure which includes air fare details. STA also has branches in the UK. Look in the listings magazines *Time Out* and *City Limits*, and the London Evening Standard plus the Sunday papers and *Exchange & Mart* for ads. Also look out for the free magazines widely available in London – start by looking outside the main railway stations.

Most British travel agents are registered with ABTA (Association of British Travel Agents). If you have paid for your flight to an ABTA-registered agent who then goes out of business, ABTA will guarantee a refund or an alternative. Unregistered bucket shops are riskier but also sometimes cheaper.

The Globetrotters Club (BCM Roving, London WC1N 3XX) publishes a newsletter called *Globe* which covers obscure destinations and can help in finding travelling companions.

To/From Europe

In Amsterdam, NBBS (a nationwide 'student' travel agency) at Rokin 38 (☎ 624 09 89) or Leidsestraat 53 (☎ 638 17 36) is popular. See the Maldives Getting There & Away chapter for a comprehensive list of tour operators.

To/From Australia

STA and Flight Centres International are major dealers in cheap air fares. Check the travel agents' ads in the Yellow Pages and ring around.

To/From New Zealand

As in Australia, STA and Flight Centres International are popular travel agents.

To/From Asia

Hong Kong is the discount plane ticket capital of the region. Its bucket shops are at least as unreliable as those of other cities. Ask the advice of other travellers before buying a ticket.

STA, which is reliable, has branches in Hong Kong, Tokyo, Singapore, Bangkok and Kuala Lumpur.

There are flights from Thiruvananthapuram (formerly Trivandrum) in India to the Maldives for around US$63 one way. Air Lanka flies from Colombo to Malé for around US$10 more.

Airfares

For sample airfares see the Getting There & Away sections of the specific chapter(s) which are relevant to your destination.

Travel Insurance

However you're travelling, it's worth taking out travel insurance. Work out what you need. You may not want to insure that grotty old army surplus backpack – but everyone should be covered for the worst possible case: an accident, for example, that will require hospital treatment and a flight home.

It's a good idea to make a copy of your policy, in case the original is lost. If you are planning to travel for a long time, the insurance may seem very expensive – but if you can't afford it, you certainly won't be able to afford to deal with a medical emergency overseas. For more information on travel insurance see the Health section in the introductory Facts for the Visitor chapter.

Buying a Plane Ticket

The plane ticket will probably be the single most expensive item in your budget, and buying it can be an intimidating business. There is likely to be a multitude of airlines and travel agents hoping to separate you from your money, and it is always worth putting aside a few hours to research the current state of the market. Start early: some of the cheapest tickets have to be bought months in advance, and some popular flights sell out early. Talk to other recent travellers – they may be able to stop you making some of the same old mistakes. Look at the ads in newspapers and magazines, consult reference books and watch for special offers. Then phone round travel agents for bargains. (Airlines can supply information on routes and timetables; however, except at times of inter-airline war they do not supply the cheapest tickets.) Find out the fare, the route, the duration of the journey and any restrictions on the ticket. (See restrictions in the Air Travel Glossary.) Then sit back and decide which is best for you.

You may discover that those impossibly cheap flights are 'fully booked, but we have another one that costs a bit more...' Or the flight is on an airline notorious for its poor safety standards and leaves you in the world's least favourite airport in mid-journey for 14 hours. Or they claim only to have the last two seats available for that country for the whole of July, which they will hold for you for a maximum of two hours. Don't panic – keep ringing around.

Use the fares quoted in this book as a guide only. They are approximate and based on the rates advertised by travel agents at the time of going to press. Quoted airfares do not necessarily constitute a recommendation for the carrier.

If you are travelling from the UK or the USA, you will probably find that the cheapest flights are being advertised by obscure bucket shops whose names haven't yet reached the telephone directory. Many such firms are honest and solvent, but there are a few rogues who will take your money and disappear, to reopen elsewhere a month or two later under a new name. If you feel suspicious about a firm, don't give them all the money at once – leave a deposit of 20% or so and pay the balance when you get the ticket. If they insist on cash in advance, go somewhere else. And once you have the ticket, ring the airline to confirm that you are actually booked onto the flight.

You may decide to pay more than the rock-bottom fare by opting for the safety of a better-known travel agent. Firms such as STA, who have offices worldwide, Council Travel in the USA or Travel CUTS in Canada are not going to disappear overnight, leaving you clutching a receipt for a non-existent ticket, but they do offer good prices to most destinations.

Once you have your ticket, write its number down, together with the flight number and other details, and keep the information somewhere separate. If the ticket is lost or stolen, this will help you get a replacement.

It's sensible to buy travel insurance as early as possible. If you buy it the week before you fly, you may find, for example, that you're not covered for delays to your flight caused by industrial action.

Air Travellers with Special Needs

If you have special needs of any sort – you've broken a leg, you're vegetarian, travelling in a wheelchair, taking the baby, terrified of flying – you should let the airline know as soon as possible so that they can make arrangements accordingly. You should remind them when you reconfirm your booking (at least 72 hours before departure) and again when you check in at the airport. It may also be worth ringing round the airlines before you make your booking to find out how they can handle your particular needs.

Airports and airlines can be surprisingly helpful, but they do need advance warning. Most international airports will provide escorts from check-in desk to plane where needed, and there should be ramps, lifts, accessible toilets and reachable phones. Aircraft toilets, on the other hand, are likely to present a problem; travellers should discuss this with the airline at an early stage and, if necessary, with their doctor.

Guide dogs for the blind will often have to travel in a specially pressurised baggage compartment with other animals, away from their owner; though smaller guide dogs may be admitted to the cabin. All guide dogs will be subject to the same quarantine laws (six months in isolation etc) as any other animal when entering or returning to countries currently free of rabies such as the UK or Australia.

Hearing impaired travellers can ask for airport and in-flight announcements to be written down for them.

Air Travel Glossary

Apex Apex, or 'advance purchase excursion' is a discounted ticket which must be paid for in advance. There are penalties if you wish to change it.

Baggage Allowance This will be written on your ticket – usually one 20-kg item to go in the hold, plus one item of hand luggage.

Bucket Shop An unbonded travel agency specialising in discounted airline tickets

Bumped Just because you have a confirmed seat doesn't mean you're going to get on the plane – see Overbooking.

Cancellation Penalties If you have to cancel or change an Apex ticket there are often heavy penalties involved, insurance can sometimes be taken out against these penalties. Some airlines impose penalties on regular tickets as well, particularly against 'no show' passengers.

Check In Airlines ask you to check in a certain time ahead of the flight departure (usually 1½ hours on international flights). If you fail to check in on time and the flight is overbooked the airline can cancel your booking and give your seat to somebody else. This is not an uncommon occurrence in the Maldives.

Confirmation Having a ticket written out with the flight and date you want doesn't mean you have a seat until the agent has checked with the airline that your status is 'OK' or confirmed. Meanwhile you could just be 'on request'.

Discounted Tickets There are two types of discounted fares – officially discounted (see Promotional Fares) and unofficially discounted. The lowest prices often impose drawbacks like flying with unpopular airlines, inconvenient schedules, or unpleasant routes and connections. A discounted ticket can save you more than money – you may be able to pay Apex prices without the associated Apex advance booking and other requirements. Discounted tickets only exist where there is fierce competition.

Full Fares Airlines traditionally offer 1st-class (coded F), business-class (coded J) and economy-class (coded Y) tickets. These days there are so many promotional and discounted fares available from the regular economy class that few passengers pay full economy fare.

Lost Tickets If you lose your airline ticket an airline will usually treat it like a travellers' cheque and, after enquiries, issue you with another ticket. Legally, however, an airline is entitled to treat it like cash and if you lose it then it's gone forever. Take good care of your tickets.

No Shows No shows are passengers who fail to show up for their flight, sometimes due to unexpected delays or disasters, sometimes due to simply forgetting, sometimes because they made more than one booking and didn't bother to cancel the one they didn't want. Full-fare passengers who fail to turn up are sometimes entitled to travel on a later flight. The rest of us are penalised (see Cancellation Penalties).

On Request An unconfirmed booking for a flight, see Confirmation

Open Jaws A return ticket where you fly out to one place but return from another. If available this can save you backtracking to your arrival point.

Children under two years of age travel for 10% of the standard fare (or free, on some airlines), as long as they don't occupy a seat. They don't get a baggage allowance either. 'Skycots' should be provided by the airline if requested in advance; these will take a child weighing up to about 10 kg. Children aged between two and 12 years can usually occupy a seat for half to two-thirds of the full fare, and do get get a baggage allowance. Push chairs (pushers, strollers) can often be taken as hand luggage, though check with the airline first.

SEA

If you have the time, money and inclination, the best way to get to any of the islands in this far flung region is by boat, preferably a private yacht. For those of us who cannot contemplate such a possibility, the seafaring options are somewhat limited. Occasionally a traveller manages to secure a job on someone else's private yacht or arrange passage on a freighter from Singapore or Colombo to Malé, but in general you cannot expect to arrive in the Maldives by sea.

There are no cruise lines plying the ocean

Overbooking Airlines hate to fly with empty seats and since every flight has some passengers who fail to show up (see No Shows) airlines often book more passengers than they have seats. Usually the excess passengers balance those who fail to show up but occasionally somebody gets bumped. If this happens guess who it is most likely to be? The passengers who check in late. Remember this is not uncommon in the Maldives.

Promotional Fares Officially discounted fares like Apex fares which are available from travel agents or direct from the airline.

Reconfirmation At least 72 hours prior to departure time of an onward or return flight you must contact the airline and 'reconfirm' that you intend to be on the flight. If you don't do this the airline can delete your name from the passenger list and you could lose your seat. You don't have to reconfirm the first flight on your itinerary or if your stopover is less than 72 hours. It doesn't hurt to reconfirm more than once. Because of continual overbooking problems, this rule is applied to the letter in the Maldives.

Restrictions Discounted tickets often have various restrictions on them – advance purchase is the most usual one (see Apex). Others are restrictions on the minimum and maximum period you must be away, such as a minimum of 14 days or a maximum of one year. See Cancellation Penalties.

Standby A discounted ticket where you only fly if there is a seat free at the last moment. Standby fares are usually only available on domestic routes.

Tickets Out An entry requirement for many countries is that you have an onward or return ticket, in other words, a ticket out of the country. If you're not sure what you intend to do next, the easiest solution is to buy the cheapest onward ticket to a neighbouring country or a ticket from a reliable airline which can later be refunded if you do not use it.

Transferred Tickets Airline tickets cannot be transferred from one person to another. Travellers sometimes try to sell the return half of their ticket, but officials can ask you to prove that you are the person named on the ticket. This is unlikely to happen on domestic flights, on an international flight tickets may be compared with passports.

Travel Agencies Travel agencies vary widely and you should ensure you use one that suits your needs. Some simply handle tours while full-service agencies handle everything from tours and tickets to car rental and hotel bookings. A good one will do all these things and can save you a lot of money but if all you want is a ticket at the lowest possible price, then you really need an agency specialising in discounted tickets. A discounted ticket agency, however, may not be useful for other things, like hotel bookings.

Travel Periods Some officially discounted fares, Apex fares in particular, vary with the time of year. There is often a low (off-peak) season and a high (peak) season. Sometimes there's an intermediate or shoulder season as well. At peak times, when everyone wants to fly, not only will the officially discounted fares be higher but so will unofficially discounted fares or there may simply be no discounted tickets available. Usually the fare depends on your outward flight – if you depart in the high season and return in the low season, you pay the high-season fare.

waves of this region. There are, however, irregular boat services from Madras and Calcutta to the Andaman and Nicobar islands and from Cochin to Lakshadweep. The Shipping Corporation of India puts out a schedule about every three months. Foreigners are required to travel 1st or 2nd class.

The Chagos Islands are accessible only by boat except for the US military base on Diego Garcia, which is completely off limits to civilians anyway.

TOURS

Most visitors to this region arrive on a package tour which usually includes the cost of airfares, accommodation and meals. For a list of tour operators covering the Maldives, see the Getting There & Away section of the Maldives chapter. See also the Cocos & Christmas islands chapters for information on packages to those islands.

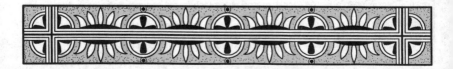

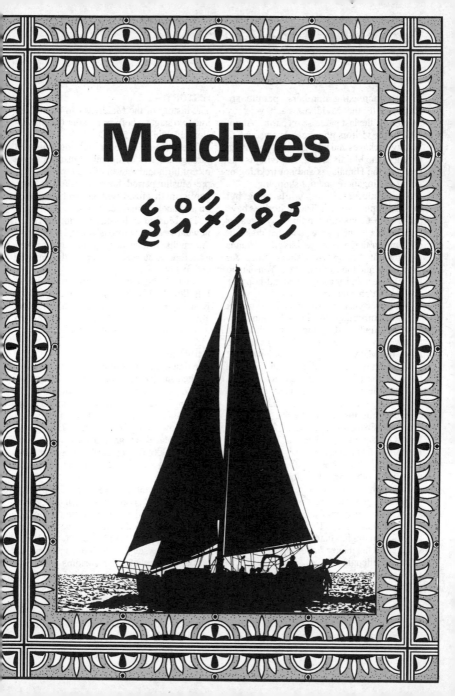

Maldives

ދިވެހިރާއްޖެ

Facts about the Country

In ever-increasing numbers, people are attracted to the Maldives each year by images of 'the last paradise on earth'. About 90% of the visitors go to resorts on seven to 14-day packages and 90% of them go diving. Going to the Maldives and not diving is like going to the Himalayas and not trekking or going to Singapore and not shopping.

The Maldives is an exhilarating but expensive place to visit. The authorities have put a stop to visitors finding any cheaper alternatives to the resorts, and that makes it difficult for the low-budget traveller. Islands are now out of bounds to visitors, except for the resorts and the capital, Malé. You can no longer breeze in for a spot of island-hopping or drop out on a deserted island.

The government restrictions are to prevent visitors 'corrupting' the local Muslim lifestyle and undercutting the tourist industry. Sadly, they also prevent anyone getting to know the Maldives and its people properly.

The paradise images that woo tourists are by no means misleading, but the first fact that most people are surprised to learn about the Maldives is that it is an independent Islamic country, not just a cluster of romantic, deserted islands off the coast of India, Sri Lanka or 'somewhere like that'. Indeed, the Republic of Maldives is a *very* independent nation. It has been looking after itself longer than most other small nations, and has a history, culture and language all of its own.

Another surprising fact is the fragmented and scattered nature of this nation's geography. It is made up of 1192 tiny islands, none of which are higher than a few metres above sea level. This makes travelling difficult, or at least challenging.

Despair not, however, as there are ways of getting around the country, though you'd better visit soon. If predicted consequences of the greenhouse effect become a reality, the Maldives will be under threat of extinction from rising sea levels; the country could vanish completely by the year 2020.

HISTORY

The history of the Maldives can be divided into two stages – before and after the conversion to Islam in 1153 AD.

The second stage is well documented through a series of sultanic dynasties to the recent birth and rebirth of the republic. The pre-Muslim period, however, is full of hazy, heroic myth mixed with conjectures based on archaeological discoveries.

The Muslim authorities are not interested in what went on before Islam and tend to use the myths of legendary queens and princes as religious stories to support the ensuing conversion.

It was foreign archaeologists such as H C P Bell early this century and, more recently, Kon-Tiki explorer Thor Heyerdahl who have attempted to explain the tangible, although insubstantial, remains of early civilisations.

Early Days

The first settlers probably arrived in the uninhabited archipelago from Ceylon (Sri Lanka) and southern India, not later than 500 BC.

Thor Heyerdahl, however, explores the theory that the existence of the Maldives was well known long before that. Rather than being isolated or ignored they were, from around 2000 BC onwards, at the trading crossroads of several ancient maritime nations.

He believes the ancient Egyptians, Romans, Mesopotamians and Indus Valley traders all called by at one time or another. Which ones settled to become the legendary sun-worshipping people called the Redin remains a mystery. The Redin left a pagan heritage of beliefs and customs involving evil spirits, or *jinnis*, which still exists today.

Around 500 BC the Redin left or were absorbed by Buddhists, probably from Ceylon, and by Hindus from north-west India. Because the islands were so small and building materials were limited each group built its important structures on the founda-

A	B
C	E
D	

A (TG), B (MB)
C (PS), E (MB)
D (MB)

Top: Bodufoludhu, Ari Atoll (Hummingbird)
Middle: Dhoni rest stop (PS)
Bottom: Sunset, from Malé (MB)

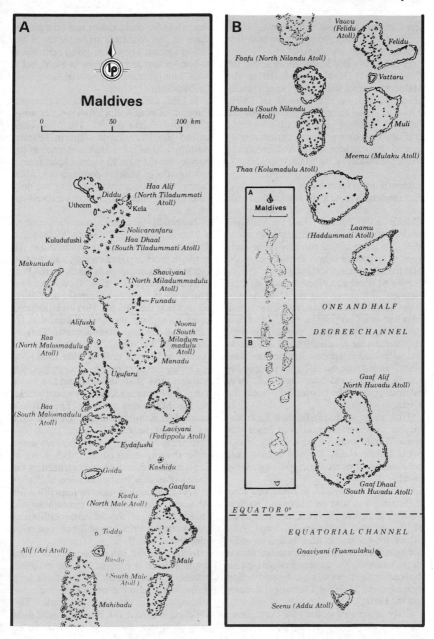

A

Maldives

0   50   100 km

Diddu
Utheem   Haa Alif
(North Tiladummati
Kela   Atoll)

Nolivaranfaru
Kuludufushi   Haa Dhaal
(South Tiladummati Atoll)

Makunudu   Shaviyani
(North Miladummadulu
Atoll)

Funadu

Alifushi   Noonu
(South
Raa   Miladum-
(North   madulu
Malosmadulu   Atoll)
Atoll)   Manadu

Ugufaru

Baa
(South Malosmadulu
Atoll)   Laviyani
(Fadippolu Atoll)
Eydafushi

Goidu   Kashidu

Gaafaru
Kaafu
(North Male Atoll)

Toddu

Alif (Ari Atoll)   Rasdu

(South Male   Male
Atoll)

Mahibadu

B

Vaavu
(Felidu
Atoll)   Felidu

Faafu (North Nilandu Atoll)

Vattaru

Dhaalu (South Nilandu
Atoll)

Muli

Meemu (Mulaku Atoll)

Thaa (Kolumadulu Atoll)

A
Maldives   Laamu
(Haddummati Atoll)

ONE AND HALF

DEGREE CHANNEL

B

Gaaf Alif
North Huvadu Atoll)

Gaaf Dhaal
(South Huvadu Atoll)

EQUATOR 0°

EQUATORIAL CHANNEL

Gnaviyani (Fuamulaku)

Seenu (Addu Atoll)

tions of the previous inhabitants, which explains why many mosques in the Maldives face the sun and not Mecca.

H C P Bell, a British commissioner of the Ceylon Civil Service, returned to the Maldives several times after being initially shipwrecked on the islands in 1879. Amongst other things, he investigated the ruins of Buddhist *dagobas* (dome-shaped edifices containing relics) dotted mostly around the southern atolls, and eventually wrote the history of the Maldives.

Conversion to Islam

Arab traders en route to the Far East had been calling on the Maldives for many years. Known as the 'Money Isles', the Maldives provided enormous quantities of cowrie shells, an international currency of the early ages. (The cowrie is now the symbol of the Maldives Monetary Authority.)

Abu Al Barakat, a North African Arab, is credited with converting the Maldivians to Islam when he killed Rannamaari, a sea jinni, who had been preying on virgins in Malé. According to the legend, young girls were chosen from the community, left in a temple and sacrificed to appease the monster. One night Barakat took the place of a prospective sacrificial virgin and drove the demon away by reading from the Islamic holy book, the Koran.

That may seem far-fetched and best treated as a parable until you learn that certain Hindu sects did practise human sacrifice, and the skulls of young women have been unearthed where the temple supposedly stood.

Whatever happened, the Maldivian king at the time was sold on Islam, and Barakat went on to become the first sultan. A series of six sultanic dynasties followed – 84 sultans and sultanas in all, although some did not belong to the line of succession. At one stage, when the Portuguese first arrived on the scene, there were actually two ruling dynasties, the Malé (or Theemuge) dynasty and the Hilali.

Early in the 16th century the Portuguese, who were already well-established in Goa in western India, decided they wanted a greater share of the profitable trade routes of the Indian Ocean. They were given permission to build a fort and a factory in Malé, but it wasn't long before they wanted more from the Maldives.

In 1558, after a few unsuccessful attempts, Captain Andreas Andre led an invasion army and killed Sultan Ali VI. The Maldivians called the Portuguese captain 'Andiri Andirin' and he ruled Malé and much of the country for the next 15 years. (Apart from a few months of Malabar domination in Malé during the 18th century, this was the only time that another country has occupied the Maldives.)

The brutal Portuguese occupation came to a bloody end in 1573 when Mohammed Thakurufaan, chief of Utheem Island in the northern atoll of Tiladummati, and his two brothers led a commando attack on the Portuguese garrison and slew the lot. Thakurufaan went on to start the next sultanic dynasty, the Utheem. He also introduced coins to replace the cowrie currency. (A memorial centre to commemorate Thakurufaan, the Maldives' greatest hero, was opened on Utheem in November 1986.)

During the next couple of centuries, the Malabar rajas of south India, and to a lesser extent the Portuguese, made frequent attacks on the Maldivian sultans. They didn't succeed in a military sense, but took over trading interests instead.

In the 17th century the Maldives came under the protection of the Dutch rulers of Ceylon. That protection was extended by the British after they took possession of Ceylon in 1796, although it was not formalised for 90 years. Because of the remoteness and unhealthiness of the islands, neither the Dutch nor the British established a colonial administration.

In the 1860s Borah merchants from Bombay were invited to Malé to establish warehouses and shops, but it wasn't long before they acquired an almost exclusive monopoly on the foreign trade. The Maldivians feared the Borahs would soon gain complete control of the islands, so

Sultan Mohammed Mueenuddin II signed an agreement with the British in 1887 which guaranteed the islands' full independence. The Maldives became a British protectorate, in return for defence facilities.

20th Century

The sultanate became an elected position rather than a hereditary one when, in 1932, the Maldives' first constitution was imposed upon Sultan Shamsuddin, who was subsequently deposed. The next sultan, Hasan Nurudin II, abdicated in 1943 and his replacement, the elderly Abdul Majeed Didi, retired to Ceylon (Sri Lanka) leaving the control of the government in the hands of his prime minister, Mohammed Amin Didi.

Amin Didi nationalised the fish export industry, instituted a broad modernisation programme and introduced a total ban on tobacco smoking.

When Ceylon gained independence in 1948 the Maldivians signed a defence pact with the British, which gave the latter control of the foreign affairs of the islands but not the right to interfere internally. In return the Maldivians agreed to provide facilities for the British forces for the defence of the islands and of the Commonwealth.

In 1953 the sultanate was abolished and a republic was proclaimed, with Amin Didi as its first president. Didi was too tough too soon however, and the new government was short-lived. Less than a year after he came to power Didi was overthrown and, during a riot over food shortages, was beaten by a mob and died on Kurumba Island. The sultanate was returned, with Mohammed Farid Didi elected as the 94th sultan of the Maldives.

While Britain, the absentee landlord, did not overtly interfere in the running of the country or impose judicial and cultural changes, it did secure permission to re-establish its wartime airfield on Gan Island in the southernmost Addu Atoll. In 1956 the Royal Air Force began developing the base as a staging post, employing hundreds of Maldivians, and undertook the resettlement of the Gan islanders. The British were infor-

mally granted a 100-year lease of Gan which required them to pay £2000 a year.

When Ibrahim Nasir was elected prime minister in 1957 he immediately called for a review of the agreement with the British on Gan, demanding that the lease be shortened and the annual payment increased.

This was followed by an insurrection against the Maldivian government by the inhabitants of the southern atolls of Addu and Suvadiva (Huvadu), who objected to Nasir's demand that the British cease employing local labour. Undoubtedly influenced by the British presence, they decided to cut ties altogether and form an independent state, electing Abdulla Afif Didi president.

In 1960, however, the Maldivian government officially granted the British the use of Gan and other facilities in Addu Atoll for 30 years (effective from December 1956) in return for the payment of £100,000 a year and a grant of £750,000 to finance specific development projects over a period of years.

In 1962, Nasir sent gunboats from Malé to quash the rebellion in the southern atolls. Afif fled to the Seychelles, then a British colony, while other leaders were banished to various islands in the Maldives.

In 1965 Britain recognised the islands as a completely sovereign and independent state, and ceased to be responsible for their defence (although it retained the use of Gan and continued to pay rent until 1976). The Maldives were granted independence on 26 July 1965 and later became a member of the United Nations.

Following a referendum in 1968 the sultanate was again abolished, Sultan Majeed Didi retired to Ceylon and a new republic was inaugurated. Nasir was elected president.

Nasir ruled for 10 years, seemingly becoming more autocratic each year. The Sri Lankan market for the Maldives' biggest export, dried fish, collapsed in 1972. Fortunately that was the year the tourist industry was born with the opening of Kurumba and Bandos resorts.

Unfortunately, the money generated by

tourism didn't directly benefit the populace. Prices kept going up and there were revolts, plots and banishments as Nasir clung to power. In response to one protest in 1974 Nasir ordered the police to open fire on a large crowd which had gathered to air their grievances.

In 1978, fearing for his life, Nasir stepped down and skipped across to Singapore reputedly with US$4 million from the Maldivian national coffers.

Former university lecturer and Maldivian ambassador to the United Nations, Maumoon Abdul Gayoom, was elected president in Nasir's place. Gayoom's style of governing was much more open, and he immediately denounced Nasir's regime and banished several of the former president's associates.

In 1980 a coup plot against Gayoom, involving mercenaries, was discovered and more banishments occurred; the list included more of Nasir's cohorts. Extradition proceedings began, for the second time, to have Nasir brought back from Singapore to stand trial for murder and theft. They were unsuccessful.

Gayoom was re-elected in 1983 and has done much to further education, health and industry, particularly tourism. He has also given the tiny country a higher international profile with full membership in the Commonwealth of Nations and the South Asian Regional Co-operation (SARC) group.

His main opposition today comes from Muslim fundamentalists who want to return to a more traditional way of life, and from powerful local business barons whose interests are often said to dictate government decisions.

In January 1986, unable to extradite Nasir, the Maldivian High Court sentenced the ex-president *in absentia* to 25 years banishment. He was pardoned in 1988 as a goodwill gesture recognising the role he played in changing the Maldives' status from that of British protectorate to full independence in 1965 (the Maldives joined the UN in the same year).

In September 1988, the 51-year-old Gayoom was re-elected for a third term as president although, as the only candidate, it was really a referendum to see if he should continue in office for another five years. More than 96% of the people voted 'yes'.

Gayoom's sense of security was shattered only a month later. A group of disaffected Maldivian businessmen attempted a coup employing about 400 Sri Lankan Tamil mercenaries. Half of these soldiers infiltrated Malé as visitors, while the rest landed by boat. The mercenaries took the airport on Hulhule Island and several key installations on Malé, but failed to capture the National Security Guard headquarters.

More than 1600 Indian paratroopers, immediately dispatched by Prime Minister Rajiv Gandhi, ended further gains by the invaders who then fled by boat towards Sri Lanka. They took 27 hostages and left 14 people dead and 40 wounded. No tourists were affected.

The mercenaries were later caught by an Indian frigate 100 km from the Sri Lankan coast. According to authorities, four hostages were found dead and three were missing.

Sixty of the mercenaries were returned to the Maldives for trial in July 1989. Several were sentenced to death. (The last death sentence to be carried out in the Maldives was in 1951.)

Ibrahim Nasir has denied any involvement in the coup attempt. The assault was headed by Abdulla Luthufi, a former Maldivian exporter of tropical fish, who had lived in Sri Lanka since 1985.

The coup attempt was the last truly significant event in Maldivian history. Things have been stable since then and the government has settled into promoting tourism more heavily and tourists are now arriving in greater numbers than ever before.

GEOGRAPHY

The Maldives are a chain of 1192 small, low-lying coral islands grouped in clusters, or atolls, about 600 km south-west of Sri Lanka. The word 'atoll' actually derives from the Maldivian word *atolu*.

With a total land area of 298 sq km, the 26 atolls stretch out across the equator in a thin strip 754 km long and 118 km wide. There are no hills or rivers in the Maldives as none of the islands rises more than three metres above sea level or is longer than eight km, though some of the atolls measure up to 40 km long and 20 km wide.

Just how many islands make up the Maldives has only recently been conclusively determined. Estimates throughout history have ranged from 1300 to 13,000. The government now says there are 1192 islands, of which only 202 are inhabited. To further confuse the issue, there are 68 resort islands which are classed as 'uninhabited by Maldivians'.

Some of the islands are simply tiny palm-covered coral sandbanks that take 10 minutes to walk around, while larger islands are covered with bamboo, banyan, mangroves and towering coconut palms.

Built of coral on the peaks of an ancient submerged volcanic mountain range, and protected from the open ocean and the destructive effects of monsoons by barrier reefs, the Maldive atolls have brilliant white sand beaches surrounded by deep, crystal-clear lagoons.

The protective reefs may not be enough, however, to save the Maldives from the disaster which scientific experts warn will befall the islands in the not too distant future. They fear the whole chain of atolls could be submerged within 30 years because of the rising sea levels caused by the greenhouse effect. Island water supplies could run out before the end of the century and already strong tidal waves have left a trail of destruction on several islands.

President Gayoom made an impassioned plea for help to the 1987 Commonwealth Heads of Government conference. The problem is now one of many receiving international attention having been given a high profile at the 1992 SAARC conference.

Coral Atolls
A coral reef or garden is not, as many people believe, formed of multicoloured marine plants. It is rather, a living colony of coral polyps, which are tiny tentacled creatures that feed on plankton.

These coral polyps, which are related to both the jellyfish and the sea anemone, are invertebrates with sack-like bodies and calcerous or horny skeletons. After extracting calcium deposits from the water around them, these polyps excrete tiny cup-shaped limestone skeletons.

A coral reef is the rock-like aggregation of millions of these animals or their skeletons. Only the outer layer of coral is alive. As polyps reproduce and die, the new polyps attach themselves in successive layers to the skeletons already in place.

Charles Darwin was the first to put forward the theory that atolls develop from coral growth that has built up around the edges of a submerged volcanic mountain peak.

In a scenario played out over hundreds of thousands of years, coral first builds up around the shores of a volcanic land mass producing a fringing reef. Then, when the island (often simply the exposed peak of a submarine mountain) begins slowly to sink, the coral continues to grow upwards at about the same rate.

This forms a barrier reef which is separated from the shore of the sinking island by a lagoon. By the time the island is completely submerged, the coral growth has become the base for an atoll, circling the place where the volcanic land mass or mountain used to be.

As the centuries pass, sand and debris accumulate on the higher parts of the reef and vegetation eventually takes root, creating islands. The classic atoll shape is roughly oval, incorporating these islands of coral rubble and enclosing others in deep-water lagoons. There are usually breaks in the reef rim large enough for boats to enter the sheltered lagoon.

CLIMATE
The year is divided into two monsoon periods which also determine the high and low tourist seasons. The north-east monsoon lasts from the beginning of December to the

end of March and marks the high season and high prices. February is the driest and busiest month – the one to avoid if you are travelling.

The wetter south-west monsoon, from the end of April to the end of October, brings the worst weather with stronger winds and storms, particularly in June. For a tourist paying US$2000 for an idyllic fortnight's holiday, visiting in the low season is probably too much of a risk. But the traveller shouldn't balk at it, especially with the prospect of better travel and resort deals.

The temperature ranges between 24°C and 33°C throughout the year, with relatively high humidity. Continual sea breezes keep the air moving and make life quite bearable, but you can't always count on the weather patterns. When I was there at the height of the dry season, it rained continuously over the whole country for more than a week. In Malé, you didn't go out for a walk, you went out for a wade. In recent years, November has been the wettest month by far, followed by May.

FLORA & FAUNA

Plants and animals are not exactly the Maldives' main drawcards, except of course for the amazing wildlife under the sea. The vegetation ranges from thick to sparse to none at all and, while there are no extensive tropical jungles, there are areas of rainforest.

The islands have sandy beaches, lagoons, mangroves, and luxuriant stands of breadfruit trees, banyans, bamboo, pandanus, banana, tropical vines and, naturally, the ubiquitous coconut palm.

Sweet potatoes, yams, taro and millet are grown. No crop is rich or plentiful, except perhaps on the atoll-island of Fuamulaku in the extreme south, where citrus fruits and pineapples grow.

Animals are few and far between, although goats, chickens and the occasional cow are kept.

Giant fruit bats or flying foxes are common to many islands; you'll see them cruising past at dusk. They are not eaten here as they are in the Seychelles. There are pet cats but no dogs, and you may come across

a rat or two. (By the way, those who have visited Bali will appreciate the irony in the Maldivian word for dog – *kuta*.)

The mosquito population varies from island to island but tends not to be too bothersome in Malé and the villages. Only occasionally will you encounter other insects, lizards and creepy-crawlies – none of which are supposed to be dangerous. On the other hand, explorer Thor Heyerdahl tells how one of his expeditioners nearly died after receiving a bite on the leg, which he believed was delivered by a large centipede.

There are more than 700 species of fish in the Indian Ocean, most of which have been seen by diving enthusiasts in the Maldives, which makes the islands one of the best natural aquariums in the world.

You don't even need to be a diver to make the most of the Maldives' underwater tourist attraction. A snorkel, flippers and a few short strokes from the beach will take you into a world of extraordinary beauty where you can swim amongst amazing multicoloured reef fish, skipjack tuna and coral gardens. While divers marvel at half the species, the locals eat the other half.

Coral

Coral is usually stationary and often looks decidedly flowery, but in fact it's an animal and a hungry carnivorous animal at that. Although in the 3rd century AD, a Greek philosopher surmised that coral was really an animal, it was still generally considered to be a plant only 250 years ago.

Corals are Coelenterates, a class of animals which also includes sea anemones and jellyfish. The true reef-building corals or Scleractinia are distinguished by their lime skeletons. It is this relatively indestructible skeleton which forms the coral reef, as new coral continually builds on old dead coral and the reef gradually builds up.

Coral takes a vast number of forms but all are distinguished by polyps, the tiny tube like fleshy cylinders, which look very much like their close relation, the anemone. The top of the cylinder is open and ringed by waving tentacles which sting and draw into the polyp's stomach, the open space within the cylinder, any passing prey. Each polyp is an individual creature, but they can reproduce by splitting to form a coral colony of separate but closely related polyps. Although each polyp catches and digests its own food the nutrition passes between the polyps to the whole colony. Most coral polyps only feed at night, during the daytime they withdraw into their hard limestone skeleton, so it is only after dark that a coral reef can be seen in its full, colourful glory.

Hard corals may take many forms. One of the most common and easiest to recognise is the staghorn coral which grows by budding off new branches from the tips. Brain corals are huge and round with a surface looking very much like a human brain. They grow by adding new base levels of skeletal matter and expanding outwards. Flat or sheet corals, like plate coral, expand out at their outer edges. Many corals can take different shapes depending on their environment.

Like their reef-building relatives soft coral is made up of individual polyps, but they do not form a hard limestone skeleton. Without the skeleton which protects hard coral it would seem likely that soft coral would fall prey to fish, but in fact they seem to remain relatively immune either due to toxic substances in their tissues or due to the presence of sharp limestone needles which protect the polyps. Soft corals can move around and will sometimes engulf and kill off a hard coral.

Coral catch their prey by means of stinging nematocysts. Some corals can give humans a painful sting and the fern like stinging hydroid should be given a wide berth.

Sharks

Sharks are not a problem for divers in the Maldives, there's simply too much else for them to eat. Nevertheless, a variety of sharks can be found around the country and just about every diving school in the Maldives has a shark-spotting dive or two on their itinerary. Usually the sharks are either shy and timid and disappear at first sight or, more often, they simply ignore divers as a harmless intruder.

Sharks are a primitive form of fish with a cartilaginous skeleton. Primitive or not they are superbly practical creatures with a sleek and highly streamlined shape. The white-tipped reef shark is a small, unaggressive, territorial shark rarely more than 1.5 metres long and often seen over areas of coral or off reef edges. Grey reef sharks are also timid, shallow water dwellers which often grow to over two metres in length. On the other hand, if you sight a hammerhead shark you should treat it with caution.

Stingrays & Manta Rays

Rays are essentially flattened sharks but their feeding habits are quite unshark-like. Stingrays are sea-bottom feeders, equipped with

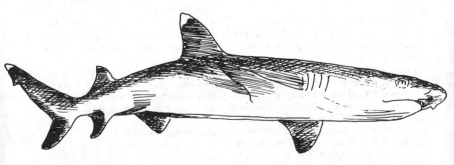

White Tipped Reef Shark

crushing teeth to grind the molluscs and crustaceans they sift out of the sand. They are occasionally found in the shallows, often lying motionless on the sandy bottom of lagoons.

While there is no need to be paranoid about them, it is a good idea to keep your eyes open if you are wading around in a shallow lagoon, as stingrays are less than impressed when a human foot pins them down to the bottom and that barbed and poisonous tail can then swing up and into your leg with painful efficiency.

Manta rays are amongst the largest fish found in the Maldives and a firm favourite of scuba divers. There's nothing quite like the feeling of sensing a shadow passing over the sun and looking up to see a couple of tons of manta ray swooping smoothly through the water above you.

They are quite harmless, feeding only on plankton and small fishes, and in some places seem quite relaxed about divers approaching them closely. Manta rays are sometimes seen to leap completely out of the water, landing back with a tremendous splash. The eagle ray is a close relative of the manta and is also often see by divers in the Maldives.

Despite their shy nature, rays do have one shark-like characteristic in that they generally give birth to live young. A baby manta ray is born neatly wrapped up in its bat-like wings.

Shells

Invertebrate creatures which inhabit shells are all in the group *Mollusca*, although not all molluscs have shells. The group is a huge one including creatures as diverse as common garden snails at one extreme and octopus at the other. The variety of shells found in the Maldives is immense and falls into several categories. *Chitons* or coat-of-mail shells are a small and ancient group. The huge variety of *Gastropods* or univalves includes most of the shells of interest to collectors and interested observers, including the ubiquitous cowries. The third category is the bivalves such as oysters,

clams and scallops. Finally there are *Cephalopoda*, which includes octopus, squid, the pearly nautilus and cuttlefish.

Collecting shells, whether from the ocean floor or from the beach is prohibited in the Maldives. You can purchase shells from souvenir shops and tourist shops on some of the inhabited islands, however, they have often been engraved or set in an earring.

Cowries Cowrie shells are noted for their gently rounded shape, their beautiful patterns and their glossy surface. They are a firm favourite amongst amateur shell collectors, but living examples are mainly seen at night, when they come out in search of food. Maldivian cowries were at one time used as currency and traded with seafarers from the Arab world and India.

Bivalves & Clams Bivalves, which include oysters and scallops, have a bivalve shell which can be closed by powerful muscles. Some bivalves embed themselves in rocks and others can swim, but most live in mud or sand.

Giant Clams are a common sight on reef flats in the Maldives. All bivalves are covered by a flap of skin known as the mantle. The edge of the mantle meets the edge of the shell and creates the shell by adding layer after layer of calcium carbonate along its edge. Only the fleshy shape of the open mantle is visible, but this comes in many different colours and makes a fascinating sight for divers. Stories abound of divers inadvertently putting their foot into the shell opening and being unable to escape when the huge clam clamps shut. As divers and snorkellers will soon realise this is obviously just a story, for the clams shut slowly and none too tightly. Their adductor muscles are certainly strong, however, and persuading a closed clam to reopen is not easy.

Crown-of-Thorns Starfish

The crown-of-thorns is a large 'thorny', brown-coloured starfish. When it finds a patch of coral to its liking it turns its stomach out through its mouth, an activity known as 'stomach eversion', wraps it around the coral and digests the living coral polyps. When the stomach is drawn back in and the starfish moves on to the next tasty coral patch, all that's left is the limestone coral skeleton. A hungry crown-of-thorns can work its way through five square metres of coral in a year. The problem is made worse by the ability the starfish seems to have to send out a message that it has found a tasty coral reef and call in its relatives. Eventually huge numbers of starfish concentrate on one area and when this happens they start to feed day and night instead of hiding during the daylight hours.

The only way to combat the crown-of-thorns appears to be to physically remove them. The Maldivian fisheries and tourism departments are aware of the presence of the starfish and a few dive schools offer divers a reward for each crown-of-thorns brought back to the resort. The problem is by no means out of control, but if you do see a crown-of-thorns while diving, you should certainly consider removing it from the reef (only if you are wearing gloves or have a bag to carry it in).

GOVERNMENT

The Maldivian parliament, the Majlis, or Citizens' Council, has 48 members. Malé, which is the capital island, and each of the atolls has two elected representatives. The president chooses the remaining eight parliamentary representatives; has the power to appoint or dismiss cabinet ministers; and appoints all judges, who administer justice under the tenets of Islam.

The president is nominated by the Majlis and the appointment is put to a national referendum. There is no choice of candidates and to vote against the candidate would be to vote against the chosen religious, as well as military and political leader. Gayoom got in with 98% of the vote. Elections take place every five years.

Local government, of the 19 administrative atolls, is in the hands of each *atolu verin*, or atoll chief. The *gazi* is the religious head of the atoll and joins the atoll chief in deciding legal matters.

ECONOMY

The Maldives has a developing economy based on fishing, tourism and shipping. This is still one of the poorest countries in the world, listed by the UN among the 25 least developed nations. Growth has been consistently strong for the last decade, with the GDP tripling between 1981 and 1991. In the 1990-91 fiscal year, the GDP was estimated to be 1048.1 million Rufiya (or around US$100 million).

Most of the population survives outside the money-based economy, subsisting on fishing, coconut gathering and the growing of millet, corn, yams and sorghum. Cropland is minimal and scattered over many small islands.

Despite efforts to increase agricultural output, nearly all the food for the increasing population has to be imported. The government plans to raise import taxes on fruits and vegetables to encourage people to grow more of their own.

With the exception of the national shipping line and the tuna-canning factory, industry in the Maldives is mostly of the cottage or handicraft type, and includes boat-building, and the making of coconut oil, coir (coconut-husk fibre) and coir products such as rope and matting. Local craft industries are encouraged to expand with assistance from the United Nations Development Programme (UNDP).

Fishing, the traditional base of the economy, employs almost 40% of the labour force and accounts for about 40% of the earnings received from exports. Skipjack tuna is the principal catch, followed by yellowfin, little tuna and frigate mackerel, as well as reef fish such as sharks.

The national shipping line, Maldives Shipping Ltd (MSL), forms the basis of the country's second largest commercial industry.

The fishing industry was dealt a blow in 1972 when the rich Sri Lankan market for 'Maldive Fish' (smoked and dried skipjack tuna) collapsed. The government, however, knuckled down and started mechanising the fishing fleet of *dhonis* and improving navigational aids, although the actual fishing is still done by the pole and line method.

The government took control of a tuna-canning factory in Laviyani atoll, and export markets for canned, frozen and salted fish were opened in Japan, Korea, Singapore and some European countries.

Towards the end of 1981, a glut of tuna on the international market sent the price plummeting. At the same time there was a glut of shipping and freight prices crashed. To make matters worse, the Gulf War between Iraq and Iran hit the Maldives shipping industry, cutting trade and reducing Maldives Shipping Ltd by two-thirds.

The country had to borrow large sums of money and ask for aid, which they managed to get without having to align themselves with a superpower. Instead of accepting an offer from either the Russians or Americans, who had both been after Gan as a military base, the Maldives turned the former RAF base over to two Hong Kong garment manufacturers and the Maldives State Trading Organisation.

The great advantage for the garment firms is that clothing made in the Maldives avoids Western quota restrictions on imports from Hong Kong. The government continues to try to attract investors with offers like tax incentives for resort developers and no foreign exchange controls.

Indians used to come to the Maldives in droves to buy up foreign goods which were cheaper in Malé. But in 1983 the Indian government slashed duty-free allowances for arrivals from Sri Lanka and the Maldives, so these days India has little trade with the islands. In one year, the number of Indian visitors dropped from almost 15,000 to just over 3000, which accounts for the closure of most of the cheap guesthouses in Malé.

Even though the average income is the equivalent of only a few hundred dollars a year, there are no beggars in the Maldives.

Tourism

It was an Italian tour operator, George Corbin, who saw the tourist potential of the Maldives when he visited the islands in 1972. (Coincidentally, *Corbin* was also the name of a French ship wrecked off Fuladu in Baa Atoll in 1602. It made a castaway of François Pyrard, who wrote an account of his experience among the 'natives'.)

Later the same year, after a promotional tour by travel writers, Kurumba Island was opened as a resort and the Italian tourists took to it like Parmesan cheese to Bolognese sauce.

As word spread around Europe, other islands close to Malé were turned into resorts. By 1977 there were 11, and six to eight resorts have been added each year since then, bringing the number to 68 (some undergoing open-ended redevelopment) at the end of 1992. By the end of 1994, there may be another five or six. Tourism receipts in 1991 totalled US$94 million and tourism is by far the largest earner of foreign exchange.

The rate of growth in the tourism market has been nothing short of stunning. The first 1097 tourists arrived in 1972. In 1981 there were 60,358 arrivals. In 1991 there were 196,112 arrivals. The 200,000 barrier was broken for the first time in 1992 – I just happened to be at the airport at the time:

An unsuspecting couple from Italy landed in Malé to be welcomed by numerous officials from various government and non-government organisations and, much to their delight and the envy of all other holiday-makers on their flight, were presented with a free holiday.

Most of the tourists who visit the Maldives are Europeans. Germans (23%), Italians (just under 20%) and British visitors (11.6% in 1990, 7.5% in 1991) are the big three, with a number of resorts being used exclusively by Germans or Italians. French, Swiss, Austrian and Scandinavian visitors make up another 22% of all the visitors to the Maldives. The Asian market is the fastest growing, with Japanese visitors expected to outnumber British visitors for the first time in 1993. The Taiwanese and Hong Kong markets are also developing very quickly, while Korea is being actively targeted as the next boom market. Visitors from Australasia, the Americas and Africa made up 2.7% of all visitors in 1991.

All land is state-owned. Initially the uninhabited islands were leased out to shopkeepers, businesspeople and *befalus* (upper-class people) for agricultural development. Agricultural leases were bought for less than Rf 1000 (US$143).

Then along came the tour operators, hoteliers and other foreign investors. Once they had approval from the government, they would finance the building and management of the resort and either take the Maldivian lessee on as a partner or pay them Rf 50,000 a year. The government gains from taxes and rents. Maldivians now own and run 38 resorts.

Since North and South Malé atolls have been developed, the government is continuing resort expansion into Alif (Ari Atoll).

POPULATION & PEOPLE

According to official estimates, there were 223,273 people living in the Maldives (57,939 of them in Malé) at the end of 1991. With a current annual growth rate of close to 3.5%, the government has projected that there will be around 290,000 at the end of the century. It is thought that the original settlers of the Maldives were Dravidian and Sinhalese people who came from south India and Ceylon. There has also been a great deal of intermarriage and mixing with Arabian and African people.

A distinguishing physical characteristic of Maldivians is their generally small stature. You can tell the difference between the locals and any Indian visitors because the latter are noticeably bigger.

The most obvious character trait of the Maldivian people is their nonaggressive nature. They laugh a lot and anger is rarely openly expressed. Expatriates in Malé will tell you that they have never seen a fight between Maldivians.

That doesn't mean to say they're completely lovable or easily pushed around. One volunteer summed it up when he said violence in Maldivian society was of a psychological, rather than a physical nature; and although the people are openly warm to outsiders, it takes a long time to get over their 'trust threshold'.

You'll find Maldivians don't have a servile attitude towards visitors. Unlike the Sri Lankans, Indians and Pakistanis, they have no experience with colonialism (except with the RAF on Gan). Apart from in Malé, Addu and Ari atolls people may not have seen a White person for several years, if at all.

You can address Maldivians by their first or last name. Since so many men are called Mohammed, Hassan or Ali, the surname is more appropriate and, in many cases, the honorary title. *Maniku* is another title used to bestow respect.

The names Manik and Didi belong, by and large, to the *befalu* or upper-class, privileged families. At the other end of the scale you have the Giravaru people, the descendants of the early settlers from southern India. They are the Maldives aborigines, treated as inferior, and are fast disappearing as a tribe though a small community resides in Malé. Their island, Giravaru, is now a tourist resort.

Many people in Malé have two jobs, particularly the young people. There is a system of bonded labour under which people must work for the government in the morning for a meagre wage and then pursue their chosen occupation for the rest of the day to make ends meet.

This system means that many government departments are overstaffed with people who do very little and don't want to be there. When you go to the Atolls Administration for instance, the service can be painfully slow and frustrating by Western standards. Patience and politeness are naturally advised.

Maldivians generally do not volunteer help and information to visitors. They'll only answer what is asked. If you ask where X is, you will be told X is in Y street; full stop. They will not tell you how to get there, or what there is to see there, or if it no longer exists. You must ask separate questions to elicit that information.

Since Islam forbids the consumption of alcohol many Sri Lankans have been brought over to fill key management positions in resorts, creating a situation resented by Maldivians who have to contend with bouts of high unemployment and low wages. Advancement in any form still tends to be determined by who, rather than what, you know, proving that the class system which existed under the sultans still unofficially applies. As an outsider, it's worth keeping this in mind when you want something.

The adult literacy rate is around 86%. In the atolls there are two types of school: the traditional Islamic *maktabs*, and the atoll education centres which offer a broader curriculum. In Malé there are medium schools which take students up to the English GCE 'O' Level standard and the Science Education Centre which teaches to 'A' Level. English is taught as a second language. Most official forms and publications are printed in both Divehi and English.

The average life expectancy in the Maldives is 52 years – an improvement on the 1977 average which was only 46 years.

CULTURE & SPORT

Sadly, but predictably, Western influences are having a greater effect on the Maldives each year. Videos are the rage, pop music blares out of stores and Michael Jackson T-shirts hang on many young shoulders.

The Divehi culture is slowly eroding and becoming harder to witness, though you can still catch a glimpse of it at the beginning and end of Ramadan and during other holidays and festivals.

Song & Dance

The *bodu beru* drum music is the best known and most performed traditional music. It is what the tourist resort will put on for a local culture night.

There are dances performed to the bodu beru where the participants begin with a slow, nonchalant swaying and swinging of the arms and end in a frenzied state, with some of the dancers entering a trance-like state. One such dance, the *tara*, finishes with the dancers hitting their heads with spikes until they start to bleed. The tara has been banned by the government.

More acceptable is the *bandiya jehun* where young women dance and beat metal pots held under their arms. It is a popular dance on Toddu, to the west of North Malé Atoll, and on Mahibadu in nearby Alif (Ari Atoll).

The author of one local tourist guide, when describing the *tharaa* form of folk music, wrote:

a line of men sit on the ground and beat hand drums (not unlike trampolines) while other men dance between them.

No trampolines accompany the *raivaru* folk song, although they would give some much needed bounce to this 'old type of poetry sung in a dragging tune'.

Most agreeable to Western ears are the love songs. You can buy cassettes of these and also bodu beru music for Rf 45 in several Malé music stores. Ask to hear the tape by Hassan Fulu. Also look out for tapes by Zero Degree Atoll who play traditional music on modern instruments and Meyna Hassan who sings modern Divehi love songs. All of these groups incorporate bodu beru into their music.

Sports & Games

With so little open space in the Maldives, it seems quite amazing that soccer and cricket are the national sports.

Soccer is an all-year affair. On every island there is a daily football match among the young men; it's sort of like an afternoon ritual. There's a league competition in Malé, played at the National Stadium on Majidi Magu, between teams with names such as 'Renown' and 'Victory'. There is also an annual tournament against teams from Sri Lanka.

Cricket, perhaps the only legacy of the British, is also played at the stadium for a few months, beginning in March. Maldivians keenly follow the fortunes of Sri Lanka, India and the other cricketing countries.

On a more traditional level there is *mandi*, a game which sounds like an Indonesian shower and looks like primitive lacrosse, in which players with long sticks have to hurl and catch a small stick; and *bai bala*, which is Maldivian tag-wrestling. There are no regular public exhibitions of either game.

You will, however, see men playing *ouvalhugon'di*, a board game with seeds.

Thin mugoali is a game similar to baseball which has been played in the atolls for more than 400 years. The cubical ball is made of coconut fronds and the bat is made of the sun-hardened lower part of a coconut leaf stem. The *mugoali* or 'bases' are made by rotating on one foot in the sand through 360 degrees leaving a circle behind. The object, as in baseball, is to accrue as many 'home runs' or *landeh* as possible.

Smoking

In the Maldives the cheapest cigarettes you will find are *bidis*, made from imported tobacco rolled in newspaper. Cigarettes generally cost from Rf 10 to Rf 12 for a packet of 20.

More pleasant to smell, and occasionally taste, is the water-cooled hookah or hubble-bubble. The mixture of tobacco flavoured by honey and coconut gives off a lovely aroma.

RELIGION

Islam is the religion of the Maldives and those who practise it are called Muslims. All Maldivians are Muslims of the Sunni sect, as opposed to the Shi'ite sect. There are no other religions or sects present or permitted in the country.

Islam shares its roots with two of the other major religions, Judaism and Christianity, and its teachings correspond closely with the Torah, the Old Testament and Gospels. The essence of Islam, however, is the Koran and the Prophet Mohammed.

Adam, Abraham, Noah, Moses and Jesus are all accepted as Muslim prophets, although Jesus is not recognised as the son of God. According to Islam, all of these prophets received the word of Allah (God), but only Mohammed received the complete revelation.

Mohammed was born in Mecca (now in Saudi Arabia) in 570 AD and had his first revelation from Allah in 610. He began to preach against the idolatry that was rampant in the region, particularly in Mecca, and proved to be a powerful and persuasive speaker attracting a devoted following. His teachings appealed to the poorer levels of society and angered the wealthy merchant class.

By 622, life for Mohammed and his followers became so unpleasant that they were forced to migrate to Medina, 300 km to the north. This migration, known as the *Hejira*, marks the start of the Islamic Calendar: 622 AD became year 1 AH.

In 630 AD Mohammed had gained enough followers to return and take Mecca. Within two decades of Mohammed's death most of Arabia had converted to Islam. With seemingly unlimited ambition and zeal the Prophet's followers spread the word, using force where necessary, and the influence of the Islamic state soon extended from the Atlantic to the Indian Ocean.

Islam in the Maldives is fundamental to all aspects of life; there's no getting away from it unless you go to a resort. It is, however, Islam of a more liberal nature than that adhered to in the Arab states; comparable, rather, to the faith practised in India and Indonesia.

Maldivian women, for example, do not have to observe *purdah*, which is the custom of keeping women in seclusion, with clothing that conceals them completely when they go out.

Children are taught the Arabic alphabet and, until their mid-teens, attend a *maktab*, one of the traditional Islamic schools where the reading and reciting of the Koran is taught.

There are mosques for the men and for the women. Most are of simple, unadorned design, both inside and out and, apart from the new Islamic Centre in Malé, they are not much to look at.

Mosque

The Five Pillars of Islam

Islam is the Arabic word for submission and underlies the duty of all Muslims to submit themselves to Allah.

Shahada, the profession of faith that 'There is no God but Allah and Mohammed is his prophet', is the first of the Five Pillars of Islam – the tenets that guide Muslims in their daily life.

This first pillar is accomplished through prayer which, in turn, is the second pillar. *Salath* is the call to prayer and Islam decrees that Muslims must face Mecca and pray five times each day. In the Maldives, salath is also called *namadh*.

The third pillar is *zakat*, the act of giving alms to the needy. Some Islamic countries have turned this into an obligatory land tax which goes to help the poor.

All Muslims must fast during the day for the month of *Ramadan*, the ninth month of the Islamic calendar.

The fifth pillar is the *haj* or pilgrimage to Mecca, the holiest place in Islam. It is the duty of every Muslim who is able, to make the haj at least once in their life.

Prayer Times

The initial prayer session is in the first hour before sunrise, the second around noon, the third in mid-afternoon around 3.30 pm, the fourth at sunset, and the final session in early evening.

The call to prayer is delivered by the *mudeem* or *muezzin*. In former days, he climbed to the top of the minaret and shouted it out. Now a cassette recording, relayed by loudspeakers on the minaret, announces the call and the mudeem even appears on TV.

Shops and offices close for 15 minutes after each call. Some people go to the mosque, some kneel where they are and others do not participate.

Ramadan

The fourth pillar of Islam is the fast during the month of Ramadan, which begins at the time of a full moon and ends with the sighting of the new moon. The Ramadan month varies from year to year but is usually sometime between February and April.

During Ramadan Muslims do not eat, drink, smoke or have sex between sunrise and sunset, and working hours are restricted. Exceptions are granted to young children, pregnant or menstruating women and those who are travelling. It is a difficult time for visitors, as cafés are closed during the day and everybody is generally on edge. The evenings, however, are long and lively.

Marriage & Divorce

A Mexican divorce is a long, drawn-out affair compared to a Maldivian divorce. All the man has to do is to say 'I divorce you', or words to that effect, three times in quick succession; notify the local minister or *gazi*; and that's the end of the marriage. No questions are asked, however, the woman is not permitted to remarry for three months to ensure that she is not pregnant to her ex-husband, and the man is required to pay for the upkeep of all the children of the marriage.

Many couples are married one day and divorced the next. He'll go fishing and that's the last she sees of him. It is not uncommon to find men who have been married more than 20 times and no surprise to learn that the Maldives has the highest rate of divorce in the world. In 1990 there were 3880 marriages and 3412 divorces in Malé alone, with most of the newly weds and divorcees aged between 15 to 19 years. As a consequence, Maldivians, unlike the Muslims of the Comoros, do not go in for elaborate, expensive weddings.

Men who can afford it are permitted to have more than one wife, but there is little reason to do this, apart from as a status symbol. Gossip is rife, but promiscuity is not. Religion, the family and the birth rate make sure of that. Birth control devices may only be used by married couples.

Circumcision

A circumcision is cause for a big celebration in the Maldives – worth going to if you can get an invitation. The celebrations for this event seem to make up for the lack of wedding ceremonies and, more to the point, for the pain experienced by the six-year-old child. In fact, the festivities are held to entertain the snipped boy. Often several boys will be done at once and there will be one big carnival to save expense.

The boys lie on their beds, or wooden platforms, each with a sheet suspended over their lower bodies while the merriment continues around them. There is singing, dancing and lots to eat – for the guests; it takes the youngsters three days to get back on their feet.

You'll know when a circumcision party is in progress by the noise and the coloured lights which often decorate the house and yard. Most circumcisions take place during the school holidays.

The government has a dim view of female circumcision recognising it for the barbaric rite that it is. It is now only rarely practised, and then only in secret, in some of the outer atolls.

Local Beliefs

In the islands people still fear *jinnis*, the evil spirits which come from the sea, land and sky. They are blamed for everything that can't be explained by religion or education.

To combat jinnis there are *fandita*, which are the spells and potions provided by the local *hakeem* or medicine man. The hakeem is often called upon when illness strikes, if a woman fails to conceive, or if the fishing catch is poor.

The hakeem might cast a curing spell by writing phrases from the Koran on strips of paper and sticking or tying them to the patient. Another method is to write the sayings in ink on a plate, fill the plate with water to dissolve the ink and make the patient drink the potion.

Other concoctions include *isitri*, a love potion used in matchmaking, and its antidote *varitoli*, which is used to break up marriages. Judging by the divorce statistics it isn't really needed, or perhaps it's overused.

LANGUAGE

The language of the Maldives is Divehi. It is closely related to an ancient form of Sinhala, a Sri Lankan language, but also contains some Arabic, Hindi and English words.

Divehi has its own script, Tana, which was introduced by the great Maldivian hero Thakurufaan after he tossed out the Portuguese in the 16th century. Tana looks like shorthand and is read from right to left (their

Ancient stone plaque with heiroglyphic script

front page is our back page). There are 24 letters in the alphabet.

The first thing you should know about the language is that Maldives is pronounced *mawl-divs* – as in 'gives' not 'dives'.

On most islands you'd be very lucky to find anyone who speaks anything other than Divehi, although you can get around Malé and Hitadu easily enough with just English. Hitadu is the capital of Seenu, the southernmost atoll, where the British employed most of the islanders on the air base for 20 years.

The romanised transliteration of the language is a potpourri of phonetic approximations, and words can be spelt in a variety of ways. This is most obvious if you study Maldivian place names. For example: Majidi Magu is also spelt Majeedhee and Majeedee; Sosun Ge could be Soasan Ge; Hitadu becomes Hithadhu and Hithadhoo; and Fuamulak can be Fua Mulaku, Foahmmulah or, thanks to one 19th century mariner, Phoowa Moloku.

To add to the confusion several islands have the same name (there are six called Viligili), and there are both traditional *and* administrative names for each of the 19

atolls. On top of all this, dialects vary throughout the country.

The government is party to these variations. There seems to be no officially correct, or even consistent, spelling of Divehi words in their English literature. For the sake of uniformity in this book I have tried to keep to the most basic spelling and have not added vowels or consonants if they do not radically affect the pronunciation.

Maldivians tend not to believe their ears when they first hear a foreigner speaking their language. However, if you persevere with it, they will delight in helping you learn a few more useful phrases, and even if you only learn a few words, the Maldivians you meet will be very appreciative of your interest.

The best phrasebook available is *Practical Divehi* by M Zuhair (Novelty Press, Malé, 1992). It is available from the Novelty Bookshop in Malé and in a number of the resort shops. Here are a few words and phrases to whet your appetite.

Greetings & Civilities
Hello/Farewell.	*a-salam alekum*
peace	*salam*
How are you?	*haalu kihine*
Very well. (reply)	*vara gada*
See you later.	*fahung badaluvang*
fine, good, great	*barabah*
OK	*enge*
Thank you.	*shukuria*

Some Useful Words
I, me	*aharen, ma*
you, she, he	*kale, mina, ena*
name	*nang, nama*
yes	*aa*
no	*noo*
expensive	*agu bodu*
very expensive	*vara agu bodu*
cheap	*agu heyo*
enough	*heo*
now	*mihaaru*
little (for people, places)	*kuda*
mosquito	*madiri*
mosquito net	*madiri ge*
toilet	*gifili*

inside	*etere*
outside	*berufarai*
water (rain, well)	*vaare feng, valu feng*

Some Useful Verbs

swim	*fatani*
eat	*kani*
walk	*hingani*
sleep	*nidani*
sail	*duvani*
go	*dani*
stay	*hunani*
dance	*nashani*
wash	*donani*

Some Useful Phrases

How much is this?	*mi kihavaraka*
What is that?	*e korche*
What did you say?	*kike*
I'm going	*Aharen dani*
Where are you going?	*kong taka dani*
How much is the fare?	*fi kihavare*

People

friend	*ratehi*
father, mother	*bapa, mama*
atoll chief	*atolu verin*
island chief	*kateeb*
VIP, upper-class person	*befalu*
White person (tourist or expat)	*don miha*
community religious leader	*gazi*
prayer caller	*mudeem*
fisherman	*mas veri*
toddy man	*ra veri*
evil spirit	*jinni*

Places

atoll	*atolu*
island	*fushi* or *rah*
sandbank	*finolhu*
reef or lagoon	*faru*
street	*magu*
lane or small street	*golhi* or *higun*
mosque	*miski*
house	*ge*

Time & Days

day	*duvas*
week	*hafta*
month	*mas*
year	*aharu*
tomorrow	*madamma*
today	*miadu*
yesterday	*iye*
tonight	*mire*
Monday	*horma*
Tuesday	*angaara*
Wednesday	*buda*
Thursday	*brassfati*
Friday	*hukuru*
Saturday	*honihiu*
Sunday	*aadita*

Numbers

1	*eke*
2	*de*
3	*tine*
4	*hatare*
5	*fahe*
6	*haie*
7	*hate*
8	*ashe*
9	*nue*
10	*diha*
11	*egaara*
12	*baara*
13	*tera*
14	*saada*
15	*fanara*
16	*sorla*
17	*satara*
18	*ashara*
19	*onavihi*
20	*vihi*
30	*tiris*
40	*saalis*
50	*fansaas*
60	*fasdolaas*
70	*hai-diha*
80	*a-diha*
90	*nua-diha*
100	*sateka*

Facts for the Visitor

VISAS & EMBASSIES

Visas are not required by any nationality except Sri Lankans. Israeli passport holders are not generally permitted to enter the Maldives, while South African passport holders should make advance enquiries to determine if they will be permitted entry or not.

You get a one-month visitor's permit (no fee) on arrival unless you're Indian, Pakistani, Bangladeshi or Italian, in which case you get a 90-day permit. It is difficult to extend this permit (see the following section) unless you continue to stay on resorts and have sufficient funds.

Maldivian Embassies

Maldivian diplomatic representatives overseas include:

Austria
    Gerald Wiedler, Peter Jordan Strasse 21-250, 1190 Vienna (☎ 343438)
Germany
    Maldivian Consul, Immanuel Kant Strasse 16, D-6380 Bad Homburg (☎ 6902624)
Japan
    Tsuyoshi Fumizono, 712, 5-10 1-Chome, Kamimeguro, Meguro-ku, Tokyo (☎ 03 7113511)
Sri Lanka
    Maldivian High Commission, 25 Melbourne Ave, Colombo 4 (☎ 586762)
Sweden
    Stephen Ericson, Gamla Brogatan 32, S-11120, Stockholm (☎ 08-247550)
Switzerland
    Marc Odermatt, Gerechtigkeitsgasse 23, 8002 Zürich (☎ 01-2029785)

Visa Extensions

If you want to apply for an extension go to the Department of Immigration (☎ 323913) on the 2nd floor in the Huravee Building next to the police station in Malé. You must first buy an Extension of Tourist Visa form (Rf 2) from one of the last two windows on the right at the immigration department. After filling the form in and having it signed and stamped by your sponsor, you must return it to the Immigration Department between 7.30 and 9.30 am. Simply walk through the door with the 'Staff Only' sign (to the left as you face the window where you bought your form), and find a staff member who will speak with you. Extensions are granted for up to an additional three months at Rf 300 for each extension (one month per extension). Be warned that overstaying your visa is not worth the expense and hassles that it can cause.

Work Visas

Work visas are issued but they are mainly for tourism-related employment. This generally means diving and other water-sport instructors or helicopter pilots. The necessary papers are only issued from outside the country, so if you do organise work while in the Maldives, you will have to leave the country for a few weeks while your application is processed.

Foreign Consuls

The diplomatic corps in the Maldives is not very large and includes:

Denmark/Sweden
    Abdulla Saeed, Cyprea, 25 Marine Drive (☎ 322451)
France
    Mohamed Ismail Manik, 27 Chandani Magu (☎ 323760)
Germany
    Farouk Ismail, 10 Faridi Magu (☎ 322669)
India
    High Commission, Orchid Magu (☎ 323015). It does not issue tourist visas for India. If you don't have one already, you'll have to go to Colombo to get one.
USA
    Rasheeda Mohamed Didi, Violet Magu (off Sosun Magu) (☎ 322581)

There is no British or Australian representation. If you lose your passport, you will have to get an identity certificate from the Department of Immigration to get yourself to Colombo or Singapore. Australian, US, UK, Canadian and most Western European nationals do not need a visa to enter Sri Lanka. Sri Lanka does have a diplomatic mission in the Maldives, as do Pakistan and Bangladesh. Libya and the PLO are also said to have official representatives in Malé.

PERMITS

A few years ago a group of Italian tourists invaded an island, threw off their clothes and tried to convert the fishing community back to sunworshipping. Ever since then all inhabited islands have been declared off-limits to travellers.

The days of casual island-hopping are over as the government resolves to keep Muslim Maldivian society separate from and untainted by Western ways. You now must apply to the Ministry of Atolls Administration, next to Air Maldives in the Fashanaa Building on Marine Drive in Malé, for a permit to visit any island, other than a resort, which is inhabited.

At the time of researching this book, the permit regulations were being changed. While there is, as yet, no official government translation of the relevant conditions, the Ministry of Atolls Administration carefully scrutinised and edited a translation of the almost completed official Divehi version kindly done for Lonely Planet by Malé based journalist and translator M Zuhair.

Essentially the regulations state that all permit applications must be submitted in writing. You must supply your name, passport number, nationality, the name of the island/atoll which you intend to visit, how long you intend to stay there, the name and address of your sponsor, the name and registry number of the vessel with which you will be travelling to your destination and the purpose of your visit.

It may also be worth approaching your country's consular representative or writing to the relevant government departments in Malé for their backing. The more official-looking names and paperwork you have, the better.

As a tourist, your sponsor should ideally be a friend on the island who will be prepared to vouch for you, feed and accommodate you. This support must be given in writing, preferably with an OK from the *kateeb* (island chief), and submitted with your application. (The letter must come from the island not from Malé.)

As it is unlikely you already have contacts in the Maldives, you will need to make friends quickly on arrival in Malé. Guest-house managers/owners and souvenir salespeople are good starting points. Most Malé residents will have friends or family on various atolls, which of course will determine your choice of island.

Getting a letter of support-cum-invitation back from the island, however, could take up to two weeks depending on how isolated it is from Malé.

The Atolls Administration itself is slow and discouraging so perseverance and patience are necessary. If you succeed, you pay Rf 10 for the permit which will specify which atolls or islands you can visit. Try to get an atoll approval that will give you authority to visit any island within it. Permits are issued only between 8.30 and 11 am on all days except government holidays. These hours are strictly enforced and absolutely no exceptions will be made.

As soon as you land on an island you must go to the island office to present the permit. Don't land without one as island and atoll chiefs are fearful of breaking these rules, so they will enforce them. Note also that it is illegal for anyone to request payment for accommodation on an inhabited island. This means that any offers mentioning money that you might hear about in Malé are, without exception, shady. While it may be tempting to try and circumvent some of these rules, keep in mind that while the worst thing that can happen to you is a fine or deportation, a Maldivian involved in any such dealings could find themselves in all kinds of trouble if found out.

Outside of Malé and the resorts the only

atoll you may visit without a permit is Seenu (traditionally called Addu Atoll). Getting there, however, is not so simple. You must fly to Gan and stay at the Ocean Reef Club – the former RAF officers' and sergeants' mess. From there causeways link the village islands of Hitadu, Maradu and Feydu.

Most resorts run day trips to inhabited and uninhabited islands, including Malé if they're close enough, mostly to buy and sell souvenirs. You do not need a permit for these trips. The same applies if you are staying in Malé and someone representing your guest-house or hotel accompanies you on your day trip.

The only other way for a tourist to legally obtain a permit for travel to the outer atolls is by joining a safari cruise (see the Maldives Getting Around chapter for more information). If you are on such a cruise with an officially registered safari company, the company should be able to make all the necessary arrangements. That said, if you hope to visit and dive at sites of historical importance, there may be a considerable increase in the amount of paper work involved.

Finally, the most obvious condition applied to a permit is also the most important:

It is prohibited for foreigners on inter-atoll trips to conduct or participate in any activity that might jeopardise the peace and harmony prevailing in the country. Legal action shall be taken against persons known to conduct such activities.

Essentially this means respect the country, the people and the culture. In addition the government reserves the right to impose a fine of Rf 100 on any foreigner travelling in the outer atolls without a permit or in any other way in breach of the conditions.

CUSTOMS

Malé International Airport is on Hulhule Island, two km across the water from the capital. Customs, immigration and health checks are relatively perfunctory if you are on the way to a resort with all the other passengers, or if it looks like you are.

Because the Maldives are Islamic, no alcohol or pornography can be brought into the country. You will get your duty-free bottle of Scotch back when you leave. Pornography may include women's magazines such as *Cleo* or *Cosmopolitan*, pictures of women in bras or even demonstrating a breast self-examination are considered offensive. Your magazine is more likely to have the offending pages ripped out than be confiscated, however.

You will be asked on the immigration form where you are staying. If you have not booked a place, put down the name of any resort, otherwise the immigration officials will take your passport from you and make you arrange accommodation somewhere before they let you leave the airport.

MONEY

The unit of currency is the rufiya (Rf), which is divided into 100 larees. Notes come in denominations of 500, 100, 50, 20, 10, five and two rufiya. Coins are in denominations of 50, 25, 10, five, two and one rufiya.

Bring your money in US dollars because that currency carries the most weight in the Maldives. Visitors must pay accommodation and most travel expenses with the greenback. Guesthouses will take travellers' cheques.

There are no currency restrictions when you change money into rufiya but you are only allowed to re-convert 10% of that amount on departure, and only then if you have the original bill of exchange. So don't get caught with too many rufiya at the end of your visit.

US$1	=	Rf 10
A$1	=	Rf 7
UK£1	=	Rf 16
C$1	=	Rf 8
DM1	=	Rf 6
1FF	=	Rf 2
Y100	=	Rf 8

The exchange rate is published daily in the *Haveeru* newspaper in Divehi script.

Banks

The six banks in Malé are clustered at the harbour end of Chandani Magu and along Marine Drive (East). They are open Sunday to Thursday from 9 am to 1 pm, and on Saturday to 11 am. They are closed on Friday. If you need to have money wired to you in Malé, don't leave it till the last minute. While it might come through quickly, travellers report of waiting penniless in Malé for two or three weeks.

While there are various methods of transferring money internationally, Swift seems to be the most efficient in the Maldives. If you want your money handed over to you in the currency in which it was sent rather than in rufiya, then stick to US dollars. You may still have to fight for it, but you should succeed.

Reconversion of currency can only be done officially if you have receipts to prove that you originally bought your rufiya at the official rate. The best places to reconvert are at the Monetary Authority on Chandani Magu or at the bank at the airport. If you have an early morning flight, change your money the day before you leave, as the airport bank may be closed.

While it is possible to exchange travellers' cheques from currencies other than the US dollar, UK pound or German mark, you would be well advised to avoid the hassles involved by sticking to the big three. Japanese yen are becoming easier to exchange and in the Italian and French resorts, you won't have any problems with francs and lire. The most common difficulty is 'transfer problems with correspondents'. In other words, they have had difficulty cashing the cheques.

There are a number of official and unofficial moneychangers in Malé. They generally stick rigidly to the official rates, but usually only buy US dollars. Many of them will change US-dollar traveller's cheques into US dollars cash with little or no commission. Ask in guesthouses, souvenir shops and hardware stores.

Black Market

Until mid-1987, there was an active black market in currency. There were plenty of unofficial moneychangers in Malé and little danger from authorities. The black market no longer exists, however, as the government has set more realistic rates for buying and selling rufiya.

Credit Cards

Major credit cards are accepted. The American Express representative is Universal Enterprises (☎ 323116) on Marine Drive.

Costs

If you are on a very tight budget then your movements in the Maldives will be extremely limited. If you stay in Malé, you will be able to get by on around US$25 a day if you are on your own. Two people could manage on around US$20. Basically you have the US$6 per person daily bed tax plus the cost of accommodation and eating. If you want to do day trips from Malé to the islands, your costs could skyrocket. See the Maldives Getting Around chapter for details.

The cheapest resorts start with doubles for around US$50 in the low season. This covers you for your room and two or three meals a day. If you want to dive, fish or take part in any of the other activities, you will have to allow more. Diving is without a doubt the single most expensive part of the holiday for people who stay on the cheaper resorts, with every dive costing from about US$25 to US$45 or more, depending on how much equipment you brought with you or what kind of diving package you arrange (ie multiple dives or single ones).

Finally, don't forget to budget for drinks. Apart from coffee or tea with meals and juice with breakfast, drinks are not free. Expect to pay US$3 to US$5 or more for a beer. The price of drinks is approximately proportional to the cost of the resort.

Tipping

There is a 10% service charge in many resorts, but not in the restaurants and cafés of Malé. Airport porters obviously expect a reasonable tip; Rf 10 or US$1 is usual.

Bargaining

Bargaining is limited to the tourist shops in and around the Singapore Bazaar in Malé and at island village stalls where prices are not fixed. Because most tourists come on brief one-off shopping excursions from the resorts, some traders will charge what they feel they can get away with, knowing there is little chance an unhappy customer will return.

SUGGESTED ITINERARIES

Around 85% of all visitors to the Maldives arrive with their itinerary more or less pre-planned. The standard practice is to book one or two weeks on a single resort as part of an all encompassing package deal. Just about everyone else who comes here on holiday arranges a resort package when they arrive at the airport or in Malé.

In the event that you are intent on spending a week or two of legal independent island hopping, you should expect major hassles at every turn and you will need a serious wad of US dollars to see you through.

One of the more appealing options for travellers who do decide to go it alone is a resort-hopping trip from the south of Ari Atoll to Malé. This requires patience and good organisation as well as time to burn but, if the sea is not too rough, it comes highly recommended from the author who personally followed this route among others. Such trips are only possible if you always make your arrangements a day in advance. This means telephoning ahead to the resort where you hope to spend the next night to ensure that they have room for you. It is also extremely important to make sure that they will be able to organise transport for you from their island to the next island on your itinerary.

Do not underestimate the importance of pre-arranging your transport away from any resort before you arrive there. All resorts in the Maldives have a limited number of dhonis and they will not under any circumstances hire them out if they are required for their longer term guests (for diving trips and so on). I literally had to wade and swim between nearby islands on two occasions because transport simply could not be arranged. You should not attempt this unless you are a strong swimmer and you have a hat and a strong sunscreen. If you put your luggage in a watertight bag full of air it should float well enough to drag if not to use as a raft. One option if you are having trouble getting any further might be to join an island-hopping tour and simply get off at another resort.

On another occasion I convinced the manager of one resort to hire out a canoe at triple the normal hire rate and send someone to pick it up from a nearby resort the next day when they had a spare dhoni for a few hours. Yet another method I used was to pay for a 'sailing lesson' and have the instructor sail me, luggage and all, by catamaran to the next resort. You should never count on these options, but when things get desperate, try them out – you just might get lucky.

Day one
>   Helicopter flight to Maafushivaru. Dhoni to Angaga resort. If there are no packaged passengers for Angaga or nearby Mirihi, you will have to pay around US$30 for a dhoni to come from Angaga to pick you up (about 1½ hours each way). If the dhoni is not at the helipad when you arrive, you might consider going across to Maafushivaru resort (five minutes by dhoni from the helipad – assuming there is a dhoni making the trip) until your transport arrives.

Day two
>   Angaga

Day three
> Resort hopping. You will probably have to pay around US$100 for a day's dhoni hire if you can convince the resort to part with one of their vessels for that long. If you start out early enough, you should be able to visit Mirihi, Thundufushi and Athuruga before settling in for the night on Moofushi (unless you want to stop earlier of course). Note that while these resorts do not cater for English-speaking guests, none of them will object to your presence if you have prebooked. Do not turn up unannounced.

Day four
> Resort hopping. For around US$30 you will be transported from Moofushi to Fesdu. From Fesdu to Maayafushi or Halaveli takes a little over an hour and should cost around US$25. Halaveli can be recommended as a 1st-class meal stop, but do not under any circumstances arrive unannounced as you will not be welcome. For the night your best option would be either Maayafushi or Bathala.

Day five
> Maayafushi or Bathala

Day six
> Maayafushi or Bathala to Kuramathi. You may find it difficult to convince either island to part with a dhoni. Kuramathi may send a speedboat to pick you up for around US$70. If you are not having any luck try to get to Madoogali or Velidu. Sometimes diving boats from Bathala stop at Velidu for lunch after a morning dive on nearby Velidu Tila.

Day seven
> You shouldn't have too much trouble getting from Kuramathi to Malé. If you spent the night on Velidu or Madoogali you can either try to get to Malé by dhoni or speedboat or, alternatively head for Nika Hotel and take a chopper from nearby Bodhufolhudu back to Malé. Never assume that there will be a flight or that there will be room for unannounced passengers.

If you have more time, you can either take in more islands or increase the amount of time spent on each island. This itinerary is clearly one of many possibilities. You can just as 'easily' spend a week or two doing the same thing in North or South Malé Atoll. Another option, which is certainly easier to organise, is to make a series of day trips out of Malé. See the Maldives Getting Around chapter for information on daily boat hire out of Malé.

WHEN TO GO
The timing of your trip will depend on your priorities. If you're looking for a few extra hours of sunshine then you should go between October and April or May, with March a notoriously sunny month. Of course, this is the season when everyone visits. If you're willing to go where the beds are, then you will find a resort, however, you may have to hunt around for a while. As you may have guessed, the resorts are also more expensive during the high season.

The rest of the months, from May to September, make up the low season. There are fewer people meaning a greater choice of resorts and lower prices to boot. Of course, you don't get as much sunshine and rain falls considerably more often. Note also that Christmas is the busiest time of all and some resorts raise their prices above the high-season standard.

Late October, early November and late March/early April mark approximate boundaries in the turn of the monsoon and are sometimes said to be associated with increased clarity and visibility for divers.

WHAT TO BRING
Despite the proliferation of palm leaves on the Maldives, the Maldivians are not great hat weavers, or even wearers. So make sure you bring some sort of head gear with you as protection against the sun because there aren't many hats for sale on the islands, and those available in tourist shops or resort shops are expensive.

There is a slight drop in temperature during the night but not enough to warrant bringing a thick jumper. Packing a light-weight sweater, however, is a good idea, and a waterproof cape or jacket is strongly advised, especially if you're not confined to a resort. Plastic bags can be useful for protecting clothes, cameras, documents and other items during sea journeys.

A duffle bag or internal frame backpack, which can be carried as a suitcase is fine for carrying your belongings. There are very few occasions when you'll do a lot of walking or have to carry your luggage too far. Backpacks can signal 'poor traveller' and you can kiss any chance of a permit goodbye.

Although nudity or topless bathing for women is strictly forbidden, skimpy bikinis and bathers are quite acceptable in the resorts. In Malé and on other inhabited islands, however, travellers should make an effort not to offend or excite the townsfolk. Men should never go bare chested and women should wear skirts or shorts that cover their thighs, and avoid wearing low-cut tops.

TOURIST INFORMATION
There is a Department of Tourism information desk in the lobby of the Nasandhura Palace Hotel on Marine Drive in Malé, which offers minimal tourist literature and advice. They'll give you a free map of Malé Island and Atoll and neighbouring Alif Atoll with a list of resorts. They have another desk at the airport.

For more specific enquiries, go to the Department of Tourism head office (☎ 323224/8) in the Ghaazee Building opposite the police station.

The adjacent Huravee Building houses the Department of Information & Broadcasting (☎ 323837) which is responsible for Maldives TV and radio. They issue a fortnightly news sheet in English and will assist with any legitimate research.

For historical, cultural and linguistic information try the National Centre for Linguistic & Historical Research on Sosun Magu a couple of blocks north of the hospital and on the other side of the road.

Overseas Reps
In addition to the Maldivian diplomatic representatives listed in this chapter you can contact the Maldives Department of Tourism, (☎ 02407-3129) Glebe House, Welder's Lane, Chalfont St Peter, Buckinghamshire, UK. While there are no definite plans yet, the possibility of setting up tourism offices in Australia and Japan has been broached.

USEFUL ORGANISATIONS
The lack of diplomatic representation is compensated for by a multinational community of volunteer workers. These people and the organisations for which they work are often good sources of information and help.

These organisations are led by the British Voluntary Service Overseas (VSO). The VSO offices (☎ 323167) are at Gongali Magu near Orchid Magu. While visitors are welcome, they prefer you to telephone first rather than just drop in.

The VSO, whose volunteers work in nursing, planning, teaching and other roles, is supplemented by six or seven Australian Volunteers Abroad (AVA). The Japanese take charge of dentistry and sports. The Danish and Americans are involved in health, while Norway and the USA run the Save the Children missions.

There are also the United Nations' agencies: UNDP, UNICEF and UNESCO. The UN Development Program (UNDP) predominates, providing aid to the agriculture, fishing and craft industries. The office (☎ 324501/2/3) is in Kulidoshi Magu.

The volunteers, together with other expatriates, can often be contacted informally at the bar of the Alia Hotel between 6 and 11 pm, if the bar is operational.

BUSINESS HOURS & HOLIDAYS
Government offices are open every day, except Friday, from 7.30 am to 1.30 pm. During Ramadan, hours are from 9 am to 1 pm.

Business hours vary. In Malé the shops at the bottom of Chandani Magu open earlier and those on Majidi Magu close later, but in general they all open between 7 and 8 am and close between 9 and 11 pm every day, including Friday. These hours are interrupted by prayer calls when doors close for about 15 minutes. The streets are quietest around the time of the last two prayer calls, between 6 and 8 pm, although lunch time from 1.30 to 3 pm is also quiet.

Holidays
Most holidays are based on the Islamic lunar calendar and the dates vary from year to year.

Ramadan
Known as *rorda mas* in the Maldives, this is the Islamic month of fasting. Ramadan is the most important religious event and will occur from 12 February to mid-March in 1994; 1 February to the first week of March in 1995; and 22 January to late February in 1996.

Kuda Id
This occurs at the end of Ramadan, with the sighting of the new moon, and is celebrated with a feast.

Prophet's Birthday
The birthday of the Prophet Mohammed is celebrated with three days of eating and merriment. The dates are: 30 August 1993, 19 August 1994, 9 August 1995 and 28 July 1996.

Huravee Day
The day the Malabars of India were kicked out by Sultan Hassan Izzuddeen after their brief occupation in 1752.

Martyr's Day
Commemorates the death of Sultan Ali VI at the hands of the Portuguese in 1558.

Fixed holiday dates are:

New Year's Day
1 January

National Day
A major event celebrating the day Mohammed Thakurufaan and his men overthrew the Portuguese on Malé in 1578, it is celebrated on the first day of the third month of the lunar calendar.

Independence Day
26 July – the day the British protectorate ended

Victory Day
3 November – celebrates the victory over the Sri Lankan mercenaries who tried to overthrow the Maldivian government in 1988

Republic Day
11 November – commemorates the second (current) republic, founded in 1968. Celebrated in Malé with lots of pomp, brass bands and parades.

Fisheries Day
10 December

POST & TELECOMMUNICATIONS
Post

The post office is on Chandani Magu, a couple of blocks north of Majidi Magu. It is open daily, except Friday, from 7.30 am to 12.45 pm and from 4 to 5.50 pm. (These hours are strange but precise.)

To send a postcard anywhere overseas costs Rf 7 and a standard airmail letter costs Rf 10. Complications start with parcel post and customs formalities. There is a poste restante service.

On the resorts you can buy stamps and postcards at the shop or the reception. Generally there is a mailbox at the reception.

Telephone

A new national telephone service started in 1988. All Malé numbers are prefixed with 32 and numbers on other islands (the resorts) with 34.

Public telephones are few and far between, but shopkeepers will let you use their phone for Rf 2 a local call. You can also call overseas from any private phone which has been registered for international calls, either through the international operator in Malé (☎ 190) or by direct dialling. Alternatively you can go to Dhiraagu (the Maldives cable & wireless company) on Meduziyaaraiy Magu, near the intersection with Chandani Magu.

Since the introduction of International Direct Dialling to the Maldives, the international telephone service has become as efficient as any in the world. By European standards it is reasonably priced: the charges are US$2.13 per minute to Singapore and the SAARC nations (sub-continent), US$3.27 per minute to the rest of Asia and the UK, US$4.52 per minute to the rest of Europe, the Middle East and Africa, and US$4.83 per minute to the Americas and Australasia.

Most resorts can be contacted directly by private phone. The atoll offices are linked to Malé and to each other by radio-telephone and between islands by CB radio. To contact someone on an island through their atoll office, you have to book the call a day in advance at the Department of P&T in Malé at a cost of Rf 5 for three minutes. Some private phones are registered for inter-atoll communications.

TIME

The Maldives are five hours ahead of GMT/UTC. They are in the same time zone as Pakistan, half an hour behind India and Sri Lanka, and three hours behind Singapore.

A number of resorts operate one to two hours ahead of Malé time to give their guests extra daylight in the evening and longer to sleep in the morning.

ELECTRICITY

Electricity supply is from 220 to 240 volts, 50 cycles AC. Plug sockets vary, so you'd better bring an adapter if you've got a lot to switch on. In Malé the electricity supply is reasonably reliable.

There is no national grid and power is supplied by generators. The fuel to power those generators is one of the resorts' major expenses. About half the islands in the country have generators and power is restricted, in most cases, to the evening between 6 and 11 pm. The other islands rely on kerosene and candles. For that reason, a torch could be very useful.

LAUNDRY

If you want shirts, dresses or trousers washed, there are two or three laundries on Majidi Magu in Malé which charge Rf 1.50 an item. Another, Adam's Laundry, can be found at the corner of Orchid Magu and Carnation Magu. On most resorts, people do their own washing by hand and hang it out on their balcony. Otherwise, if you ask at the reception, your washing can be done for you (for a price).

WEIGHTS & MEASURES

We have used metric measurement in this book. For those unaccustomed to this system there is a metric/imperial conversion chart at the end of the book.

BOOKS

If you plan to do a lot of reading – and often there is little else to do – just take a couple of your own books because you'll probably be able to swap them later with other travellers.

The following selection of books should provide some background on the Maldives.

History

The historian of the Maldives is H C P Bell, a former British commissioner in the Ceylon Civil Service who first visited the islands in 1879 courtesy of a shipwreck.

He returned twice, in 1920 and 1922, to lead archaeological expeditions and published several accounts including *A Description of the Maldive Islands* for the *Journal of the Royal Asiatic Society* (Ceylon Branch, Colombo, 1925).

In 1940, three years after his death, the Ceylon Government Press published his main work *The Maldive Islands: Monograph on the History, Archaeology & Epigraphy*. Original copies of the book are rare, however, there are copies in the two Malé libraries. The National Centre for Linguistic & Historical Research of the Maldives, based at the National Library, is reprinting the book.

Much of Bell's research on pre-Muslim civilisation has been supported, challenged and expanded by Kon-Tiki explorer Thor Heyerdahl in *The Maldive Mystery* (George Allen & Unwin, London, 1986).

Heyerdahl spent several months during 1982-83 digging around the southern atolls. With the apparent blessing of the Maldives government, he unearthed evidence of early Buddhist, Hindu and sun-worshipping prehistoric societies, each succeeding the other before the arrival of Islam in the 12th century.

Heyerdahl's discoveries are exhibited at the National Museum in Sultan Park. His theories on early navigators and traders have not exactly been embraced by Maldivian authorities, who seem to have a 'we don't really wish to know that' attitude. In fact some non-Maldivian critics have pointed to Heyerdahl's tendency to jump to conclusions without any solid backing, and the more vociferous of those critics have even gone as far as to discredit his work as nothing more than fiction.

For history of the Muslim period, look at Ibn Battuta's *Travels in Asia & Africa 1325-54*, reprinted in paperback by Routledge Kegan Paul in 1983. Ibn Battuta was a great Moorish globetrotter.

Another historical text is *The Story of*

Mohamed Thakurufaan by Hussain Sala-huddeen (1986), which tells of the Maldives' greatest hero who liberated the people from the Portuguese. It is available in Malé from Novelty Bookshop.

Travel & Diving Guides

There are one-off glossy guides in several European languages published during the 1980s, as well as coffee-table photographic collections by German and Italian photographers.

A much more practical and down-to-earth guide is *Maldives* by Australian writer Stuart Bevan (Other People, Australia, 1987). Bevan spent five years on the islands, collecting a wealth of information in the process, but the book is officially banned as the Maldivian authorities took offence to some quips he made about prayer calls.

Officially approved is *Papineau's Travel Guide to the Maldives* (MHP Publishing, Singapore, 1987). It's informative, has nice pictures and a decent text, but is not very practical.

Berlitz's tiny guide on Sri Lanka has an even tinier supplement on the Maldives.

The Islands of Maldives (Novelty Press, Malé, 1983), written by the former director of the Department of Information Hassan Ahmed Maniku, is more a list of the islands than a guidebook. Maniku attempts to sort out the eternal confusion of how many islands there are, what they are called and whether or not they are inhabited. Then he leaves it up to you to count them. The book has no pictures, illustrations or commentary.

Surprisingly, there have not been many books published on the marine life or diving in the Maldives. *Land of 1000 Atolls* by Irenaeus Eibl-Eibelsfeldt (World Publishing, New York, 1966) explores the underwater world around the Nicobar and Maldive islands.

More recently Dr Charles Anderson, a British marine biologist living in Malé since 1983, has put together *Maldives, the Diver's Paradise*, *Living Reefs of the Maldives* and the *Diver's Guide to the Sharks of the Maldives*: three great pictorials to whet your appetite before heading for the depths. Also by Dr Anderson in conjunction with Ahmed Hafiz are the identification guides *Common Reef Fishes of the Maldives* parts one, two and three. All six books are published by Novelty Press in Malé, and some if not all can usually be found in resort shops and in bookshops in Malé.

Maldives Diving Guide & Logbook (North Malé Atoll) by Tim Godfrey (Novelty Press, Malé, 1992) is a handy book showing the most important dive sites in the most heavily touristed atoll. Included in the book are detailed maps of a number of the sites, with brief descriptions where necessary, and a built-in diver's log. Tim, an Australian who has spent a number of years as a dive instructor in the Maldives, is currently working on similar books covering South Malé Atoll and Ari Atoll.

General

A well-respected work is *People of the Maldive Islands* by US anthropologist Dr Clarence Maloney (Orient Longman, New Delhi, 1980). Covering past and present, this is the best general reference on the country and is not too academic. Unfortunately, it is not readily available, and has been banned in the Maldives.

More accessible, much cheaper and just as readable is *The Fascinating Maldives* by Mohamed Farook (Novelty Press, Malé, 1985). It sells for Rf 12 at the Novelty Bookshop. Farook, naturally, presents a favourable image of Maldivian society, but it's an honest account.

Maldives: A Nation of Islands, published by the Department of Tourism in 1983, has plenty of colour plates, though the text goes in for a lot of back-patting and hailing of national achievements. It makes an attractive gift and you can buy it at any souvenir or resort store for about Rf 60.

As well as the explorers, seafarers and several shipwreck victims of days gone by, the odd modern adventurer or two has also bumped into the Maldives. Author and sailor Alan Villiers tells of his brigantine forays in *Give Me a Ship to Sail* (Hodder & Stoughton,

London, 1958); and sportsman, explorer and former US ambassador to Colombo, Philip K Crowe, has an essay on Malé in his *Diversions of a Diplomat in Ceylon* (Van Nostram, New York, 1957).

Not much fiction has been set around the Maldives. There is only a sea adventure penned by Hammond Innes called *The Strode Venturer* (Collins, London, 1965). The setting of the story ranges from a London boardroom to the RAF bases on Gan and Addu atolls. The southern atoll's bid for independence in the early 1960s is worked into this adventure yarn. If you don't find it among Innes's other available paperbacks, there is a faded hardback copy in the National Library in Malé.

Bookshops

Malé has several bookshops and two libraries but the range and access is limited.

Asrafee Bookshop on Chandani Magu near the corner of Majidi Magu is the only outlet for paperback fiction. It offers a small selection of Western novels (as opposed to Eastern; not Zane Grey and Louis Lamour).

Novelty Bookshop on Faridi Magu is better for Maldivian titles, some of which they publish. Again, there is not a large choice.

There are other bookshops which deal only in school books and stationery.

Libraries

Many of the books in the collection at the National Library, on Majidi Magu in Malé, came from the RAF Gan library when the British air base closed in 1976. More were appropriated from the estate of exiled former president Nasir. The selection is slowly being expanded although the library staff tend to buy up any new fiction the Asrafee Bookshop gets in.

The library is open daily except Friday from 9 am to noon and from 2 to 5 pm. Non-residents can't borrow books, but are welcome to sit and read in the library.

Travellers and tourists can, however, borrow from the private Mohamed Ismail Didi (MID) Library on Ameer Ahmed Magu.

It's open from 2 to 10 pm every day, except during Ramadan when it closes between 5.30 and 8 pm. You can join the library for Rf 12 with a monthly subscription of Rf 4. When borrowing books, foreigners are required to leave Rf 100 as a deposit or their passport as security. 'The library shall hold itself responsible for the safe keeping of such documents', a notice promises.

The MID Library has a weird and wonderful assortment of literature including old editions of *National Geographic*, UN agency reports, soccer and cricket programmes, ancient press cuttings and magazines. There is also a good reference section for history and tourist books on the Maldives. It is worth visiting just to see the house, which is run by the son of the late M I Didi.

The British Voluntary Service Overseas (VSO) have a book exchange scheme. If you have any paperbacks you want to swap, contact their office (☎ 323167) and they will direct you to the volunteer who is in charge of the exchange. Most resorts also have a small selection of swapable paperbacks left behind by past guests.

MAPS

Because of the scattered nature of the islands, the Maldives are difficult to map. Until 1992, the islands had not been accurately counted, and although it has now been determined that there are 1192 islands in the country, it has not yet been properly mapped.

Tourist maps of Malé, the island and atoll, are available from the Department of Tourism office on Marine Drive. There are also three or four different maps available in tourist shops and resort shops. None of the available maps seem to position all the resorts correctly, but this doesn't matter that much, as you will never have to find your own way to any of the resorts (or indeed have the opportunity unless you are in a private yacht). Unfortunately, the only map found by the author which did place all the resorts close to their correct locations is not for sale; only covers North Malé, South Malé and Ari atolls; has no scale; and is intended only as reference for passengers on Hummingbird Helicopter flights. You don't need, and won't be able to find, maps for the individual islands because they are so small.

The navigation charts are important and the British Admiralty is the best source. Failing that, try the Ministry of Fisheries in the Ghaazee Building, opposite the police station. Olhuveli resort has used high-powered satellite-tracking technology to map out parts of South Malé Atoll for their high-speed launches, but they would be unlikely to want to sell this to anyone at an affordable price.

MEDIA
Newspapers & Magazines
The Maldives has two daily papers, the *Haveeru* (evening) and the *Aafathis* (morning). The *Haveeru* has a circulation of 1000 and is available only in Malé. It usually has around eight pages, one of which is devoted to news in English. The cinema advertisements are also in English and you should be able to understand the prayer times. Horoscopes and exchange rates are in Divehi. The *Aafathis* is also eight pages long, with two pages devoted to English-language news. Both papers cost Rf 1.

Until mid-1987 *Haveeru* was written by hand, then copied and printed. There was only one typewriter with Divehi characters in the whole country and it was used by the president's office. New 'nationalised' typewriters are now being used.

Every fortnight the Department of Information & Broadcasting publishes an English-language *News Bulletin*, detailing local news and international events where there is a Maldivian interest. It is available free from the department offices.

Furadhaana is a weekly government newspaper published in Divehi.

Hindi film papers and magazines are popular, and copies of *Time* and *Newsweek* are available from Novelty and Asrafee bookshops and on resorts.

Radio & TV
The Voice of Maldives radio is broadcast to the whole country for 11 hours each day. The news, in English, is read at 6 pm for 10 minutes, following a half-hour pop music show from Radio Australia. A new transmitter and studios were built with Australian aid.

TV Maldives, which started in 1978, broadcasts for up to five hours a day during the week, with an extended service on weekends. It only transmits within a 30-km radius of Malé. There is a daily 20-minute news bulletin in English at 9 pm. Generally there is an English-language film on Monday evenings at 9.45 pm, and an English-language series is also broadcast once or twice a week ('Beverly Hills 90210' was on when I was visiting last).

FILM & PHOTOGRAPHY
If the Maldives is a paradise for anyone other than divers, it's photographers. The photographer given the most exposure for his shots of Maldivian islands is probably Michael Friedel of Munich. You'll see his photos in brochures and on postcards. Also keep an eye out for the underwater photography of Japan's Katsutoshi-Ito.

For amateur photographers the best advice you can be given on photography in the Maldives is to follow the time-proven rule for photography in tropical light: shoot early or late as the sun is often high overhead between around 10 am and 3 pm and photos taken at that time tend to be flat or washed out. At the best of times exposure settings can be critical. It's very easy to end up with over-exposed photos and you should beware of backlighting from bright sunlight and of reflected light. A polaroid filter can work wonders when you're photographing over the sea.

Remember: don't take pictures of people while they're praying; and don't photograph the Muleeaage (president's office) which is on Meduziyaaraiy Magu opposite the Hukuru Miski (mosque), or the Theemuge, (president's residence) which is on Orchid Magu, or the airport, or any police barracks.

Underwater Photography
Of course the urge to take underwater photo-

graphs is going to come upon many snorkellers and divers in the Maldives. In recent years underwater photography has become a much easier activity to be engaged in. At one time it required complex and expensive equipment whereas now there is a variety of reasonably priced and easy-to-use underwater cameras available. Very often it's possible to rent cameras, including underwater video cameras, from diving operators on the reef.

As with basic cameras above surface level the best photos taken with the simplest underwater cameras are likely to be straightforward snapshots. You are not going to get superb photographs of fish and marine life with a small, cheap camera, but on the other hand, photos of your fellow snorkellers or divers can often be terrific.

More than with other types of photography, the results achieved underwater can improve dramatically with equipment expenditure, particularly on artificial lighting. As you descend natural colours are quickly absorbed, starting with the red end of the spectrum. You can see the same result with a picture or poster that has been left in bright sunlight for too long, soon the colours fade until everything looks blue. It's the same underwater, the deeper you go the more blue things look. Red has virtually disappeared by the time you're 10 metres down. The human brain fools us to some extent by automatically compensating for this colour change, but the camera doesn't lie. If you are at any depth your pictures will look cold and blue.

To put the colour back in you need a flash and to work effectively underwater it has to be a much more powerful and complicated flash than above water. Thus newcomers to serious underwater photography soon find that having bought a Nikonos camera they have to lay out as much money again for flash equipment to go with it. With the right experience and equipment the results can be superb. Generally the Nikonos cameras work best with 28 or 35 mm lenses, longer lenses do not work so well underwater. Although objects appear closer underwater

with these short focal lengths you have to get close to achieve good results. Patience and practice will eventually enable you to move in close to otherwise wary fish. Underwater photography opens up whole new fields of interest to divers and the results can often be startling. Flash photography can reveal colours which simply aren't there for the naked eye.

Photo Shops

Colour film is available in several shops, but it is often safer and cheaper to go to the photographic studios. B&W film and video film are also available. Resorts which specialise in diving usually have underwater photographic equipment to rent.

Fototeknik, opposite the Olympus Cinema on Majidi Magu, is the Kodak agent. Kodak Gold 100 ASA 36/24 exposure film costs Rf 100/80. Kodachrome 64 ASA 36 exposure slide film costs Rf 160, but it is not developed in the country. Colour developing and printing generally costs Rf 150/110 for 36/24 exposures. A 100 ASA slide film costs Rf 100 to develop. There is another Fototeknik shop on Marine Drive close to the Nasandhura Palace Hotel. It also has an agent on Bandos resort.

Reethi-foto and Fotogenic are also on Majidi Magu. Both are marginally cheaper than Fototeknik. They all do repairs.

You can buy film at the shops on all resorts, however, it is very expensive.

HEALTH

See the general introductory Facts for the Visitor chapter for information on predeparture health preparations for the Maldives and the other islands covered in this book.

Although it is continually being upgraded, the Maldives health service is very limited and relies heavily on volunteer doctors, nurses and dentists from overseas.

The main Central Hospital is on Sosun Magu in Malé. There are also hospitals on Ugufaaru, the capital of Raa; Kuludufushi in Haa Dhaal; Hitadu on Seenu; and, the latest, in Muli on Meemu. They all suffer from inadequate supplies of drugs and staff. The other atoll capitals each have a health centre staffed by a health worker who has had basic training.

The AMDC (☎ 325979), Dharmavantha Magu, is a clinic run by Swiss doctors who generally come out to the Maldives on short-term contracts. The quality of care is said to be high, but it has prices to match, and you must pay cash at the time of your appointment with the doctor.

There's a volunteer Japanese dentist in Malé who does cheap, professional dental work. Fees for a medical consultation and treatment are not high.

The atoll hospitals and health centres can treat minor illnesses, while Malé's Central Hospital, which has Russian doctors, can deal with routine operations but post-operative treatment is not up to Western standards.

This basically means that getting seriously ill in the Maldives is not recommended. Cases that require specialist operations must be evacuated to Colombo or taken home. Check your insurance policy to see if you are covered for the worst. You'll come across several Maldivians saving up to go to Colombo or New Delhi for treatment.

Emergency evacuations from resorts are coordinated by the National Coast Guard and Hummingbird Helicopters. Inter-Atoll Air company's flying boat can also be called upon. Flying Swiss Ambulance still has a plane in the Maldives, but it has been sitting idle for some time, and the company is no longer operational in the Maldives.

Remember, if you're planning to go diving, make sure that your travel insurance covers you for diving. Some experienced divers would even go as far to suggest that you are covered for the cost of a low altitude flight to Singapore (see the section on Diving in the Atolls chapter for more information on health).

Vaccinations
The health regulations require that you are immunised against cholera and yellow fever if arriving from an infected area. Vaccinations against tetanus and hepatitis are advisable if you are travelling further afield than Malé or one of the resorts.

If you have come from Sri Lanka or India, looking the worse for wear, you could find yourself having a blood test, vaccination and one-week's quarantine in Malé before you get the OK by the immigration department to visit the country. This is unlikely, however, since officials tend to concentrate on Indian and Sri Lankan visitors, many of whom arrive with insufficient funds.

Health Precautions
Drink only rainwater or water which has been boiled or sterilised. Never take a chance on the water served in Malé cafés or water from village wells. It's a good idea to include iodine solution or water-purification tablets in your first aid kit. Bottled water is also available.

Bring with you from home any medication you think you will need. There are numerous pharmacies in Malé, with the most convenient all situated around Majidi Magu and Sosun Magu near the hospital.

Common Ailments
Malaria has officially been wiped out in the Maldives. According to the World Health Organisation there has not been a case of malaria in the Maldives since 1981. For this reason very few doctors will recommend taking anti-malarials for a trip to the Maldives, however, this must be a personal decision. The proximity of Sri Lanka, a country where malaria is still rife, is probably the only reason you would consider it.

The strength of the mosquito squadrons varies from island to island. They are not a problem in Malé and the resorts are generally mosquito-free around living areas. To combat the mosquitoes use coils if you can put up with the smell, fast ceiling fans if you can put up with the draught, or air-con if you can put up the money.

As in India and Sri Lanka, diarrhoea and stomach ailments are common in the Maldives. The biggest danger though is most likely to come from infected cuts. If you plan to do a lot of diving or snorkelling, there is an increased risk from coral cuts. Refer to the Health section in the general Facts for the Visitor chapter.

WOMEN TRAVELLERS

On the resorts women do not have to make too many adjustments. You should be aware, however, that topless bathing is strictly forbidden in the Maldives. The fine for breaking this law is US$1000 each to both the woman concerned and the resort or safari boat where she is holidaying. Nude bathing attracts an even higher fine. Wearing most bathing attire is perfectly acceptable.

In Malé, Addu Atoll and the inhabited islands frequently visited by tourists, shorts which cover the thighs and T-shirts or blouses which are not too low cut are acceptable dress, while in more out-of-the-way parts of the country, slightly more conservative dress may be in order.

The main reason for dressing up a little is so as not to offend the locals, but it also makes your life considerably easier. Most Maldivian men do not often see women in bikinis or low-cut skirts, shorts and blouses, and they see it as a sign of promiscuity.

Women holidaying alone or together on the resort islands may have to cope with Western men who have seen many women in bikinis before and still don't know how to behave themselves.

DANGERS & ANNOYANCES
Security

The Maldives police consists of a civilian and a military force. The latter are involved in guarding the president, airport and other sensitive subjects, and although they sport the usual olive green fatigues, berets and Kalashnikov AK47s and M16s, they maintain a low profile and do not disturb visitors.

The civilian police are relatively efficient but hard to identify. The only uniform apparent on many is a light blue shirt. Unless there's a chevron or two on the sleeve, you can't tell if you're looking at a police officer.

The Maldivian justice system is often surprising to visitors who take the time to look into it. While you can applaud the fact that it is not as barbaric (to Western senses) as that in some Arab countries, some of the methods are questionable.

In the Maldives, instead of chopping off hands for theft or dishing out 50 lashes for drinking whisky, those who fall foul of the law are banished to an island other than their home island, or put under house arrest for years at a time.

There are of course stories of former prisoners, banished for various reasons, who claim to have thoroughly enjoyed their exile, however, for most offenders this is a devastating punishment since they are taken away from their families and friends for years at a time.

On an island in the extreme north of North Malé Atoll lives a German traveller who was banished there in 1976 after being convicted of the murder of his girlfriend. He is now married to a local woman, has two children and has resisted all attempts by the West German government and consul to have him extradited to serve his sentence at home. He was pardoned by the Maldivian government upon his conversion to Islam.

Theft

Crimes of violence and theft are not a pressing problem in the Maldives. There are occasional thefts from resort rooms and on island village tours, but tourists generally are safe.

Each year 2000 criminals are convicted, of whom more than half are banished.

ACTIVITIES

Ironically, when people think of a holiday on a tropical island they dream of all the time they can spend doing nothing, just lazing around in the sun. But in fact, in the Maldives, you'll never be lost for something to do. Club Med is the most striking example, where you can be on the go almost nonstop from the moment you arrive on the island until the time you leave. But Club Med is by no means alone in this. Every resort has a diving school which keeps a majority of the guests occupied either in the depths or snorkelling on the surface. There are also

Top: Launching a new dhoni (PS)
Bottom: Seafood anyone? (PS)

Top: Malé from the air (Hummingbird)
Bottom: Himmafushi, Tari Village & Huraa (Hummingbird)

Top: Dhoni crew (MB)
Middle: Fishermen unloading the catch (TG)
Bottom: Harbour scene, Malé (MB)

Top: Grand Friday Mosque, Malé (PS)
Bottom: Shop front, Malé (MB)

island-hopping day trips, trips to the capital Malé, and night fishing trips. A helicopter flight over the atolls or even a game of golf on Gan in Addu Atoll way down in the south of the country are among the more unexpected offerings.

Snorkelling

If you can swim then you can also snorkel and the Maldives is simply one of the best places in the world for this activity. Some islands are much better than others for snorkelling, at some there's virtually none to speak of while at others there's a wonderland waiting just a few steps out from the beach. Those resorts that don't have a reef just offshore offer snorkelling trips.

If you've never tried snorkelling before you'll soon pick it up and many resorts give brief free snorkelling lessons in their swimming pools or in shallow parts of the lagoon. Every resort will have snorkelling equipment which you can borrow or rent. Of course if you've got your own that certainly makes life somewhat easier and you won't

have the risk of finding that you've got an odd-shaped face which most masks won't fit.

There are three pieces of equipment for snorkelling, each of which is also used for scuba diving.

Mask First and most essential there's the mask, this is what lets you see underwater. The reason you can't see underwater normally is that your eyes won't focus in water. Fish eyes were designed to focus underwater, human eyes weren't. The mask introduces an air space in front of your eyes so you can focus just as well as the fish.

Masks cost anything from $10 to hundreds of dollars and, as with most things, you get what you pay for. Any mask, however, no matter how cheap, should have a shatterproof lens. That's the one essential to check before you try a mask on. Next you must make sure the mask fits and this is highly dependent on the shape of your face. Some people find almost any mask fits easily, others find oval masks fit better, others prefer square ones. If the mask doesn't fit well it

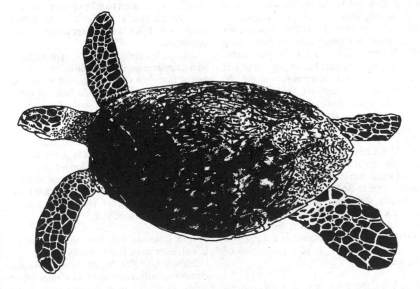

Hawksbill Turtle

will gradually fill with water and you'll have to stop periodically to clear the water out, which can be annoying. To check if a mask fits well, simply fit it to your face, but without the strap around the back of your head. Breathe in through your nose and the suction should hold the mask on your face if the fit is good.

If you're shortsighted and serious about snorkelling or scuba diving you can get the mask lens ground to your optical prescription or, rather easier, get stick-on optical lens to attached to the inside of the mask lens. If you wear contact lenses you can wear these with a mask, although there is the risk of losing them if your mask is accidentally flooded. Actually the altered focal length of light underwater often compensates quite well for shortsightedness – I wear glasses all the time but never miss them when underwater.

Snorkel With your mask on you can now see fine underwater, but every time you want to breathe you must raise your head out of the water. This will be the instant that fish you were quietly observing shoots for cover. A snorkel lets you breathe with your face down in the water. It's simply a curved tube with a mouthpiece which you grip in your teeth. The tube curves round beside your head and you breathe in and out through your mouth. When you dive underwater the snorkel tube fills with water which you expel, once back on the surface, by simply blowing out forcefully. The snorkel tube has to be long enough to reach above the surface of the water but should not be either too long or too wide. If it is too big then you have more water to expel when you come to the surface and it's not pleasant to find that first gulp of fresh air is mostly seawater. Also, each breath out leaves a snorkel full of used air. Normally, this only slightly dilutes the fresh air you breathe in but if the snorkel is too big you could breathe in too large a proportion of carbon dioxide.

Fins Fins, the third item of a snorkeller's equipment, are not absolutely necessary. If they're there it's always nice to have fins but if not you can still snorkel fine without them. As with masks, fin selection is very much a matter of personal preference. What fits and suits one person another person simply cannot get along with. Fins either fit completely over your foot or have an open back with a strap around your heel. The latter type generally offers more adjustment and more comfort. If you're serious about your underwater activities then you should really buy fins in conjunction with wet-suit boots. These make the fins more comfortable and fit better and can also be used for walking across reefs.

Diving

Scuba diving is the main attraction in the Maldives. Every resort has a diving school, and there are plans to open up a diving school in Malé. The main consideration with scuba diving is that it requires knowledge and care. You can sling a mask and snorkel on and be a snorkeller in minutes. Adding an air tank on your back and diving in is asking for trouble. If you want to take up scuba diving you should first complete a good diving course which leads to an approved diving certificate.

Although learning to scuba dive requires some application it is not difficult to learn and it does not require any sort of superhuman strength or fitness. In fact one thing you quickly learn is that doing things with the minimum expenditure of energy is what diving is about. Your diving time is limited by your tank of air and the more gently you do things the longer that air is going to last. It's remarkable how much longer the same tank of air will last with an experienced diver compared to a beginner. Women often have an advantage over men in this area – they don't breathe so much air.

Diving Courses Full-time diving courses last about a week and typically cost around US$250 to US$500. A good course will have classroom instruction and underwater experience in a pool or a shallow part of the lagoon, followed by some real dives in the sea. The best way of finding out if the course is good is to ask somebody else who has done it. Resorts, with a reputation to protect, usually ensure their dive school operators know what they're about. Of course you can also learn to dive before you leave home. Diving courses in your home town are likely to be part time rather than full time, but they allow you to make the most of the underwater world in the Maldives as soon as you arrive.

What do you learn in a diving course? One thousand ways to kill yourself underwater was one succinct description. Actually it's the reverse of that, a diving course should teach you to anticipate possible problems and avoid them. Much of the course is designed to drum into you things which have to become second nature when you're underwater – things like always keep breathing, don't hold your breath as you ascend, how to adjust your buoyancy; all these soon become straightforward techniques. Of course you also spend some time learning how to grapple with those tricky decompression tables.

Certificates The end result of your diving course is not just a basic knowledge of scuba diving it's also a certificate to prove you know it. A certificate is like a driving licence. You can't walk into a car-rental agency and rent a car without a driving licence, nor can you go out on a diving trip without a diving certificate. Once you have a recognised certificate, however, you'll be welcomed by diving operators all over the world. Certificates in the Maldives are generally issued by PADI (Professional Association of Diving Instructors) or CMAS (an international nonprofit organisation founded by Jacques Cousteau). PADI is the largest and the best known internationally but either organisation's certificate is quite acceptable.

As well as successfully completing the course you must have a diving medical examination before your certificate can be issued. Certain medical conditions, such as asthma, do not go with diving. It would be wise to have a diving medical test done

before you travel to the Maldives, as once you are on your resort, it is considerably more complicated to organise (unless you are on one of the more exclusive resorts which has a resident doctor).

Don't let having a certificate lull you into thinking you know everything. Like with any activity, experience is vitally important. As well as your diving certificate every diver has a log book in which they should record every dive they make. If a proposed dive is deep or difficult a good dive operator should check your log book to ensure your experience is sufficient. A high proportion of diving accidents happen to inexperienced divers 'getting out of their depth'.

Equipment Dive schools in the Maldives can rent out all diving gear but most divers prefer to have at least some of their own equipment. The usual minimum is mask, snorkel, fins and boots. These are items for which most divers have personal preferences and are happiest using their own equipment. They are also relatively light and compact to pack. Other necessary scuba diving equipment includes:

Air cylinders
    Don't bother bringing your own.
Buoyancy vest or Buoyancy Control Device (BCD)
    These are readily available but some divers prefer to have their own.
Depth gauge & tank pressure gauge
    These are readily available but again some divers like their own familiar equipment.
Regulator
    Many divers like to have their own regulator with which they are familiar and confident.
Weight belt & weights
    There is absolutely no reason to bring lead weights with you.
Dive computer
    These new-fangled devices allow you to increase your bottom time considerably by constantly measuring your depth. If you are approaching your time limit for a particular depth the computer starts beeping. Ascending a few metres will then allow you to continue your dive. Many dive schools in the Maldives use computers, however, you should never rely solely on a computer and should always keep an eye on your other gauges and your watch.

Wet suit
> The waters of the Maldives and other islands in the Indian Ocean may be warm but a wet suit is still necessary for comfortable diving. Having a properly fitting wet suit is also important, gushes of cold water rushing down your back are never comfortable. On the other hand, a wet suit is relatively bulky to carry around and if you normally dive in colder waters your regular suit may be too thick for the Maldives.

Sailing

Sailing is a popular activity in the Maldives whether it's cruising through the atolls in your own yacht or taking a turn round the lagoon in a resort catamaran. Most resorts have one or two catamarans and beginners can usually organise lessons on their island.

Windsurfing

Like sailing, windsurfing has taken off in the Maldives. The shallow, protected lagoons around most resort islands make it the ideal place for beginners, while for experienced windsurfers, there is nothing like having an entire lagoon to yourself.

Surfing

Although the Maldives have been surfed for almost two decades, it has only come to the attention of the international surfing crowd in the last couple of years. For the better part of the year offshore winds are predominant, which means that if you know where and when to go, you'll be riding clean, fast, hollow waves all day long. Of course, in a country as scattered as the Maldives, finding those waves is easier said than done, and with the hassles involved in getting permits before you can even begin to look for them, you need to have time and money to burn if you want to go it alone.

Understandably, those people who do surf here are very wary about telling anyone where to look for the ride of your life, however, if you want to know more about either resort-based or safari-boat-based surfing, you should contact Atoll Adventures (☎ 328810, fax 314788), PO Box 2059, Malé, whose operations manager, Tony Hinde, is a Sydney surfer who was ship-wrecked here in the early '70s and has surfed all over the country ever since. Atoll Adventures Australian agent is Foster Travel Service (☎ (056) 822155, fax (056) 822965), 10 Station Rd, Foster, Victoria 3960, Australia. It offers eight and 15-night surfing packages with airfares (Singapore Airlines), transfers, accommodation, meals and of course transport to the offshore waves every day. Eight days costs A$1960 ex-Melbourne, Sydney, Brisbane and Adelaide and A$1810 ex-Perth. Fifteen nights costs A$2550/2740 in the low/high season (from May to July/August to October). From Perth the equivalent rates are A$2390/2590. Special group tours for up to 35 nights can be arranged.

Island Hopping

Every resort offers guests the opportunity to visit some of the nearby islands. Usually this is accomplished by a half or full-day's island-hopping trip. In general you will visit an inhabited island, another resort and an uninhabited island. While it is interesting to see how the locals live on a fishing island, you should be aware that most of the islands visited by tourists on these island-hopping tours, have been sadly influenced by the Western shopping mentality.

Inevitably, as the tourist boat arrives at the jetty, there is a scurry of activity on the island as every second or third house along the main street is converted into a shop in the hope of selling imported Balinese T-shirts, Sri Lankan carved wooden elephants, tortoise-shell, sea-shell and coral products to the tourists. More recently, tourists have come across children asking for 'one dollar'. Visitors who do decide to take part in an island-hopping tour have a responsibility to help reverse these trends. There are many skilled artisans and craftspeople in the Maldives, but if the tourists continue to buy the mass-produced imported rubbish, these people will have no incentive to show their culture to the world.

Night Fishing

Most resorts organise weekly night fishing

trips. Usually, about a dozen people go out in a dhoni for two or three hours with a handline each and a bucket full of bait. On a typical evening you would expect over 80% of them to catch something, and everyone would get a few nibbles. Apart from the numerous reef fish which go for the bait, you can catch barracuda and, if you're trawling, the tuna may take an interest.

Night fishing trips generally cost around US$10 to US$15 per person. You can usually arrange to have your catch prepared by the chef. Tari Village is said to be the only resort where you can cook your fish yourself.

Big Game Fishing

This is not a budget traveller's activity, and is a great deal harder to justify than night fishing. Yellow fin tuna, sailfish and marlin are the fish they go after, sometimes returning to the island after a day on the water with a fish weighing 100 kg or more. A day on a big-game fishing boat usually costs around US$660 with a maximum of four fishing passengers to split the cost. Half a day costs around US$330, but if you are serious about your fishing, that won't be long enough.

Helicopter Flights

For information on helicopter joy rides see the Getting Around chapter.

Other Activities

There are a number of other activities on offer at various resorts around the Maldives. Olhuveli resort has a chamber which allows nondivers to descend hundreds of metres under the sea. A few resorts boast 'banana riding'. About a dozen guests climb onto a giant, inflatable banana and hang on screaming for dear life as they are dragged around the lagoon at high speed by a speedboat. Water-skiing is available on some islands, while one or two have glass-bottomed boats for those who want to see the reef without getting their feet wet. Parasailing and jetskiing are becoming more popular, and more islands are bound to have the facilities before long.

HIGHLIGHTS

The main highlight in the Maldives is undoubtedly the underwater world. Whether it's snorkelling over a multicoloured coral reef alive with fish of just as many colours and varieties, or diving with sharks and mantas, or on the wreck of the *Maldive Victory* off Hulule airport, the underwater world becomes for most people the most overwhelming memory of the Maldives. If for even a fleeting moment you have ever considered diving, then consider it again: this is some of the most exhilarating diving in the world. For more information see the diving section of this chapter. There is also information on a few selected dive sites in the most heavily touristed atolls in the Atolls chapter.

For a great splurge you might look into a 15-minute helicopter joy ride over the atolls. This is a great photo opportunity (a skylight filter on your camera lens is a good idea), and generally the pilot tries to fly over or near any resorts that the passengers are staying on. There are also helicopter day trips including lunch on a desert island and a visit to one of the most expensive resorts in the Maldives, Nika Hotel. For more information see the Getting Around chapter.

For those with the time, money, and inclination, a visit to Addu Atoll is a great side trip or entire holiday in itself. While the resort on Gan is not enough reason on its own to fly so far, it is the best opportunity for tourists to come into contact with uncommercialised Maldivian culture. You had better hurry though, as with the expected influx over the next few years, that could all change.

ACCOMMODATION
Resorts

While every resort has its distinctive character and appeal, there are three or four different classes of resorts in the Maldives. The most natural resorts are those which put their guests in thatched bungalows, cabanas, bures, rondavels, units, huts or whatever the brochure wants to call them, with an attached bathroom and shower, and a verandah of

sorts usually facing the beach. These include Bathala, Halaveli, Angaga, Ihuru, Rihiveli, Nika Hotel, Cocoa Island and Emboodhu Finolhu among others.

Then there are the international resorts which could just as easily be in the Caribbean, Fiji, Tahiti or on Australia's Great Barrier Reef – places such as Kurumba, Embudu Village, Moofushi, Mirihi, Maafushivaru and others.

The third kind is less easy to stereotype, and includes resorts such as Little Hura, Fesdu and Tari Village. These resorts all have a definite Maldivian flavour, yet they have not tried to make their islands look like fishing villages. Only about seven resorts (including Tari Village) have two-storey accommodation.

Finally there is Olhuveli, in a class all of its own. Perhaps things have changed, but it was nothing less than a luxury concrete monstrosity at the time of writing.

Water Supply One of the major complaints is about the salty bore-water showers. Almost all of the resorts used to pump the water from the ground and filter it through sand. Sometimes it was heated, which resulted in a pungent smell, but mostly it was (is) left cold. The water is never freezing of course, but it is difficult to wash in as soap and shampoo won't lather. (Unless you use Shower Gel, you end up with stiff and sticky hair.)

Today over half the resorts now have desalination plants and others collect rainwater in barrels. A few provide fresh water 24 hours a day, while some restrict it to a few hours in the evening or the morning. Occasionally the desalination systems break down or there are long periods without rain, and then it's back to the bore water and sea water.

There are, however, always flasks of fresh drinking water available in the rooms and at meals.

Rates All rates quoted are the 'fixed individual tariff' (FIT) for one day's/night's full-board unless otherwise stated. As you will see, the price increases for the high season vary remarkably from resort to resort. In some cases it's only a matter of a few more dollars, in others, the rate more than doubles.

It is important to realise that you will always, without exception, get cheaper rates through overseas packages and with the independent tour operators in Malé (some of whom are connected with guesthouses) than you will if you try to organise your stay yourself. There are also some excellent 'special offers' and stopover deals during the low season. Refer to the Maldives Getting There & Away chapter and try a couple of travel agents at home to compare prices.

Resorts fall into low, medium and high-price ranges. The low range represents all resorts with doubles costing from US$50 to US$80 for full board. In the low season (from May to September) these resorts include Hembadoo, Helengeli, Meerufenfushi, Kandooma, Baros, Ziyaaraifushi, Lohifushi, Maayafushi, Nakatchafushi, Bathala, Fihalhohi, Fesdu Fun Island, Little

Hura, Bolifushi and Dhigufinolhu in order of price.

In the high season only Hembadoo, Helengeli, Meerufenfushi, Kandooma, Ziyaaraifushi and Fesdu Fun Island offer low-range prices.

Middle-range resorts (exactly half of the resorts) charge anywhere from US$80 to US$149 for doubles. The high-range resorts charge US$150 or more for a double. In the low season these resorts include Athuruga, Thundufushi, Ihuru, Vabinfaru, Gangehi, Veligandu Huraa, Kuda Rah, Rihiveli, Gasfinolhu, Madoogali, Club Med/Farukolufushi, Makunudhoo, Olhuveli, Kudahithi, Nika Hotel, and Cocoa Island in order of price. During the high season another 12 resorts join the fray, and Nika Hotel becomes the most expensive resort by raising the double rate to an impressive US$440 per night. Note that many resorts push their rates through the roof over the Christmas period.

There may be extra charges for air-con and it's a good idea to check what recreational facilities are included in the cost. Diving, for instance, is rarely included in the package. Club Med, however, is the most notable exception to this and Fun Island Resort offers a free introductory dive to beginners.

Also remember that each resort charges a boat transfer for taking you to and from Hulhule Airport. This starts at US$12 for the closer islands and goes up to as much as US$200 (return) for the more distant ones, or even more for the very popular helicopter transfers. Generally children under two years old travel free and those aged up to 12 years, for half-price.

Before booking a resort you should find out whether it has the following: fresh water, hot water, an international clientele or mainly German or Italian groups, a full range of activities and facilities, and which of them are included in the full-board rates.

If it is difficult to find more information than this guidebook provides, it may suggest that the resort is used exclusively by European tour operators such as Club Vacanze or Jet Reisen. The Malé contact number and address listed should provide such informa-

tion. There are continual changes among the contact people, some of whom are owners or operators while others are merely agents.

Hotels & Guesthouses

Apart from the resort islands, the only official accommodation is provided by two hotels, the Ocean Reef Club on Gan and guesthouses on Malé.

Unless you want air-con or have an expense account there is no reason to stay at the hotels. Some resort tourists, however, may find themselves at a hotel on the first night if bad weather prevents the boat transfer to the resort. The rooms are basic and soulless. You'll find several guesthouses that are just as good for a third of the price.

All accommodation may be paid for in US dollars or in Maldivian rufiya. The rates quoted should include the US$6 per night government bed tax, but double-check. The prices are for a bed only, not a room and vary from around US$15 for a single at the bottom end to US$55 for a double at the other end. Unless you enquire first, you could end up sharing a room with strangers. Some of the better guesthouses have special double rates.

The government does little to promote guesthouses. In 1983 there were more than 100 guesthouses in Malé, but since the Indians stopped visiting for duty-free sprees, more than half have closed. Others have been hit for not declaring bed tax, while some suffered when inter-island travel was restricted, which also curtailed their sideline travel services. Finally, in 1987 when the black market for the US dollar ended, the guesthouses increased their rates considerably.

Still, there is a large choice and conditions range from overcrowded hovels to spacious, clean units. Your biggest problem will be pronouncing some of the names.

Check to see that rooms have a ceiling fan; it makes all the difference in the cramped and stuffy rooms at the bottom end of the market. Guesthouses usually offer only cold-water showers. Bring a sleeping sheet; it will prove more comfortable in some places and safer in others.

See the Malé chapter for more information on guesthouses and hotels, and the Atolls chapter for details of resort accommodation.

Island Villages
If you are fortunate enough to stay in an island village, you will be housed where there is room, and not necessarily with your 'friend'. In many cases, particularly on the smaller islands, where you stay will depend on the kateeb (island chief), and it may well be at his home.

Protocol As a matter of protocol, guests should introduce themselves to the kateeb upon arrival or shortly after. If the island is the atoll capital, guests should also introduce themselves to the atoll chief. The other person to make yourself known to is the gazi (champion of the faith), the island's religious leader and judge.

It is always best to dress as smartly as possible when meeting officials. In some ways it helps to justify the respect that will be shown to you at the outset. Wear a shirt rather than a T-shirt, shoes not thongs, and long trousers or a skirt instead of shorts or a sarong. Don't worry about this too much if you arrive by fishing dhoni after spending eight hours at sea. It just helps, that's all.

Homes On the main islands, official visitors are usually put up in the atoll chief's house. These are modern but basic abodes built out of concrete rather than coral. Informal guests will be offered a room with a family.

The average home and surrounding low walls are made from coral stone and mortar. Wooden beams support a palm-thatched or corrugated iron roof. Beds are nothing out of the ordinary, and the mattresses and pillows are filled with coconut matting.

Hanging by rope from the beams or trees are the *undorlis*, which are swinging wooden platforms also known as bed-boats. The undorli is a combination lounge suite and hammock and takes the place of both in Maldivian homes. A variation is the *joli*, made from rope and wood, which is like sitting in a string shopping bag. Often you'll find a three or four-seater joli outside the front or back door.

Toilet Less relaxing for Western guests is the *gifili* – the bathroom and toilet. In most cases, the toilet is a hole in the ground surrounded by shrubs or a thatched fence. Some places have a manufactured Asian-style drained latrine.

On some islands the beach is still used as a toilet, even though the government is trying to discourage the habit. One part of the beach is reserved for women and another part, some distance away, for men. It is not used until after dusk. The sea is supposed to wash the beach clean by the next morning, but I'd check before snorkelling.

Washing is done around the well, not in it. Water for showering or cleaning is drawn by a large tin can on the end of a long pole. Some homes have a well out the front, comparable to the kitchen sink, and another out the back for bathing only.

Other Information Several islands have a generator, but the use of electricity is generally restricted to between 6 and 11 pm, and only used for radios and lights. Apart from this, lighting is provided by candles and hurricane lanterns.

All meals will be provided by your host but to begin with, you may be expected to dine separately from the family. This could be because they think you would prefer to, maybe for religious reasons, or it might simply signify special treatment along with a special menu. Don't worry about it. One more thing, don't drink the water unless you are sure it is rainwater. Never drink well water.

Legally, you are not permitted to pay for accommodation in an island village. There are a few people in Malé who can organise transfers and short or long stays on inhabited islands in just about any part of the country so long as you have time to wait in Malé while they organise your permits for you. Often the rates offered for accommodation on such islands are very reasonable (US$15 to US$25 per night), however, it must be reiterated that it is against the law to pay for it. For more information see the Permits section.

FOOD

One of the biggest surprises about the Maldives is the scarcity of luscious fruits and vegetables. It spoils the paradise image, but is perfectly understandable as there's just not the room or soil depth on the tiny coral atolls to produce anything much at all. Only the coconut thrives; mostly everything else is imported.

The quality of meals at the resorts has been the topic of regular complaint by jetsetting tourists who expect a lot better for their money. In fact, the resort operators have made efforts to improve the quality of food on the islands, and tourists on most resorts seem to be fairly happy with their lot. In general, the Italian resorts serve the best food, as their guests are apparently the most discerning (or is that the fussiest?).

Maldivian food is rarely served to tourists, which is a real shame, but the opinion is that Western stomachs will not cope with the spices. A few islands have a Maldivian night every week or so, but always offer a Western meal as an option for those who are not interested. Rihiveli resort has taken it a step further by asking guests to go without cutlery on their Maldivian night.

Fish and rice are the staple foods of the Maldivian people; meat and chicken are saved for special occasions. Their diet in general is poor which probably contributes to their short life expectancy.

If you're going to eat local food, prepare your pallet for fish curry, fish soup, and variations thereof. There is usually not much choice in what you eat, but here is a list of dishes found in the Maldives.

Fish

mas
  fried fish; usually refers to skipjack tuna or bonito

valo mas
  smoked fish

mas huni & hana kuri mas
  dried, tinned, fried or cold fish mixed with onion, chilli or spices

mas riha
  fish curry

kandukukulhu
  a special tuna curry

garudia
  the staple diet of fish soup, often taken with rice, lime, and chili

rihakuru
  garudia boiled down to a salty sauce or paste

Fruit

kurumba
  a young or new coconut; applied to any coconut

donkeo
  little bananas

bambukeyo
  breadfruit

bambukeyo hiti
  breadfruit used in curries

bambukeyo bondibai
  breadfruit used in desserts

don ambu
  mango (green mangoes boiled with sugar are delicious)

falor
  papaya or paw paw

Miscellaneous

bai
  rice

roshi
  pancake bread; eaten with soups and curries

modunu
  a simple salad

aluvi
  potato

paan
  bread

bis
  egg

kiru
  milk

hakuru
  sugar

sai
  tea; always white and sweet unless you
  ask for it otherwise

Hedhikaa is the selection of sweets and
savouries, including *gulas, kuli boakiba,
bondi bai, kastad* and *foni boakiba*, that is
placed on the tables in Malé cafés.

gulas
  fish ball; deep-fried in flour and rice
  batter
kuli boakiba
  spicy fish cake
bondi bai
  rice pudding; sometimes with currants
kastad
  sweet custard
foni boakiba
  gelatin cakes and puddings

The Maldivian equivalent of the after-dinner
mint is the *arecanut*. It is chewed by one and
all after any meal or snack. The little oval
nuts, from the areca palm, are sliced into thin
sections and chewed with betel leaf, cloves
and lime (from limestone). Unlike betel nut,
it doesn't give you red-rotten teeth but it's
still an acquired taste.

DRINKS
There is a reasonable selection of imported
soft drinks in Malé. Foreigners who do not
have a liquor permit are not allowed to drink
alcohol in Malé. Permits are only issued to
foreigners resident in the country, and there
appear to be no exceptions to that rule. The
permits are also specific and forbid anyone
from sharing their monthly entitlements with
any other person even in their own homes.
While the police do not conduct checks particularly frequently, it does happen, and you
will be in trouble if you disregard the regulations.
  On resorts alcohol is freely available to
non-Muslim guests. If you are spending your
holiday on a safari boat, you will only be
allowed to drink in resorts which you will be
able to visit most evenings, as the boats often
anchor in a lagoon off a resort island.

Raa is the name for toddy tapped from the
crown of the palm trunk at the point where
the coconuts grow. Every village has its
toddy man or *raa veri*. The raa is sweet and
delicious if you can get over the pungent
smell. Drink it immediately after it is tapped
from the tree or leave it to become more
alcoholic as the sugar ferments.

ENTERTAINMENT
On most of the resorts there is usually some
kind of entertainment at least three or four
evenings a week. It may vary from a band
playing to a magic show. Some resorts organise games evenings with anything from
table tennis to *boules*, chess or snooker. In
Malé, however, the options are limited for
visitors. For information see Malé.

THINGS TO BUY
Around the time of the 10 December fisheries holiday, the government holds a craft fair
in Malé. Each atoll sends examples of its best
work to the capital by dhoni. The quality
pieces are sold to dignitaries in advance of
the public opening, but remain on display
until the end of the exhibition. There is still
a large choice left, though the prices are
higher than in the shops.
  Gaddu and Fiyori islands in Gaaf Dhaal
(South Huvadu Atoll) are the best sources of
fine woven reed mats known as *kunaa*. They
are naturally dyed with black and brown
patterns and used as prayer mats or bed and
chair covers. The *tundu kunaa* are special
mats. There is occasionally a small selection
available for purchase by tourists in the souvenir shops in Malé. Usually the quality of
any commercially available mats is not particularly high, although it may be worth
hunting around if you are interested.
  Red, black and yellow lacquer work is a
feature of all sorts and sizes of wooden
boxes, urns, walking sticks and other items.
Baa (South Malosmadulu Atoll) always wins
this category at the fair. Baa, particularly the
capital island Eydafushi, is also known for
making the traditional brown and cream *feli*
cloth. It is difficult to find the cloth in Malé
shops as the locals there now prefer polyester

from Singapore and Hong Kong. The felis I found for sale in Malé were dusty and moth-eaten.

Alifushi, in Raa (North Malosmadulu Atoll), harbours the country's best boat-builders. They even export dhonis to other islands. Model dhonis come in all sizes, materials and prices. Just make sure you can get it home without breaking it.

It is worth looking around Malé's tourist, craft and general shops for little caches of antique gold and silver jewellery. There seem to be the remnants of many a family heirloom scattered around, including heavy bracelets, rings, mesh belts, necklaces, and small, intricately engraved boxes. The price will depend on how enthusiastic you look and sound to the shopkeeper. Prepare yourself for a long bargaining session.

Ribudu Island in Dhaalu (South Nilandu Atoll) is famous for making gold jewellery, and Huludeli, in the same atoll, for silver jewellery. Old clocks and wooden chests feature prominently among other curios.

General household items which can make good souvenirs or gifts are anything made from a coconut shell, such as toddy holders and cups; woven palm leaf baskets; *sataa* mats; and folding carved Koran rests.

Other popular souvenirs are sea shells, shark and dolphin teeth, or mother-of-pearl, coral and tortoiseshell goods. Laviyani (Fadippolu Atoll) is tops for making black coral and mother-of-pearl handicrafts. In the name of responsible tourism, however, you should avoid buying any of these shell and coral products, especially anything made of tortoiseshell. The turtles are supposed to be protected and the sale of shell products restricted, but the rules have little effect when money is involved. If tourists stop buying the products, however, maybe the reason for killing these creatures will be removed. Thankfully tortoiseshell products are a banned import in many countries, including Australia.

You can also buy the Maldives' national instrument, the bodu beru drum, but it is cumbersome to carry. The best ones come from Felidu, the capital island of Vaavu

(Felidu Atoll). Check the drum skin to see if you might have trouble getting it past your own customs.

On a more mundane level, printed T-shirts are proving a lucrative sideline for Malé souvenir shops and even some island fishing villages that are visited regularly by raiding parties of resort tourists. The shops and villages buy a batch of Chinese cotton T-shirts, dye on the designs and sell them for around Rf 25 to Rf 40. There are, however, a couple of shops in Malé which have gone to a great effort to produce high quality T-shirts with beautiful (or at least interesting) designs on them. In particular have a look at the T-shirts on sale at Pink Coral on Faamudheyri Magu, Lemon on Chandani Magu and Banana Boat on Faridi Magu. Hummingbird Helicopters also has a couple of interesting T-shirts (designed by Pink Coral), although these are generally only for sale to passengers.

The Maldives used to be a duty-free haven and Malé was constantly overrun by plane loads of Indians and Sri Lankans on smuggling excursions. Although there is a new duty-free complex in Malé, it is not worth buying luxury goods there. The Indians still come, though not in such great numbers, to buy polyester material for saris. They get it for a third of what they would pay back home.

In Malé there are numerous tailors (one opposite the Nivico Guest House) who will stitch you a shirt in a day for Rf 50 (short sleeves) or Rf 75 (long sleeves). You need two metres of material.

Music by local artists is another good souvenir. 'Maldives Fantasy' by Meyna Hassan and 'Dhoni' by Zero Degree Atoll are two contemporary favourites with locals and visitors alike.

Conservation Note

The Maldivian government is stepping up its campaign to cut down on the sale of tortoiseshell products. The export of unfinished coral and shells is forbidden and hefty fines are doled out to those who breach these regulations. It is also illegal to remove shells and coral from beaches or during dives.

To further discourage you from buying environmentally unsound souvenirs, many governments (including the Australian government) strictly forbid the import of tortoiseshell, coral and shells.

Getting There & Away

Aside from a few yachties, just about everyone who comes to the Maldives arrives by plane. However you're travelling, it's worth taking out travel insurance. Keep a close eye on the fine print in any policy before you sign up. If you are going to be diving, or are even contemplating it, remember that if you were unfortunate enough to have a serious diving accident you may have to be flown to Singapore at low altitude. Simply stated, everyone should be covered for the worst possible case.

Most visitors to the Maldives come on chartered flights from Europe as part of a resort package. The most popular, regular and direct connections are with Sri Lanka, south-west India and Singapore.

AIR

The quickest and cheapest way into the country is with Air Lanka or Indian Airlines. The former runs a return service from Colombo to Malé five days a week, and the latter from Thiruvananthapuram in Kerala, on the south-west coast of India, twice a week. A one-way ticket costs US$72 to Colombo and US$63 to Thiruvananthapuram but, Indian Airlines offers a 25% discount for travellers under 30 years of age.

Singapore Airlines calls at Malé twice a week either en route to Zürich or terminating in Malé. The Singapore/Malé leg costs around US$600, but for residents of Singapore there is a return excursion fare for around US$890.

To/From the USA & Canada

There are no direct flights from North America to the Maldives. The most direct route would be from San Francisco via Singapore with Singapore Airlines. From the east coast your best bet would be to fly via London or Frankfurt. See the introductory Getting There & Away chapter for information on sources of good value airfares.

To/From the UK

The only non-charter flight from London is with Emirates airline, via Frankfurt and Dubai or Colombo. In low season the fare for this flight is UK£297/495 one-way/return and in high season it is UK£319/594 one-way/return. You must fly via Colombo, Singapore or Europe for connections. For information on sources of good-value airfares see the introductory Getting There & Away chapter. Also see the Tours section at the end of this chapter for names and addresses of tour and package-deal operators in the UK and around the world.

To/From Europe

From Germany you should expect to pay DM1650 to DM1900 return depending on the season, if you fly on a scheduled flight. For a better deal, try your luck with a Last Minute flight (these can be organised at most major airports in Germany). If anything is available, you could well save DM500 to DM600 on the return fare.

Vienna's Lauda Air operates one flight every two weeks from Vienna, but on a charter basis. Pakistan's PIA now flies to Malé, as does Bulgaria's Balkan (from a number of European cities via Sofia).

Singapore Airlines flies out of Zürich once a week and there is a possibility of increasing that service. Malé can now be included as a stopover with Singapore Airlines on the way from Australia to Europe.

Several of the European services stop en route at Bahrain or the United Arab Emirates to pick up Western oil and construction workers heading for some R&R.

In Amsterdam, NBBS (see the introductory Getting There & Away chapter for details) is a popular travel agent.

To/From Australia

Singapore Airlines flies to the Maldives, via Singapore, from most of the state capitals in Australia. Return fares from Melbourne via

Singapore to Malé, for example, are A$1868 in the low season, and A$2200 in the high season. Air Lanka does the cheapest deals out of Australia with the return fare to Malé via Colombo costing from A$1399 to A$1440 depending on the season.

To/From New Zealand
New Zealanders have to fly via Singapore to get to the Maldives.

To/From Asia
Hong Kong is the discount plane ticket capital of the Asian region. Its bucket shops are at least as unreliable as those of other cities. Ask the advice of other travellers before buying a ticket.

STA, which is reliable, has branches in Hong Kong, Tokyo, Singapore, Bangkok and Kuala Lumpur.

Charter Lines
The other flying alternatives are with the following charter lines: Balair from Zürich and Milan; Condor from Düsseldorf, Munich and Frankfurt: and LTU from Düsseldorf and Munich as well as Zas from Cairo and EVA from Taipei. Each of these airlines runs anything from one to three flights a week in the high season. With Condor you can purchase a one-way fare, but only in Germany.

Round-the-World Tickets
Round-the-World (RTW) tickets have become very popular in the last few years. The airline RTW tickets are often real bargains, and can work out no more expensive, or even cheaper, than an ordinary return ticket. Prices start at about UK£850, A$1800 or US$1300.

The official airline RTW tickets are usually put together by a combination of two airlines, and permit you to fly anywhere you want on their route systems so long as you do not backtrack. Other restrictions are that you (usually) must book the first sector in advance and cancellation penalties then apply. There may be restrictions on how many stops you are permitted and usually the

tickets are valid for 90 days up to a year. An alternative type of RTW ticket is one put together by a travel agent using a combination of discounted tickets.

Arriving in the Maldives by Air
Malé International Airport is on Hulhule Island two km across the water from the capital. Customs, immigration and health checks are relatively perfunctory if you are on the way to a resort with all the other passengers, or seem to be.

Flights are met by a gang of assorted tour operators and an even greater variety of ferries. There is a tourist information counter next to the bank, but don't count on either being open if you arrive after hours.

There will be tour agents and touts waiting for resort tourists but, if you're prepared to wait around until the crowds disperse, there may be one who will arrange a room for you in a Malé guesthouse from as little as US$15 a night. If not, take the ferry for Rf 10 across to the capital or, if you have the money, take a chance on a resort vacancy. It is always best to phone ahead to a resort before heading out there on the hope that they may have room.

Whatever you end up doing to get away from the airport, someone will want to take your passport and ticket from you. Local operators and resorts do this in order to facilitate visa renewals and flight ticket reconfirmations. All reports suggest that this system does make life easier for tourists and that people really do get their documents back in time to fly, however, you are not obliged to give your documents up to anyone. They will probably insist, but if you refuse often enough, they will accept your decision.

There are plans to develop the old RAF runway on Gan in Addu Atoll to allow international flights to bring tourists in to the Ocean Reef Club, but for the time being they are just plans.

There is a public telephone at the airport. It costs Rf 1 to call Malé.

Leaving the Maldives by Air
Reaching the airport under your own steam

is not quite as easy as leaving it. You have to allow plenty of time if you go by ferry, as they only run regularly at peak times, or you'll have to hire a dhoni for around US$5. From 6.30 to 7.30 am you may be able to travel free of charge to Hulhule on the ferries used by the airport staff, although this is frowned upon if you are not invited.

If you are visiting other islands, and depending on fishing dhonis, allow a week to get back to Malé and Hulhule.

There is a good café and restaurant at Hulhule. In the departure lounge, there is a duty-free and souvenir shop. Believe it or not you can buy alcohol at the duty-free section. There is a drinks counter in the lounge as well, but you are better off in the café, as the departure lounge is stifling, crowded and boring.

Departure Tax Airport departure tax is US$7 and must be paid in dollars. Pay it at the window just outside the terminal building before you pass through security into the building.

SEA
Cargo Ship
Travelling to and from the Maldives by cargo ship is rarely done, but if you have time on your hands (and a lead-lined stomach) it is a possibility.

Several ships travel each month between Malé and Colombo or Tuticorin, south of Thiruvananthapuram in south-west India, exporting fish and returning with spices, vegetables, biscuits and the like. In Tuticorin seek out Albert & Co shipping agents; and in Colombo ask for Cargo Boats Shipping Lanes.

Although no shipping agent seems to be enthusiastic about taking passengers, you can try approaching ARU Enterprises on Orchid Magu in Malé about passage to Tuticorin. Another place worth checking is Mariya Shipping on the same street.

If you're travelling to Sri Lanka, call first at Matrana Enterprises Ltd on Majidi Magu, Malé (near the Olympus Cinema). They run an 800-tonne boat twice a month to Sri Lanka, via Gan Island. The voyage lasts from three to four days and they will take one to three passengers, depending on available space. The 'cabin' is an empty locker room with a mattress thrown in and the food is the basic curry and rice shared with the 15 crew.

The Maldives government operates a number of ships to Singapore, from where around 80% of the islands' imports come, but they do not carry passengers. Some of the other container ships which come in from Singapore have been known to carry passengers occasionally, but this generally only seems to happen if you are introduced to the ship's captain over a beer.

Yachts
Yachts, of course, present a more romantic but more remote opportunity. If you're looking for a yacht in the Maldives, your best bet is to check with the Atolls Administration in Malé where skippers must go to get cruising permits. But don't hold your breath. The other meeting places used to be at the Nasandhura Palace Hotel and the Alia Hotel in Malé, but both these establishments closed down their bars in late 1992, leaving Malé without a foreigners' watering hole. This situation may change in late 1993, but then again, it might not.

If you arrive in the country by yacht, you must use the customs jetty on arrival and berth No 7 for disembarking.

The regulations say:

Foreigners are not allowed to land at Malé without permission in the night after 10 pm. Anchorage between Malé and Funadoo Island is strictly prohibited.

TOURS
Package holidays vary from one travel agent to another and from one month to the next, so check a few agents for the best deal. Some tour companies also offer a stopover in the Maldives, with Singapore Airlines, for two or more nights at a choice of resorts. It costs around US$50 per day which covers full board and airport transfers.

About 90% of visitors to the Maldives go

to just one resort on a 10 to 14-day package holiday where absolutely everything is arranged for them. These holidays begin at around US$250 a week for full-board (air-fares excluded). Discounts of up to 30% are offered on the more expensive packages during the low season and there are general reductions available on diving courses, fishing and watersports.

Kuoni London offers a basic, low season, 14 day holiday on Baros, the largest and cheapest resort, for UK£959 including flights and accommodation. In the high season the rate is UK£1212.

In Australia, packages from Sydney start at around A$1700/2150 for low/high season, on a twin share basis. For example, a seven night, all-inclusive Club Med package costs A$2135/2170 in the May to October /February to April months. A five night, half-board package on Bandos costs A$1699 return plus A$90 per extra night. A five-night, full board, package on Emboodhu Finolhu costs A$1769 plus A$104 for each additional night. It is cheaper from Perth, but either way it is considerably cheaper to go to the Maldives on a package than to book your resort when you get there.

There are also separate dhoni safari holiday packages to consider. These can be booked in advance by phone, or when you arrive in Malé. For more information see Safari Cruises in the Maldives Getting Around chapter.

Following is a fairly comprehensive list of some of the major agents around the world which offer package deals to the Maldives. More often than not, you will be unable to buy directly from these agents, however, if your own travel agent comes up with only one or two possibilities, show them this list and ask them to try again – it is just possible that something more competitive may turn up.

Australia
    Foster Travel, 10 Station Rd, Foster, Victoria 3960
    Island Affair Holidays, Singapore Airlines House, 17 Bridge St, Sydney, NSW 2000
    Taprobane Tours (WA) Pty Ltd, PO Box 386, Victoria Park, WA 6100

Austria
    Astropa/Meridian Touristik International, Meridian Reisen und Touristik GMBH, Kartner Ring 17/2 A-1010 Vienna
    Jumbo Touristik, Stefan Senft Reisebüro, Schellinggasse 7 1010 Vienna
    Kuoni Travel Ltd, Brauhausgasse 7-9, 1050 Vienna

Belgium
    Jetair Belgium, 8400 Oostende
    Odysseus Travel, 2510 Mortsel – Antwerp

Finland
    Finnmatkat, Mannerheimintie 5 C, 00100 Helsinki

France
    Jet Tours, 22 Quai de la Megisserie, 75001 Paris
    Voyages Kuoni, 95 Rue d'Amsterdam, 75008 Paris
    Planet Voyages, 45 Rue de Richelieu, 75001 Paris
    Slam Voyages, 17 Rue du Faubourg Montmartre, 75009 Paris
    MVM Paris, 70 Rue Pernety, 75014 Paris
    Air Tour, Société Française de Tourisme Aérien, 36 Avenue de l'Opéra, Paris
    Maine Montparnasse Voyages, 16 Rue Littre, 75006 Paris

Germany
    Air Tours International, Adalbertstrasse 44-48, 6000 Frankfurt 90
    NUR Tourist GMBH, Hochhaus am Baselerplatz, Postfach 11, 6000 Frankfurt 11
    Kreutzer Flugreisen GMBH, Neuhauserstrasse 6/1, 8000 Munich 2
    Transair, Bismarckstrasse 102, 4000 Düsseldorf 1
    Tjaeborg, All Kauf Reisen, Korchenbroicherstrasse 4, 4050 Mönchen-Gladbach 1
    Meiers Welt Reisen, Monschauerstrasse, 4000 Düsseldorf 11
    Jet Reisen GMBH, Kaiserstrasse 64 D, 6000 Frankfurt 1
    Aquarius Reisen, Jahnstrasse 15, 6000 Frankfurt 1
    Airconti Flugreisen GMBH & Co, Neuhauserstrasse 34, 8000 Munich 2
    Touristik Union International GMBH & Co, Karl-Weichert-Allee, 3000 Hannover 61
    Jahn Reisen, Elsenheimerstrasse 61, 8000 Munich 21

Hong Kong
    Hong Thai Citizens Travel Services Ltd, 7/F Bank of Credit & Commerce Building, 25-31 Carnarvon Rd, Tsim-Sha-Tsui, Kowloon, Hong Kong
    Club Mediterranea, 2/F BCC House, 10 Queens Rd, Hong Kong
    Kwan's Travel Services Ltd, 7/F Bank of Credit & Commerce Building, 25-31 Carnarvon Rd, Tsim-Sha-Tsui, Kowloon, Hong Kong

Italy
> Tourisanda, Via Sede Centrale, Via Poerio 2a, 20129 Milan
> Franco Rosso International, Via Roma 366, 10121 Turin
> International Incoming Centre, Via L Settembrini, 00195 Rome
> I Viaggi del Sesante, Via Vittorio e Oriando, 75-00185 Rome
> Viaggi Kuoni SPA, Via Benedetto Croce 6, 00142 Rome

Japan
> Inpac Japan Co Ltd, 804 Royal Mansion Kanasugi 2-2-12, Shiba, Minato-ku, Tokyo
> Sanwa Air Service co Ltd, Orchid Tours, 3rd floor Mohri Building, 5-4-7 Chome, Ginza Chuo-ku, Tokyo 104
> Vivre International Inc, Meisei Building, 8-9 Sakuragaoka Cho, Shibuya-ku, Tokyo 150
> Miki Tourist Co Ltd, Senbikuya Building, 8-8-8 Ginza Chuo-ku, Tokyo
> JTA Japan, 106 Amagi Roppongi Building, 7 Chome, Minato-ku, Tokyo
> Sun Travel Co Ltd, 1-34-2 Komagome, Toshima-ku, Tokyo
> Play Guide Tours Inc, 4-9-6 Akasaka, Minato-ku, Tokyo

Netherlands
> Sportreizen Service, Nijvberheidsweg 14, NL 4731 CZ Oudenbosch
> Eis Bruijstens, Wibaustraat 100, 1001 AD, Amsterdam

Norway
> Travel Club, Uten Grenser As, Devregt 2A, N-0170 Oslo 1

Singapore
> Tradewinds, 77 Robinson Rd, 02-06, SIA Building, Singapore 0106

Sri Lanka
> Hemtours, 24 Sir Ernest de Silva Mawatha, Colombo 3
> Tourlanka Ltd, 40 Barnes Place, Colombo 7
> Ceylon Tours Ltd, 67 Parsons Rd 4, Colombo 2
> Aquarius Paradise Travels Ltd, Galadari Meridien Hotel, 64 Lotus Rd, Colombo 1
> Walter Tours Ltd, 130 Glennie St, Colombo 2
> Gemini Tours, 40 Wijerama Mawatha, Colombo 2
> Jet Travel, Ethukala, Negombo

Sweden
> Fritids Resor, Brottninggatan 31, 103 27 Stockholm
> Vingressor, Svevagen 25, 10520 Stockholm

Switzerland
> Kuoni Travel Ltd, Neue Hard 7, 8037 Zürich
> Irene Tourism & Travel, Dufourstrasse 82, 8008 Zürich
> Imholz Reise AG, Birmensdorferstrasse 108, 8036 Zürich
> Manta Reisen AG, Zentralstrasse 72, 8003 Zürich
> Hotel Plan, Habsburgstrasse 9, 8031 Zürich
> Beach Travel AG, Blumenrain 16, 4001 Basel
> Esco Reisen, Dufourstrasse 9, 4010 Basel
> Airtour Suisse AT, Obere Zollgasse 75a, Ostermundigen, 3072 Bern
> Indi Tours AG, Oberdorfstrasse, 8914 Aeugst
> Tropic Tours AG, Alte Obfelderstrasse 8, 8910 Affoltern am Albis

UK
> Hayes & Jarvis Travel Ltd, 6 Harriet St, Knightsbridge, London SQ1X 9Q
> Kuoni Travel Ltd, Kuoni House, Dorking, Surrey RH5 4AZ
> Thompson Tour Operations Ltd, Greater London House, Hampstead Rd, London NW1 7SD
> Wings Faraway Holidays, Wings House, Broxbourne, Hertfordshire EN 10 7 JD
> Speedbird, Alta House, 152 King St, London W6 OQU
> Indian Ocean Hideaways, 7 Haymarket, London SW1Y

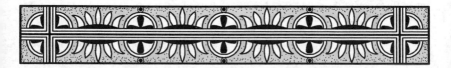

Getting Around

AIR

Air Maldives has two planes: an 18-seat Skyvan made by Short Brothers, Belfast, and a Dornier 228. There are flights to Gan Island, in the southernmost Addu Atoll, every day, with two flights on Saturday. There are flights to Kadhu Island in Laamu on Monday, Wednesday, Thursday and Saturday and to Hanimadu Island in Haa Dhaal Atoll in the far north of the country on Tuesday, Wednesday, Thursday and Sunday. The flight to Kadhu and Hanimadu costs Rf 450 one way.

The Gan flight is often fully booked well in advance and costs Rf 800 one way. (Residents pay Rf 700.)

The two-hour flight to Gan provides a great opportunity for photographing the amazing array of islands and atolls. The seats in the 3rd or 4th row, depending on the flight, are particularly good, as the windows protrude like bubbles from the body of the plane in such a way that you can effectively stick your head out the window and look straight down. The row number varies. Request one of these seats when you check in (the right side is best when flying south and the left side when flying north).

The timetable may be disrupted by weather, official duties or extra flights added during school holidays and so on.

It is possible for groups to charter one of the planes for photo flights at a rate of US$700 for 30 minutes or US$1400 per hour.

Helicopter

One of the highlights of any trip to the Maldives is a helicopter flight over the atolls. More and more visitors, particularly to the more distant resorts in Ari Atoll, are choosing to fly to one of the eight helipads rather than take the long and often rough dhoni trip. Six of the helipads are in Ari Atoll. From north to south they are at Rasdu, Bodhufolhudu, Kandolodhu, Embudu,

Maafushivaru and Ari Beach. The other two pads are at Kuredu in the north of Laviyani Atoll and Guraidu (Guraidhu) in the south of South Malé Atoll.

There is no fixed timetable of flights, however, there are generally several flights every day. The most frequently used helipads are at Ari Beach and Bodhufolhudu, while Kuredu is used rarely, as it serves only one resort. The one-way fares from Malé are as follows:

Guraidu	US$69
Rasdu	US$123
Kandolodhu	US$127
Bodhufolhudu	US$129
Embudu	US$137
Maafushivaru	US$137
Ari Beach	US$142
Kuredu	US$179

Also on offer are 15-minute sightseeing flights from the airport and from most of the helipads. These have become extremely popular, so it is a good idea to ask at the reception of your resort soon after you arrive if you are interested. The cost of these flights is US$59 per person, plus the cost of the transfer from your resort to the nearest helipad and back.

So-called 'Robinson Crusoe Excursions' are another interesting option. These generally begin at the airport in the morning, with a flight to Bodhufolhudu. From the helipad, you take a dhoni to a nearby desert island, where you spend the day doing whatever you do on a desert island. At the end of the day the dhoni brings you to Nika Hotel, where you can change before visiting the village of Guraidu and flying back to Malé. Hummingbird charges US$149 for the day, with a buffet lunch on the desert island included in the price. Transfer from your resort to the airport and back is separate. A similar picnic tour is being planned to Guraidu and another to Kandolodhu.

Also available on request are helicopter diving excursions to Ari Beach. Flights start at Malé or Guraidu and include two dhoni dives and lunch at Ari Beach resort. The helicopters never fly above around 350 metres, so there is no danger in flying so soon after diving.

For more information about helicopter flights ask at the reception at your resort or contact Hummingbird Helicopters (☎ 325708, fax 323161), 4th floor, MHA Building, Orchid Magu, Malé. Note that Hummingbird is a British-run company using Australian, South African, British and Bulgarian pilots to fly their US and Russian helicopters.

SEA
Dhonis & Vedis
The dhoni is the traditional all-purpose vessel of the Maldives. They come in all sizes and superstructures but are basically the same shape. (When they have the prow attached they look like ancient slave

galleys.) Most are engine-powered, but only the ferries have done away with sails.

Fishing dhonis offer the best opportunity for rides to those atolls that are accessible within a day's journey from Malé. For instance, from Malé to Felidu Island in Vaavu takes around six hours and costs Rf 150.

The departure time and duration of a voyage depends on the weather and sea conditions which vary considerably within and between the atolls. Be warned that this can make the trip exciting or terrifying, invigorating or sickening.

Fishing dhonis do not carry a radio, lifeboats or rescue gear. Capsize and you are history. This advice won't save your life, but if you wrap your luggage in a plastic bag it should protect your gear from getting wet on deck. You can buy giant, clear plastic bags from general stores on Majidi Magu in Malé.

To travel to the outer atolls, you must take a *vedi*. Vedis are larger, square-shaped wooden cargo boats used for trading between Malé and the outer atolls. A trip down to Seenu (Addu Atoll), the most southerly and distant atoll, takes two days and costs Rf 300. Your bunk is a mat on a shelf, the toilet is the sea and fellow passengers may include chickens.

You will need a permit to persuade a dhoni or vedi skipper to take you to any island which is not a resort. If you have made any friends in Malé they will usually introduce you to a fishing and supply boat from their island or atoll in Malé harbour. But if you have to find your own, the vessels are identified by their atoll administrative letter marked within a square on the bow. These are:

Haa Alif	(A)	Meemu	(K)
Haa Dhaal	(B)	Faaf	(L)
Shaviyani	(C)	Dhaalu	(M)
Noonu	(D)	Thaa	(N)
Raa	(E)	Laamu	(O)
Baa	(F)	Gaaf Alif	(P)
Laviyani	(G)	Gaaf Dhaal	(Q)
Kaafu	(H)	Gnaviyani	(R)
Alif	(I)	Seenu	(S)
Vaavu	(J)		

To/From Resorts Around Malé

There is a greater choice of vessel within Malé (Kaafu) Atoll with regular supply and excursion dhonis running back and forth from nearby resorts to the capital.

The closest resorts to the capital and therefore the cheapest to visit are Kurumba, Bandos and Club Med. You can telephone the resort or contact its Malé office to find out times, costs and conditions. Fares range from US$20 to US$150 return. For the more distant resorts you will have to stay a night or two if there are vacancies.

The United Nations club runs a day trip to a nearby resort each Friday, weather permitting, for a nominal fee. It is supposed to be for UN staff, expats and guests but there's no harm in asking. You can call the UNDP (☎ 324501-3) or go to their offices on Kulhidoshu Magu.

Finally you can charter a covered dhoni from the Nasandhura Palace Hotel side of Marine Drive by bargaining with individual boat owners or through a boat-hire agency. Expect to pay US$100 per day as a minimum. If you are a 1st-class bargainer you may get it down to US$80, but the dhoni crew will not be happy about it, and you will then be expected to buy them lunch and possibly pay extra for fuel.

ZSS (☎ 322505), on Marine Drive, hires speedboats (for up to five passengers). These are expensive with daily rates varying from US$500 to US$700 depending on how far you want to travel and how many hours you mean by 'a day'.

Often the cheapest way to visit the resorts from Malé, particularly the more distant ones, is to go to the airport to catch boats waiting to transfer tourists off incoming flights. Check plane arrival times first. Another option is to ring the resort you are hoping to visit and ask if you can hop on their supply boat. While they will probably say no, if you agree to buy lunch on the island, they may agree.

Safari Cruises

If you only have a week or two to spend in the Maldives and want to get around, this is the best way. A few tour companies offer cruises around the atolls neighbouring Malé. They charge from US$44 to US$200 or more per person per day aboard a dhoni with a cabin or a custom safari boat. The prices vary according to the boat you are on and the number of people booked in the group. Diving generally costs around US$45 extra per day per person for two dives per day.

The operator arranges the permits to visit approved island villages. You sleep on board or camp out on uninhabited islands.

Trips usually last a week and cater for six to 10 people. Voyages Maldives (☎ 322019, 323017), on Faridi Magu, are well recommended as are Phoenix Hotels & Resorts (☎ 325498) on Marine Drive. They both go to Vaavu or Alif (Felidu or Ari atolls) in the south and Laviyani (Fadippolu Atoll) in the north.

Sun Travel & Tours (☎ 325975), on Maaveyo Magu, and Rasja Travel & Trading (☎ 321488), on Husnuheena Magu, operate on a much smaller scale than the other two companies, however, they are more likely to be able to help individual travellers who arrive in the country without a safari booking, and their rates can be just as competitive.

You can book safaris through adventure tour operators in Australia, Europe and the USA.

Yacht Cruises

After going through customs at Malé, private yachts need to apply for a Cruising Permit from the Atolls Administration. Apart from resort visits, you must sleep on board.

According to one yachtie, the Maldives are comparatively awkward to sail around. I was told that it is difficult to anchor in the deep water surrounding most islands and the resorts don't welcome yachts.

ROAD
Car

Apart from the occasional delivery van on one or two of the larger resorts, there are motor vehicles only at the airport, on Malé and on Addu Atoll. The better part of the road network is compressed coral, sand and earth, however, the number of paved roads in Malé is gradually being increased.

The roads flood easily after heavy rain, turning into rivers full of hidden potholes. Maldivians are supposed to drive on the left-hand side of the road, but in practice they go around the potholes any which way they can and the cars rarely get out of second gear. There is, however, a major reconstruction project underway to seal the roads.

Thanks to the RAF, who flew away for good in 1976, Addu Atoll has some paved roads but they are in a bad shape.

Cars are status symbols and traffic congestion is a problem in Malé. The government has slapped a 200% import tax on cars to reduce the influx. If you borrow a private car, you first have to get your licence approved by the Department of Transport.

Taxi

Taxi services operate on both Malé and Addu, but are only really necessary to get to and from the airport boats. You can walk around most islands in under an hour.

A taxi in Malé costs Rf 10 a trip, except after midnight when you should pay Rf 20. Call Regular Taxis (☎ 322454) or Express (☎ 323132).

Motorcycle & Bicycle

Motorcycles are becoming more popular, though a greater curse, in the Maldives. Those who can't afford the motor just have a bicycle.

There are almost 30,000 bicycles in Malé. It's fun to see Maldivians riding their bikes in the rain and almost disappearing into hidden potholes amid hoots of laughter from their friends.

There are no motorcycles or bicycles for hire in Malé on an official basis. You may be able to organise a reasonable deal with a guesthouse if you are staying there, perhaps even having the cost of the bicycle included in the room rate. Make sure there is a *bati* (light) fitted on the front. These lights are Chinese-made and cost only Rf 10 each. They must be on at 6 pm whether it's dark or

not, otherwise you can be arrested (although it's more likely that you will just be told to get off the bike and push it). If your light doesn't work, keep tapping it in case you pass a police officer.

To add to the fun, or confusion, the one-way and no-entry signs are sited in an uncertain way at intersections and you're never sure which street they apply to.

In Addu Atoll, you can hire bicycles, motor scooters, and larger motorbikes from the Ocean Reef Club. The hire rates had not yet been decided when the author of this book visited Gan, as the resort was not yet open.

RESORT OPERATORS

Each resort has an office or agency in Malé. The main operators are:

Universal Enterprises
    38 Orchid Magu (☎ 322971) and Marine Drive East. They run Baros, Fesdu, Kuramathi, Kurumba, Veligandu Huraa, and Nakatchafushi resorts.
Safari Tours
    Chandani Magu (☎ 323524). They run Dhiggiri, Alimatha, Boduhithi, Ellaidu and Kudahithi resorts.
Dhirham Travels
    Faamudheyri Magu (☎ 323372). They run Gasfinolhu, Fihalhohi and Vabinfaru.

The agents for the other resorts are given in the Atolls chapter when the resort island is discussed.

TOUR OPERATORS

Perhaps most important for the unattached traveller are the few independent travel agencies.

Paradise Travel & Tours (☎ 321502), on Lonuziyaarai Magu, Malé (attached to Sunrise Lodge) has good connections with a number of resorts. The staff will take their time to go through all the resorts in your price range and book your choice for you at a better price than you can arrange yourself. They can also organise fishing trips and dhoni hire from Malé at very competitive rates.

Sun Travel & Tours (☎ 325975), on Maaveyo Magu, Malé, could also prove very helpful. The owner, Mohammed Arif, prides himself on the fact that he or someone from his office meets every flight into the islands to snap up more independent visitors than any other agency. Apart from being able to offer good prices on a number of resorts, they can also organise safaris at good rates.

Imad Agency (☎ 322964), 39/2 Chandani Magu, may be worth trying to find out about special deals. Voyages Maldives (☎ 322019, 323017), on Faridi Magu, has reasonable deals, as well as representing Balair, Sterling and Monarch charters. It is the specialist in dhoni safari cruises.

Rasja Travel & Trading (☎ 321488), Husnuheena Magu, Malé, is a smaller agency with fewer connections, however, those that it does have are pretty good. The owner, Abdul 'Absy' Rasheed, insists that he can beat anyone on safari prices.

Malé

Travellers in search of a desert island paradise will be slightly disappointed in Malé.

The island capital is packed to the edges with anywhere from 55,000 to 65,000 residents or more depending on who you ask. To help accommodate everyone, the boundaries of the island have been extended twice over the past 30 years through land reclamation. Despite Malé's size of one single sq mile, it never strikes you as overcrowded or bustling. It's more like a small town, neatly laid out and tidy; although it's developing at a fast rate and losing a little of its character with each new building. The first five-storey building, an office block, was built in 1987. By the beginning of 1993 there were another two buildings that size in use and more under construction.

Since anyone who arrives in the Maldives without a pre-arranged package may have to spend some time here getting organised and cleared for inter-atoll travel, it is worth getting to know the place and people well.

Orientation

As well as expanding, Malé (pronounced 'Mah-leh') is changing rapidly with constant rebuilding. Government and commercial offices shift around and new developments spring up. As it only takes 30 minutes to walk from one end of the island to the other, the inconvenience is minimal.

The capital is divided into four districts, from west to east: Maafannu, which covers most of the western end of the island from the Singapore Bazaar area of Chandani Magu, is where you'll find the Theemuge (president's home), a few embassies, guesthouses and the residential areas of Malé's poorer citizens; Machangolhi, which runs east-west across the middle of the island, boasts the popular cafés and restaurants of Majidi Magu, the district's main street; Galolhu, a crowded residential maze in the south-east part of Malé, is a confusing and interesting place to explore; and Henveiru,

the north-east pocket of Malé, is renowned for the beautiful houses of the *befalu* (upper class) along Ameer Ahmed Magu and the fine buildings on Marine Drive overlooking the harbour.

Magu is the Maldivian word for a wide, unpaved coral street. A *goalhi* is a narrow lane, and a *higun* is a longer, wider goalhi.

Business activity on Malé is concentrated towards the north end of the island, around Marine Drive and the harbours. The other principal streets are Chandani Magu, which divides Malé from north to south, and Majidi Magu, which divides it from east to west.

The fishing and cargo port is to the west of Chandani Magu, the tourist and yacht harbour to the east. The reclaimed land is mainly to the south, and a new harbour was inaugurated in the south-east corner of the city in late 1992 to help ease the load on the already overextended old port.

Information

For information on foreign consulates, bookshops, libraries, telephones, hospitals and pharmacies refer to the Maldives' Facts for the Visitor chapter.

Tourist Offices The head office of the Department of Tourism, in the Ghaazee Building on Ameer Ahmed Magu, is the best place to go for specific enquiries. The department has a general information desk in the lobby of the Nasandhura Palace Hotel on Marine Drive, and another at the airport. Travel agents in Malé can also supply you with information on resorts and, to a lesser extent, the outer atolls.

The Atolls Administration office, where you must get permits to visit uninhabited islands and the outer atolls, is next to Air Maldives in the Fashanaa Building on Marine Drive.

Voyages Maldives is on Faridi Magu east of the Novelty Bookshop. For the addresses of other resort operators and travel agents

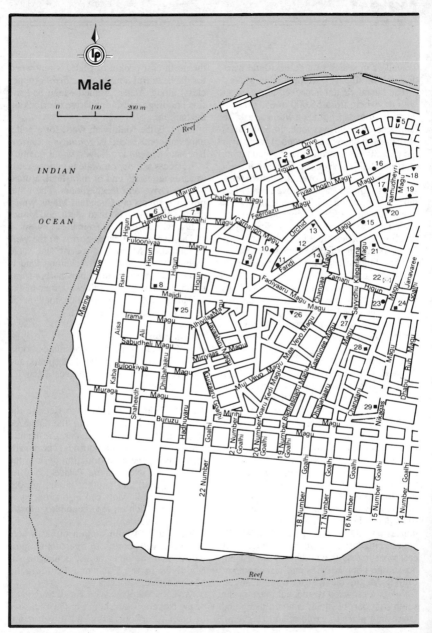

Malé

INDIAN

OCEAN

Reef

Reef

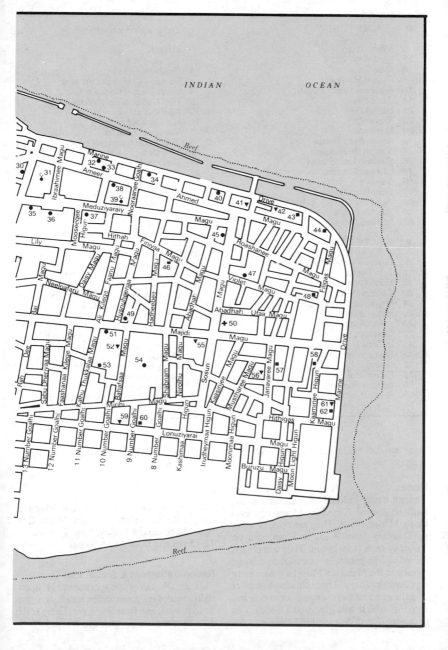

INDIAN OCEAN

Reef

Reef

■ PLACES TO STAY

6	Mermaid Inn
7	Hotel Alia
8	Male Tours Inn
9	Fehivid Huvaruge
12	Sunshine Guest House
14	Transit Inn
21	Marvel Rest
28	Kosheege
29	Mazaage
43	Nasandhura Palace
44	Maagiri Guesthouse
46	Burunee Guesthouse
48	Lifsham Guesthouse
53	Selvio
57	Sony Guesthouse
58	Reedhoo Kokaa
60	Sunrise Lodge
62	Noofaru Lodge

▼ PLACES TO EAT

2	Bukharei Hotel and Bukharei Cinema
13	Twin Peaks
18	Moon Cafe
20	Cooling Point
24	Majeedhee Uafaa and Junction Hotel
25	Hotel de Shark
26	Indian Restaurant
27	Quench
41	In Time
42	Queen of the Night
52	Orange
55	Camy Cool Spot
56	Lantern Restaurant
59	South Restaurant

61	The Dragon Restaurant

OTHER

1	Customs
3	People's Choice Supermarket
4	Local Trading Centre
5	Fish Market & Fish Market Hotel
10	Adam's Laundry
11	Novelty Bookshop
15	Voyages Maldives
16	Theemuge (president's home),
17	Pink Coral
19	Banana Boat
22	Post Office
23	Asrafee Bookshop
30	Maldives Monetary Authority on Chandani Magu
31	Islamic Centre & Grand Friday Mosque
32	Ministry of Atolls Administration
33	Department of Tourism
34	Bank of Maldives
35	Dhiraagu
36	National Museum & Sultan Park
37	Sri Lankan High Commission
38	Department of Immigration & Department of Information & Broadcasting
39	Hukuru Miski
40	Universal Enterprises (Amex rep)
45	National Centre for Linguistic & Historical Research
47	USA Consulate
49	Olympus Cinema
50	Central Hospital
51	Fototeknik
54	National Stadium on Majidi Magu.

refer to the Maldives Getting Around chapter.

Money

The six banks in Malé are clustered at the harbour end of Chandani Magu and east along Marine Drive. They are open Sunday to Thursday from 9 am to 1 pm, and on Saturday from 9 to 11 am. They are closed on Friday. In general it is easier to change money at the Maldives Monetary Authority on Chandani Magu. There are also a number of authorised moneychangers around town, some of which will give you US$ cash in exchange for US$ travellers' cheques. Try

some of the hardware shops, souvenir shops and guesthouses.

Post

The post office is on Chandani Magu a couple of blocks north of Majidi Magu. It is open daily, except Friday, from 7.30 am to 12.45 pm and from 4 to 5.50 pm.

National Museum & Sultan Park

This small, two-storey museum is open daily, except on government holidays, from 9 am to noon and from 3 to 6 pm. Entry is Rf 5. The entrance is guarded by a WW I

German torpedo, donated by a Royal Navy warship.

You'll be followed rather than guided by a caretaker who makes sure you don't touch or take anything. Exhibits consist mainly of the sultans' belongings – threadbare clothes, weapons and throne. These exhibits are poorly labelled and, as the museum staff speak only Divehi, there is no-one to explain the story or significance of what's on display.

Given this, perhaps, the best attractions are Thor Heyerdahl's recent archaeological discoveries of stone figures and carvings from pre-Muslim civilisations, which feature in his book *The Maldive Mystery*.

The Maldivians, however, do not seem to be so proud of the relics. They are on display but are tucked away in a side room without any identification labels or numbers.

The park surrounding the museum was once part of the grounds of the sultan's palace. It is small but on the crowded, compact treeless island, it is an oasis. It would be a nice place to spend a quiet hour reading or writing but it's only open to the public on Friday.

Islamic Centre & Grand Friday Mosque

Built in 1984 with help from the Gulf States, Pakistan, Brunei and Malaysia, this *miski* (mosque) dominates the sprouting Malé skyline. The first thing you see when sailing towards the capital is the gold dome glinting in the sun. (The gold is actually anodised aluminium.) The *munnaaru*, or minaret, is the tallest structure in Malé.

Visits to the Grand Friday Mosque must be arranged to fit in around prayer times and between 9 am and 5 pm. (The mosque closes to non-Muslims 15 minutes before prayer and for the following hour.) Before noon and between 2 and 3 pm are the best times to visit.

Invading bands of resort tourists and casual sightseers are not encouraged but if you are genuinely interested and suitably dressed, you'll get in. You will be asked to remove your shoes and to wash your feet in the huge ablution blocks. Do not wear shorts or short dresses to visit the mosque.

Once inside the mosque, someone will accompany you to the prayer hall, which can accommodate up to 6000 worshippers and has beautiful carved wooden side panels and doors.

The centre also includes a conference hall, library and classrooms.

Hukuru Miski

In order to visit nearby Hukuru Miski, the oldest mosque in the country, you have to apply to the Department of Religious Affairs (☎ 322266) for permission.

Built in 1656, the mosque is famed for its intricate carvings. One long panel, actually carved in the 13th century, commemorates

---

House Names

Although the street names in Malé will be strange to your ears, the house names shouldn't be. The Maldivians seem to have a great passion for bestowing an English name on their homes. Most houses are modest abodes but it seems the smaller and plainer the house, the grander and more flamboyant the name. The selection of English words covers all kinds of images.

Some Maldivians prefer rustic titles like Crabtree, Hillman, Forest and G Meadow (the G stands for Galolhu, which is the district that the house is in). Others are specifically floral like Sweet Rose and Luxury Garden. Marine titles and anything with blue in it are also popular, such as Sea Speed, Marine Dream, Dawn Dive and Blue Haven, while the sun gives rise to the likes of Sun Dance, Radiant and Plain Heat.

There are also exotic ones like Paris Villa, River Nile and Aston Villa, but I liked the more esoteric Remind House, Pardon Villa and Mary Lightning, or those that sound like toilet disinfectants – Ozone, Green Zest and Frenzy.

Shop names, on the other hand, are straight to the point – Kleen Laundry, Fair Price, Goodwill and Neat Store. ■

the introduction of Islam to the Maldives by Abu Al Barakat in 1153 AD.

Apparently worshippers have to face the corner of this mosque when kneeling to pray because the foundations face the sun instead of Mecca.

In the graveyard of Hukuru Miski, overlooked by the imposing blue and white munnaaru, is the tomb of Abu Al Barakat adorned with medieval pennons (flags) and protected by a coral wall. The gold-plated tombstones mark the graves of former sultans.

There are more than 20 miskis, often little more than a coral building with an iron roof, scattered around Malé. Hukuru Miski, near the Grand Friday Mosque, is on Meduziyaaraiy Magu.

Singapore Bazaar

The Singapore Bazaar is the nickname given to the conglomeration of stores along, and around the bottom end of, Chandani Magu (the main north-south street), Faamudheyri Magu, Faridi Magu and Orchid Magu. Aside

from the enormous duty-free shop, a couple of hardware shops and a few cafés, most of the shops here are in the souvenir business. In general the stock does not vary much from one shop to the next. See the Things to Buy section in the Maldives Facts for the Visitor chapter for more on a couple of worthwhile shops in this part of town.

Cannons

An interesting diversion (or excuse for a walk around Malé's coastline) is to see how many ancient cannons you can spot. They have been cleaned up, decorated and proudly placed along the waterfront. The cannons are the only remnants of the ignominious 15-year occupation of Malé by the Portuguese. Their brutal regime came to an end in 1573 when the great hero Thakurufaan and his two brothers led a Maldivian raid on the foreign garrison, killing everyone within it.

Places to Stay – bottom end

Guesthouse prices do not actually vary that much in Malé, however, there are still a number of places where a double room is available for under US$40 per night. The cheapest of these is *Mazaage* (☎ 324669), on Nikagas Magu, which offers several dark and dank ground-floor rooms for US$10 per person with breakfast. They have a video recorder. *Kosheege* (☎ 323585) in an unnamed sidestreet off Chandani Magu near Majidi Magu (see map) has singles/doubles for US$15/25.

Only slightly more expensive and considerably more pleasant is *Selvio* (☎ 324671) in a sidestreet off Kalhu Thukkalaa Magu, one block south of Majidi Magu (see map). They have singles/doubles for US$20/30. *Fehivid Huvaruge* (☎ 324470), 3 Funa Goalhi, near where Faridi Magu joins Orchid Magu, has five rooms and 18 beds. The going rate per person hovers around US$15 a night. The toilet and well are communal.

Nearby is the *Sunshine Guest House* (☎ 322336), 26 Faridi Magu. It also has five rooms and a score of beds for US$15 in the low season and US$25 in the high season.

Noofaru Lodge (☎ 322731) on Marine

Drive, near the corner of Hithigas Magu in the south-east corner of Malé, has reasonable doubles for US$35. Single rates are negotiable.

Reedhoo Kokaa (☎ 322505), Fiyaathoshi Goalhi; *Malé Tours Inn* (☎ 326220), on Majidi Magu close to the corner of Shaheedh Ali Higun; and *Lifsham Guesthouse* (☎ 325386), Gulisthaan Goalhi, all have double rooms for US$35. Single rates are negotiable.

Places to Stay – middle

The middle-range guesthouses in Malé generally price their rooms around US$40 to US$50 a double with breakfast. While they are only a few dollars more expensive than some of the bottom-end places, there is a notable improvement in the standard of accommodation. Prices for singles vary from US$10 to US$15 cheaper, more or less according to how full the guesthouse is.

One of the friendliest places around is *Sunrise Lodge* (☎ 321502), Lonuziyaarai Magu. The manager, Naseer, can help you organise accommodation in a number of resorts at very competitive prices. If you are staying in Malé for a while, ask him about going fishing for barracuda. Singles/doubles cost US$25/40. Another good bet is *Transit Inn* (☎ 320420), Maaveyo Magu, which has very pleasant and spacious rooms and a rooftop patio with a sea view. Doubles cost US$45.

The pink-painted *Mermaid Inn* (☎ 323329), at the west end of Marine Drive overlooking the harbour, used to have a liquor licence but is no longer an inn. It has two single and eight double or triple rooms. They are clean, smartly furnished, carpeted and have attached bathrooms. A double room costs US$40 per night. *Sony Guesthouse* (☎ 323249), Janavaree Magu, has six double rooms for US$45 per night and is popular with visiting sports teams.

Very close to the Nasandhura Palace Hotel on Marine Drive are *Maagiri Guesthouse* (☎ 322576) and the clean and airy *Gadhoo* (☎ 323222). Both of these places have singles/doubles for US$30/40 including breakfast. The Maagiri sells a lunch pack of local snacks (hedhikaa) for around US$2, which is really convenient if you are spending the day on a dhoni, as the best place to get a good deal on a dhoni is at the Nasandhura jetty. You can buy the lunch packs whether you are staying at Maagiri or not.

Places to Stay – top end

There are only two hotels in Malé. They may be top-end in price but certainly not in standard. Until late 1992, both had the only bars and licensed restaurants in Malé. The owner of the Nasandhura closed the bar voluntarily (so they say), and the Alia closed its bar in February 1993 and it is possible that the hotel will also close.

Although long-awaited renovations are underway, the single-storey *Nasandhura Palace* (☎ 323380) is anything but a palace. Because it is close to the airport it relies heavily on arriving and departing tourist parties. Rooms with air-con cost US$55/75 for a single/double including breakfast. The restaurant menu is à la carte.

There is little to choose between the Palace and the *Hotel Alia* (☎ 322080) at the other end of Marine Drive on Haveeru Higun. There singles/doubles cost US$56/83, breakfast is US$3 and dinner or lunch is US$7. They also charge US$5 during the day and US$7 at night for airport transfers.

While there are a few guesthouses in the top-end price range, it is questionable whether paying the extra dollars is really worth it. *Burunee Guesthouse* (☎ 322870), Finivaa Magu, and *Marvel Rest* (☎ 326294), a block south of Faridi Magu near Chandani Magu (see map), both have a reputation for attracting repeat customers, which is always a good sign. Both charge US$55 for a double room with bathroom. Breakfast is included.

Places to Eat

There are three sorts of places to eat in Malé: cafés or tearooms, small European-style restaurants or cafés, and hotels.

Resort rates are all full-board, but you can

visit the resorts near Malé for meals only. Lunch or dinner costs anything from US$15 to US$50 depending on how extravagant you are feeling.

Cafés There must be 100 cafés in Malé and you'll find them on almost every street. They open as early as 5 am and close as late as 1 am, particularly around the port area where they cater for fishers. Although many are called the something 'hotel', they do not offer accommodation in any form.

As far as the Maldivians are concerned, cafés are male domains, but foreign women are not hassled or refused service. They are just stared at.

The cafés are all similar in décor, service and price. Personal preferences will depend on factors such as proximity to your guesthouse or who is serving and managing the place. A good meal costs between Rf 15 to Rf 25.

The cafés close their doors for 15 minutes at prayer times but if you're already inside, there's no problem. You won't have to stop talking or eating or anything and they certainly won't throw you out.

On the tables you will find a selection of sweet and savoury tidbits called hedhikaa, which include small bowls of rice pudding, tiny bananas, wobbly gelatin pieces of indeterminate colour and taste, curried fish cakes, and frittered dough balls, which are sometimes empty, sometimes filled, and almost always spicy.

Meals include omelettes, soups, curried fish, roshi (unleavened bread) and sauce. The Maldivians tear up the roshi, mix it in a bowl and have it for breakfast or lunch.

A cup of sai, which is sweet white tea, or a glass of sweet flavoured milk (powdered or condensed) always accompanies meals and is served instantly by one of two or three scurrying young waiters. There is no coffee, but you can order your tea black (kalu sai); and just say hakuru naala sai if you want it without sugar.

Tea costs Rf 2 and the hedhikaa are Rf 1 to Rf 3. Help yourself to the prepared selection on your table which is replenished when

you leave. The waiter totals up what you have eaten by counting the number of empty and partly empty plates and writes the amount on a scrap of paper. Pay the waiter or the person at the door.

My favourite café is the *Fish Market Hotel* above the fish market on Marine Drive. Its fish curries (mas riha) are out of this world, and the atmosphere sets the place apart: most of the patrons are fishing folk, and tourists are a real rarity. If you like spicy food, don't miss this one. Another place too good to miss if you are in Malé for a few days is the nearby *Bukharei Hotel*, also on Marine Drive behind the cinema of the same name. This is also a favourite among the fishers and harbour workers. On the other side of town is *South Restaurant* on Lonuziyaarai Magu behind the stadium. The selection of hedhikaa is consistently good, and the restaurant has the unusual distinction of being the only place of its kind in Malé with women serving the tables.

The *Majeedhee Uafaa* and the neighbouring *Junction Hotel*, on the corner of Majidi Magu and Chandani Magu, are a couple of old favourites. In the centre of town on Faridi Magu, just along from Voyages Maldives, is the *Fareedhee Uafaa*.

The popular *Moon Cafe* is opposite the banks on Orchid Magu, and in the small lane behind is the *Hotel Daan Buma*. *Camy Cool Spot* on Majidi Magu near Sosun Magu is a relatively new place doing a booming trade. Of all the hedhikaa I ate, the spiciest were here.

Closer to the harbour, is the aptly named *Dawn Cafe* which is busy very early in the morning. On Marine Drive near the Nasandhura Hotel is the very popular *Queen of the Night* which caters for the night owls.

The *Hotel Dunthari*, on Majidi Magu near the Bank of Maldives, and the *Evening Glory* on Janavaree Magu are worth checking out. Try the *Hotel de Shark* opposite the mosque on Dhilbahaaru Higun in the north-west quarter of town as well.

For excellent, take-away hedhikaa, try *Orange* on Bahafsaa Magu near the main entrance to the stadium. It is a little more expensive than those at most of the other places, but the hygiene standards at Orange are higher than most of the other places, and you can still easily put together a big meal for US$2 or US$3.

Cooling Point on Faridi Magu is the ideal place to rehydrate after a few hours in the sun. A delicious, thirst-quenching and nourishing glass of coconut juice (kurumba) costs Rf 5. They also sell white bread rolls with two or three different fillings if you need a break from hedhikaa.

Western-Style Restaurants There are two basic types of Western-style restaurants: day parlours and night spots. Day parlours are popular with tourist parties from the resorts.

Hidden in the lane next to the Habib Bank on Chandani Magu is a much cheaper alternative. It is decked out as a Wild West cantina, but for some strange reason is called *Top Cream*.

The dinner spots are mostly on Majidi Magu. They all try to be small, candlelit and intimate, but sometimes turn out to be cold, gloomy and loud. You can get a three-course meal for under Rf 50.

The most established restaurant is *Twin Peaks* on Orchid Magu. This is the place where young Malé males take their girlfriends to woo and impress them, and where diplomats, government officials and voluntary workers go to relax. The menu includes tomato soup, mixed salad, curry, various pasta dishes, seafood, ice cream and coffee.

On Majidi Magu, a couple of blocks west of Chandani Magu, is *Quench*, which has both indoor and outdoor tables under a thatched roof. The menu includes hamburgers, egg and chips, spaghetti, sandwiches and fruit juice. It also does Indian meals.

The only Indian restaurant in Malé is on Majidi Magu and, just in case there is any confusion, it is called *Indian Restaurant. The Dragon Restaurant* on Marine Drive a couple of blocks south of Majidi Magu specialises in Thai food. For Chinese food try the *Lantern Restaurant* on Janvaree Magu off Majidi Magu.

For the closest thing to Western-style fast food, try *In Time* on Marine Drive not far from the Nasandhura. It serves a selection of hamburgers, fried foods, pasta dishes and Maldivian food (not too spicy for the tourists). The food is actually quite good, and it is certainly one of the cleanest restaurants you'll find here. The only problem is that the place tends to be freezing because the air-con is always on full blast.

Self-Catering The *Local Trading Centre*, behind the fishing harbour on Haveeru Higun is the best place to buy what little fruit is grown in the country. Prices vary with the seasons.

The modern alternative, complete with close-circuit cameras and turnstiles, is the *Green & Fresh Supermarket* opposite the Top Cream café on Chandani Magu. It stocks imported fruit and vegetables as well as tinned versions. There's also a good grocery shop called *Sanco Fresh* opposite the Nivico guesthouse on Chandani Magu.

Finally there is *People's Choice Supermarket* on Haveeru Higun, not far from the customs jetty. An enormous, corrugated iron warehouse, People's Choice stocks mainly imported goods at highly inflated prices. You can buy anything from Vegemite to Arnott's Assorted Biscuits to Kellogg's Rice Bubbles, as well as an impressive selection of household utensils, sporting goods and hardware. Most of the patrons appear to be expats, however, more and more Maldivians are acquiring a taste for imported luxuries.

Entertainment
There may be no nightclubs, dance halls or discos in town, but Malé is a surprisingly lively place from about 8 pm to late in the evening. Majidi Magu bustles with late-night shoppers and cafés full of people, while music and general family commotion spills over the walls of every house.

For the traveller, the only real entertainment choices are dining out, going to the cinema or going out to one of the nearby resorts for a drink. People who drink alcohol in Malé without a permit are breaking the law. There are four cinemas, the *Olympus, National, Star* and *Bukharei*, which show three-hour Hindi sagas or B-grade action adventures in English. Occasionally a reputable feature is shown.

The theatres, however, are under threat from the increasing popularity of video cassette recorders. There are numerous video outlets and some guesthouses have VCRs. Tape rental is Rf 15 a night. Any sexual or violent scenes may have been censored.

'Cultural' exhibitions are sometimes put on at the Olympus cinema or at the Maldives Centre for Social Education just off Majidi Magu on Malé's western shore.

Except during holidays and festivals the only daytime diversions are football and cricket matches, often against teams from Sri Lanka, at the National Stadium on Majidi Magu. Tickets cost Rf 7 or Rf 10 for centre seats with a better view. There are no water sports to speak of around Malé.

Top: Storage Island between Malé & airport (MB)
Upper Middle: Approaching Malé (MB)
Lower Middle: Hulule Airport, Maldives (MB)
Bottom: Surfing in the Maldives (MB)

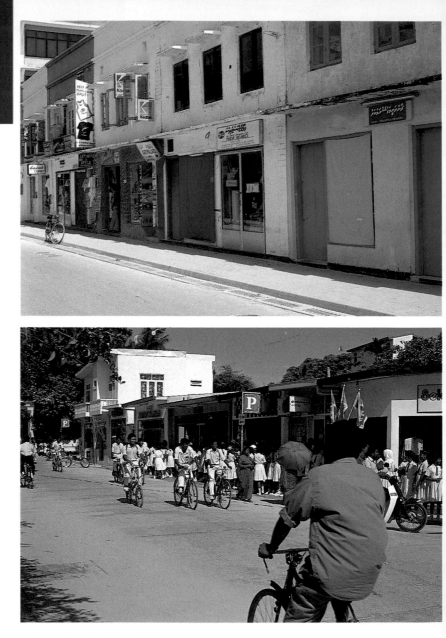

Top: Chandani Magu (MB)
Bottom: Majidi Magu (MB)

The Atolls

The Maldives is a collection of 26 atolls – listed in this chapter from north to south, firstly by the administrative title and secondly by the traditional name. The letter in brackets is the administrative code letter by which fishing dhonis are identified, and the distance listed is from Malé to the atoll capital. Note that locals are far more familiar with the traditional names.

Before you visit any inhabited atoll, other than a resort, you must have a permit from the Ministry of Atolls Administration in Malé. (See also the Permits section of the Maldives Facts for the Visitor chapter.)

The capital island is often not the largest as far as population or size goes, but it houses the atoll office. This is where you can radio-telephone any local person in the atoll and where you must present your permit. It is staffed by the atoll secretary or deputy chief (if the atoll chief is not around), and a radio operator. Each island has a kateeb (island chief), an island administrative office and a court. Contact with other islands in the atoll is by CB radio.

The lifestyle on most of the islands is fairly similar and it would be difficult to pick which islands to visit, if indeed the choice were offered. Gnaviyani (Fuamulaku) and Seenu (Addu Atoll) in the south are definitely worth considering.

Allow plenty of time to travel to and from any island, especially if you have an international flight to catch in Malé. The availability of transportation depends on when the fishers come and go, which in turn depends on the weather and how much fish, money, or how many supplies are needed. It's a different story of course if you're on a package tour staying at the resorts (as almost everyone who visits the Maldives is) because island transfers are arranged around international and domestic flight arrivals and departures.

Uninhabited islands are those which have vegetation and presumably could be, or have been, inhabited. They do not include the hundreds, if not thousands, of precarious tiny coral islets and sandbanks scattered around and between the islands.

RESORTS

A word or two about the 68 resorts. Like the villages or islands themselves, there is little to choose between resorts, and if you come on a package holiday the choice could be limited to six or less depending on where you are coming from (more if you are from Germany or Italy).

Except for those in the 'you-have-to-be-a-millionaire-to-stay-there' bracket, resorts are not noted for their solitude. During the low season you may be one of just a handful of guests on the tiny isle for most of the holiday, but in the high season you might also be stuck there with another couple of hundred sun, sand and sea worshippers. The quietest months are June, May and July in that order, when less than 50% of the beds in the country are occupied. At the other end of the scale, in January, February, March and December over 70% of the beds are occupied. In recent times it seems that August is almost as busy.

Most of the resorts are centred around the capital island of Malé in Kaafu (North Malé and South Malé atolls). New resorts will continue to open in Alif (Ari Atoll), where construction seems to be permanently ongoing. The government is planning to hand some of the resort islands back to the people, to ease the overpopulation on Malé, but this may be wishful thinking because the economy depends so much on the tourist dollar. See also Accommodation in the Maldives Facts for the Visitor chapter for details on rates and also the details on individual resorts following in this chapter.

Note that the same place may legitimately be spelt in various ways in the tourist brochures, maps and government publications that you might refer to.

Accommodation

See the Accommodation section of the Maldives Facts for the Visitor chapter for information on the different kinds of places to stay, the water supply and the accommodation rates.

Activities

The standard resort recreations are diving, snorkelling, dhoni sailing, windsurfing, water-skiing, volleyball, badminton, tennis, table tennis, day/night fishing, discos, videos, cultural shows (ie bodu beru), island hopping (including visiting Malé if your resort is close enough), and board games. Most resorts have a shop selling souvenirs, T-shirts, sunblock (expensive), postcards, film and chocolate. There is usually a reasonable collection of books left behind by past guests. The best selections are in the German resorts (and are in German of course). For more information on resort activities see the Maldives Facts for the Visitor chapter.

Diving The Maldives offer one of the best diving regions in the world. Most visitors who come to the country are on an under-water pilgrimage. The variety of marine life is extensive, and visibility is best during the high season from September to May.

Charges, with all equipment provided, range from around US$25 to US$45 for one dive, or upwards from US$250 for a week-long diving package. Diving courses giving you an internationally recognised certificate start at US$180 at Club Med, but usually cost around US$330 to US$360, and in some cases closer to US$500. Costs will be cheaper if you bring your own mask, snorkel and fins.

Many resorts hire out underwater photography equipment as well as all the basic gear. If you're not staying at a resort and don't have your own flippers etc, you can buy them from Shabim Emporium, near the post office on Marine Drive.

Nondivers who are considering taking up the sport, should only do so if they approach it with the right attitude. There is no question that it is dangerous (and not because of the sharks). A small number of divers (instructors included) are lost every year in the Maldives, and more still have frightening or dangerous experiences.

I had never dived before travelling to the Maldives to update this book for Lonely Planet. To save time, I completed the theory side of my course in Australia, only requiring four more dives to complete my Open Water Certificate. Within three days of arriving I was certified (many nondivers would say certifiable), and ready to experience some of the underwater wonders on offer. I am not in a position to compare my experiences in the Maldives with diving in other countries, however, I can say that, after 15 more dives, that I am permanently hooked on the sport.

The undisputed highlight of my trip to the Maldives came just a couple of days before my return to Australia. I had been invited by a diving instructor I had met to join him at his favourite dive site on his day off. After a 'giant stride' off the side of the dhoni, we found ourselves in fast flowing waters on the outside of the reef. We dropped about five metres to the reef, then hauling ourselves along the bottom, cm by cm against the current, we descended to around 30 metres below the surface. We let go of the reef and relaxed (as much as an inexperienced diver can be expected to relax) allowing ourselves to 'drift' with the current.

The 'vis' was not as good as I had been used to on my earlier dives, but I had never been so deep before. As I peered ahead into the darkness, my instructor friend suddenly grabbed my arm and pointed excitedly at something he had seen. Gradually, as the current carried us forward, I began to make out a number of moving forms. Sharks! When we were no more than four or five metres from them, we grabbed onto a couple of rocks and started counting. Seventeen in all, mainly white tips around 1.5 metres (five feet) long and one giant grey reef shark maybe 2.5 metres (eight feet) long.

The whole episode lasted around 15 or 20 minutes. Only one of the 36 photos I took of the sharks worked out, and pretty badly at that, but it is an experience that I will never forget.

Mark Balla

Before taking a diving course you should have a full diving medical check-up, see Diving Health in the general Facts for the Visitor chapter.

There is a lot of theory involved in gaining your diving certificate. While most of this theory is just plain common sense, it is nonetheless, extremely important that you understand, learn and remember it all. The most important rule for any aspiring scuba diver is to take the course seriously. If you follow your trainer's instructions in every detail the risk involved in diving is reduced to what any experienced diver would call minimal. For more information on diving including equipment, courses and underwater life, see the Maldives Facts for the Visitor chapter. For information on specific dive sites see North Malé, South Malé and Ari atolls in this chapter.

Most dive schools in the Maldives follow either the methods of PADI or CMAS, see the Maldives Facts for the Visitor chapter. Both organisations are internationally recognised, and both use qualified professionals as instructors. While there are undoubtedly a number of differences between the two organisations, the most obvious to a beginner is in the equipment. PADI requires all its students to have two regulators (the device through which you breathe), while CMAS requires only the instructor/guide to have a second regulator. NAUI and VIT are variations of the PADI system with two regulators per dive.

Atoll to Atoll

HAA ALIF
North Tiladummati Atoll (A)
280 km from Malé, 16 inhabited islands, 23 uninhabited islands, 0 resorts,
population 12,031

Almost 2000 people live on **Diddu**, the capital island, which also offers good anchorage for passing yachts. **Huvarafushi**, the next largest island, is noted for its music,

dancing and sporting activities, and would appear to be the more interesting community. It has a fish-freezing plant.

Utheem (Utimu) is the birthplace of Mohammed Thakurufaan, the sultan who threw out the Portuguese in 1573. A memorial centre to this Maldivian hero was opened in 1986. It has a small museum. Bamboo is grown on Utheem to make fishing rods.

Kela was the northern British base during WW II, mirroring Gan at the other end of the archipelago. The mosque here dates from the end of the 17th century. Yams and *cadjan* (mats made of coconut palm leaves) are the island's products.

HAA DHAAL
South Tiladummati Atoll (B)
240 km from Malé, 17 inhabited islands, 16 uninhabited islands, 0 resorts,
population 12,890

Nolivaranfaru is the capital, however **Kuludufushi** is the main island with more than 3500 people, electricity, a community school and a hospital. The islanders have a reputation throughout the country for being hard workers. They specialise in rope making and shark fishing.

Faridu Island, at the heady elevation of three metres above sea level, is the highest point in the Maldives. It is difficult to land on.

An interesting attraction of Haa Dhaal, particularly for divers, is that because the area has suffered several severe storms this atoll is a graveyard for ships. Quite a few vessels have gone down in these waters over the years, particularly around the tip of **Makunudu** on the western side where there are three English shipwrecks as well as the *Persia Merchant*, wrecked in 1658.

SHAVIYANI
North Miladummadulu Atoll (C)
192 km from Malé, 15 inhabited islands, 26 uninhabited islands, 0 resorts,
population 9022

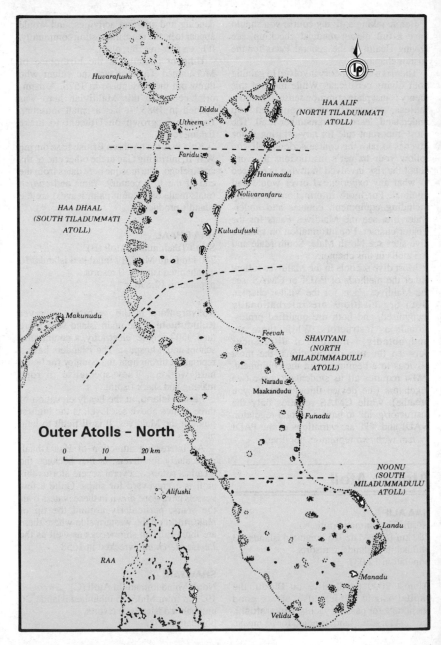

Huvarafushi

Kela

HAA ALIF
(NORTH TILADUMMATI
ATOLL)

Diddu

Utheem

Faridu

Hanimadu

Nolivaranfaru

HAA DHAAL
(SOUTH TILADUMMATI
ATOLL)

Kuludufushi

Makunudu

Feevah

SHAVIYANI
(NORTH
MILADUMMADULU
ATOLL)

Naradu
Maakandudu

Funadu

Outer Atolls – North

0   10   20 km

NOONU
(SOUTH
MILADUMMADULU
ATOLL)

Alifushi

Landu

RAA

Manadu

Velidu

The ruins of an ancient mosque and 13th century tombstones lie on the pretty capital island of **Funadu**. The most populous island with almost 1000 inhabitants is **Maakandudu** which specialises in the production of jaggery, a coarse brown sugar made from date palm sap. This island has been ravaged by storms and diseases throughout history, which may be why another island is called **Feevah**.

Naradu, with its inland lakes, is said to be the most beautiful island.

NOONU

South Miladummadulu Atoll (D)
150 km from Malé, 14 inhabited islands, 57 uninhabited, 0 resorts, population 8437

Manadu is the chief island but **Holudu** and **Velidu** islands are the busiest. The main attraction for any visitor would be the relic on **Landu** supposedly left by the fabled Redin people who are part of Maldivian folklore and magic. It is a 15-metre-high mound known locally as *maa badhige* 'great cooking pot'. Thor Heyerdahl writes extensively about the tall, fair-haired Redin in his book *The Maldive Mystery*. He believes them to have been the first inhabitants of the Maldives as long ago as 2000 BC.

RAA

North Malosmadulu Atoll (E)
145 km from Malé, 16 inhabited islands, 65 uninhabited islands, 0 resorts, population 11,303

Ugufaru is the capital of this atoll which has the highest percentage of fishers among its population of any of the atolls. The island of **Alifushi** (see the Outer Atolls – North map) is where the best dhonis in the Indian Ocean are built, even if the builders now often use wood imported from Bangladesh. The islanders also supply crafts to every atoll.

Kandoludu (Kandoludhu) is the main island and said to be overcrowded with almost 2000 people. Alifushi, **Inguraidu** and **Innamadu** are also boatbuilding and carpentry centres. The Arab seafarer Ibn Battuta, an important figure in Maldivian history, visited **Kinolhas** in 1343.

BAA

South Malosmadulu Atoll (F)
105 km from Malé, 13 inhabited islands, 51 uninhabited islands, one resort, population 7716

Baa is famous for its lacquer work, woven cotton *felis* (the traditional sarong) and political or criminal exiles. **Eydafushi**, the capital and principal island, is also the feli centre. **Tuladu** is the second largest island, while **Tulusdu** and **Fehendu** are tops in lacquer work boxes and jars.

Fuladu island has had two famous, or rather infamous, foreign residents. In 1602 François Pyrard, the French explorer, found himself a castaway on the island after his ship the *Corbin* was wrecked. Albert Gray, a colleague of H C P Bell, wrote about Pyrard's voyages. (A signed copy of the book is in the MID Library in Malé.)

In 1976 a German traveller was banished for life to the island after he was convicted of murdering his girlfriend in a Malé guesthouse. He is now married with two children. (The US magazine *New Look* carried a feature on him in the April 1986 edition.)

Fuladu and its neighbours, Goidu and Fehendu, have also been open prisons for many other exiles since 1962.

Hassan Ahmed Maniku noted in his book (or rather catalogue) *The Islands of the Maldives* that in February 1963 more than 3.8 million flying fish 'landed' on Goidu, the separate atoll in the south (also known as Horsburgh). Whether they landed by themselves or with the help of fishers's nets, he does not say. Maniku also said of the island:

There is a heap of gravel and sand in almost the centre of the island measuring 41 feet in circumference and three feet high, which has never been investigated.

Heyerdahl wasn't able to oblige.

Resorts
Kunfunadhoo (Kunfunadhu) was a medium-

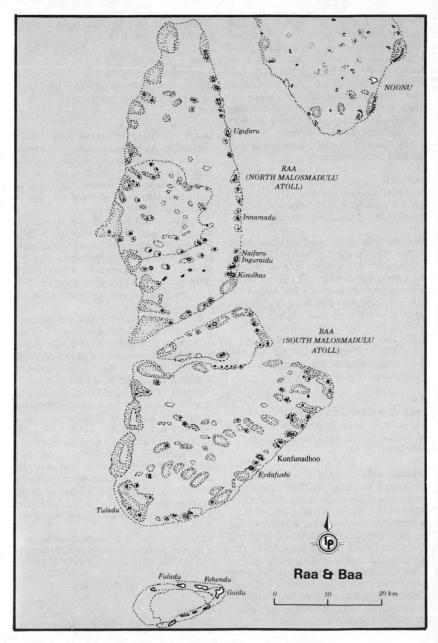

NOONU

Ugufaru

RAA
(NORTH MALOSMADULU
ATOLL)

Innamadu

Naifaru
Inguraidu

Kinolhas

BAA
(SOUTH MALOSMADULU
ATOLL)

Kunfunadhoo

Eydafushi

Tuladu

Raa & Baa

0   10   20 km

Fuladu   Fehendu

Goidu

range resort 100 km from the airport. It has been closed for redevelopment and should reopen in late '93 or early '94. The developers have planned a luxury resort with all facilities, including a hairdressing salon. It will certainly be one of the most expensive and up-market resorts in the country. The contact address in Malé is Bunny Holdings (BVI) Ltd (☎ 322335), Shoanary, 1st floor, Marine Drive.

LAVIYANI
Fadippolu Atoll (G)
120 km from Malé, four inhabited islands, 53 uninhabited islands, one resort, population 7725

All four islands are relatively crowded. **Naifaru**, the capital, has a reputation for concocting local medicines and making handicrafts from coral and mother-of-pearl. **Hinnavaru** is the next busiest island. Generally the atoll is a strong fishing centre, with a tuna cannery on **Felivaru**. A fish-processing plant was opened in November 1986.

Resorts
Kuredu Island Resort (☎ 230337) is 130 km

from Hulhule Airport, which makes it the most remote of the resorts. It was established in 1976 as a base for divers so the accommodation was rough and secondary to the sport. Known then as Kuredu Camping Resort it was the cheapest resort in the islands. It has since been enlarged and upgraded to 250 rooms. Singles/doubles/triples cost US$80/95/120 in the low season and US$100/120/145 in the high season. Transfer from Malé is generally by speedboat and costs US$80 per person (return). Helicopter transfers can be organised for groups.

Kuredu Island is comparatively large by Maldivian standards and is very popular with Germans and Scandinavians. It is also known as a good base for big-game fishing. The resort is operated by Champa Trade & Travels (☎ 321751) on Marine Drive in Malé.

KAAFU
North Malé & South Malé Atolls (H)
11 inhabited islands, 63 uninhabited islands, 43 resorts, population 10,133

North Malé and South Malé, the twin atolls of Kaafu, cover over 100 km of ocean from north to south and are made up of countless sandbanks and islands of which only 11 are inhabited. **Malé**, the capital island of the Maldives, is in the south of North Malé Atoll but does not come under the atoll administration.

The atoll capital, also in North Malé Atoll, is the island of Thulusdu. Kaafu also includes the island atoll of **Kashidu**, the most populated island, to the north in the Five Degree Channel. The islanders there are big toddy tappers.

Maafushi (in South Malé Atoll) has a big children's reformatory, which opened in 1979, where the nation's delinquents undergo skill training and rehabilitation. Until 1964 the British governor's residence was on Dhoonidhoo, just north of Malé. His house is now used for prominent political prisoners.

The oil tanks you can see from Malé are on Funadu Island. Also close to Malé is the

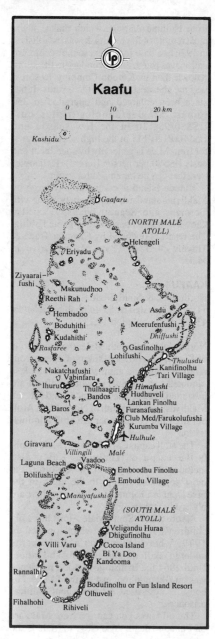

Kaafu

0   10   20 km

Kashidu

Gaafaru

(NORTH MALÉ ATOLL)

Helengeli

Eriyadu

Ziyaarai-fushi

Makunudhoo

Reethi Rah

Asdu

Hembadoo

Meerufenfushi

Boduhithi

Dhiffushi

Kudahithi

Gasfinolhu

Rasfaree

Lohifushi

Thulusdu

Nakatchafushi

Kanifinolhu

Vabinfaru

Tari Village

Iharu

Thilahaagiri

Himafushi

Bandos

Hudhuveli

Lankan Finolhu

Baros

Furanafushi

Club Med/Farukolufushi

Kurumba Village

Hulhule

Giravaru

Villingili

Malé

Laguna Beach

Vaadoo

Bolifushi

Emboodhu Finolhu

Embudu Village

Maniyafushi

(SOUTH MALÉ ATOLL)

Veligandu Huraa

Dhigufinolhu

Villi Varu

Cocoa Island

Bi Ya Doo

Kandooma

Rannalhi

Bodufinolhu or Fun Island Resort

Olhuveli

Fihalhohi

Rihiveli

Kuda Bandos Reserve, which was saved from resort development by the government so people could enjoy it in its natural state. You do not need a permit to visit.

Just 15 minutes by dhoni to the west of Malé is the island of Villingili, a one time resort which was closed down to make room for a telecommunications station. The old resort buildings are abandoned and decaying and the beaches are deserted. Plans are afoot, however, to settle as many as 9000 people on the island creating a kind of outer suburb of Malé. Once this happens, it is unlikely that tourists will have any reason to visit the island.

Diving

Kaafu is the most touristed atoll in the Maldives, so it follows that it is the most dived as well. Following is a list of some of the better known dive sites close to Malé in North Malé Atoll and a brief description of what you might expect to find.

Potato reef – nine to 15 metres
    a particularly large variety of fish; two very friendly moray eels which love having their 'chins' tickled by divers; giant grouper which have come to expect divers to hand feed them

Aquarium – 10 to 20 metres
    small reef sharks; schools of snapper and giant wrasse

Manta Point I – 10 to 20 metres
    from July to December expect to see loads of mantas: this is their breeding ground. There is a large, open cave at around 20 metres.

Manta Point II – 15 to 25 metres
    more mantas as well as reef sharks, stingrays and, because of the nearby channel, very large fish

HP Reef – 15 to 25 metres
    one of North Malé Atoll's most mesmerising dive sites with canyons and caves supporting a spectacular array of soft corals; teeming with fish

New Reef – 15 to 30 metres
    You won't often see so many small and large fish in one place; also keep your eyes open for batfish, sharks, barracuda and lion fish.

Devil's Reef – 15 to 30 metres
    There are hard and soft corals to blow your mind. Keep a close watch on your air pressure, as time really flies down here.

Nurse Point
    caves with soft gorgonians (coral) and nurse sharks

Banana Reef – 15 to 20 metres
> hot spot for sharks; used to be particularly popular for shark feeding, but the authorities are trying to discourage this dangerous (and very exciting) activity

Maldive Victory
> wreck of a cargo ship sunk on Friday 13 February 1981; wheelhouse at around 15 metres, propeller at a little over 30 metres. Another of the favourite photo spots is the ship's head. Corals have taken to the ship forming a truly fascinating combination.

Palm Reef – nine to 20 metres
> friendly schools of batfish which love being hand fed and then escort divers all the way back to the surface

North Malé Resorts

Helengeli (☎ 444615) is a low-range resort, 51 km from the airport. It's operated by the Helengeli Reservations Office (☎ 325587), Marine Drive, Malé. It is the most northerly of the Kaafu resorts and singles/doubles/triples cost US$40/50/80 in the low season and US$50/70/100 in the high season. Transfer from the airport by dhoni takes around three hours and costs US$60 return. The resort is fairly basic, albeit pleasant, with 30 thatch-roofed bungalows and saltwater showers.

Scuba charges on the resort are around

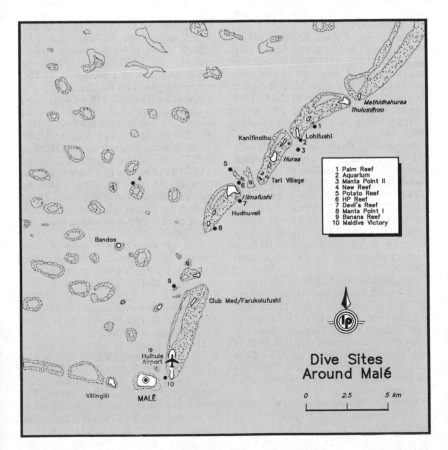

1 Palm Reef
2 Aquarium
3 Manta Point II
4 New Reef
5 Potato Reef
6 HP Reef
7 Devil's Reef
8 Manta Point I
9 Banana Reef
10 Maldive Victory

Dive Sites
Around Malé

0   2.5   5 km

US$175 for unlimited dives. The island has a good house reef over two km long, so you need not venture far for some good diving.

Eriyadu (☎ 444487) is 38 km from the airport and, probably because of the distance, is one of the cheaper resorts. It is operated by AAA Trading Co (☎ 322417), Ibrahim Hassan Didi Magu, Malé and singles/doubles/triples cost US$55/90/105 all year round. Transfer by dhoni takes three hours and costs US$50 return per person. It takes around one hour by speedboat and costs around US$100 per person (one way). This 46 bungalow resort is surrounded by a wide beach with plenty of trees. Most of the guests are German and Swiss with a few Brits and Norwegians.

The Diving Center Eriyadu offers Barakuda and CMAS training. CMAS one-star certification costs US$340 all-inclusive and takes around five days to complete. Among the packages available for divers are six dives for US$170, 10 dives for US$280 and seven days' unlimited diving for US$265. Every boat trip costs an extra US$8.

Makunudhoo (Makunudhu) (☎ 446464), 35 km from the airport, is a high-range resort operated by Gelina Maldives (☎ 324742), 7 Orchid Magu, Malé. Singles/doubles cost US$195/250 in the low season and US$250/300 in the high season, and the resort, which opened in 1983, has 31 bungalows. It is popular with passing yachties because of the good anchorage. PADI Open Water certification by the dive school costs 2500 Rf.

Ziyaaraifushi (☎ 443088), which is operated by Phoenix Hotels & Resorts (☎ 323181), Fasmeeru, Marine Drive, Malé is a low-range resort 35 km (2¼ hours by boat) from the airport. Singles/doubles cost US$45/65 in low season and US$50/70 in high season. Transfer to the island by dhoni costs US$40 per person (return). The resort has more than doubled in size in recent years to 79 bungalows.

Reethi Rah, or *Medhufinolhu*, (☎ 441905) is 33 km from the airport. The operator is M Shaazeewin, (☎ 323758), Faridi Magu,

Malé, and the resort is managed by Kuoni. Singles/doubles are US$62/99 in the low season and US$77/120 in the high season. Reethi Rah means 'beautiful island'. There are 50 bungalows, most of them in blocks of four units (motel-style) with cold-water showers.

The Mistral School of Windsurfers operates here and the resort is the Eurodivers diving base. A single 'discovery' dive for beginners costs US$19, while a single dive for certified divers costs US$28. The PADI Open Water course costs US$330, which includes nine dives. Speciality courses through to assistant instructor level are available on request. Packages of five (US$128), 10 (US$242) and 15 (US$345) are available, as well as six days' unlimited diving for US$248. These prices are inclusive of all equipment, but, US$9 should be added to the cost of each dive, or a package of 12 boat trips can be purchased for US$96.

Hembadoo (Hembadu) (☎ 443884), a low to medium-range resort 31 km from the airport, is operated by Transit Inn, (☎ 322016), Maaveyo Magu, Malé. Singles/doubles range from US$35/50 to US$85/105 in the low season and US$50/65 to US$100/120 in the high season, and the resort has 44 bungalows. The guests are mainly German, Austrian and Swiss. Transfer from the airport is generally by dhoni which takes a little under three hours and costs US$40 return.

Asdu (☎ 445051) is a medium-range resort 37 km from the airport. The operators address is c/o Shoanary (☎ 322149), Henveiru, Malé. Singles/doubles cost US$60/90 in low season and US$90/130 in high season. It's a small resort, with 30 bungalows, and offers sightseeing trips to a local fishing village on Dhiffushi.

Meerufenfushi (☎ 443157) is a low-range resort, 40 km from the airport, operated by Champa Trade & Travels (☎ 326545), Malé. It is quite likely that the resort will be closed down during the life of this edition. The government hopes to include Meerufenfushi in its decentralisation programme by opening the island up to settlers from Malé.

Singles/doubles cost US$35/55 in low season and US$50/75 in high season.

For some strange reason Meeru is known locally as Sweetwater Island. Tourists certainly won't find the unheated bore water gushing forth from the resort's showers all that sweet. **Meeru** is Kaafu's most eastern island and, covering 28 hectares, is one of the country's largest. The resort, with 164 rooms, is one of the biggest and boasts a large lagoon which attracts sailboard enthusiasts. Most of the visitors are German, however, visitors also include reasonable numbers of other nationalities.

Eurodivers runs the dive school on Meeru. Courses available include pretty much everything from Open Water to Dive Master with the Open Water Certificate costing US$396 (boat trips included). A single all-inclusive dive costs US$40 or US$31 if you have your own gear. A five-dive package costs US$155/188 with/without your own equipment. Ten dives cost US$291/362 with/without your own equipment.

Boduhithi (☎ 445905) is medium to high-price range depending on the season. It's 29 km from the airport and is operated by Safari Tours (☎ 323524), Chandani Magu, Malé. Singles/doubles cost US$90/130 in the low season and US$110/165 in the high season. Return transfer to the island costs US$70 per person by speedboat and takes 45 minutes. Transfer by dhoni costs US$40 per person. There are 86 cabanas, with freshwater showers, surrounding the island and the resort, which is also known as Coral Isle, caters mainly to Italian tourists.

Kudahithi (☎ 444613) also operated by Safari Tours is a small and luxurious high-range resort 28 km from the airport. A double in the high and low season is US$255. Transfer from the airport is by speedboat, takes 45 minutes and costs US$75 per person (return). Kudahithi is one of the most exclusive islands with only six cottages, one of which is called the Sheik's Room and has a huge bath where you can do your own diving. The others are titled the King, the Rehendi (queen), Captain's Cabin, Safari Lodge and Maldivian Apartment. There's no

diving here but you can go across to Boduhithi.

Nakatchafushi (☎ 443847), in the low price range, is 22 km (1½ hours by dhoni) from the airport. It's operated by Universal Enterprises Ltd (☎ 322971), 38 Orchid Magu, Malé. Singles/doubles cost US$55/65 in low season and US$130/140 in high season. This 51-room resort has individual round bures each with air-con and hot fresh-water showers. One of the most attractive features is the terrace bar over the water.

The diving school is run by the German organisation, Atoll Watersports. The PADI Open Water course costs US$360 including certification. Boat trips cost an extra US$11 for one trip per day and US$16 for two trips per day.

The hiring rates for sailboards, boats and instruction are comparitively high at Nakatchafushi. It's US$12 an hour to windsurf and US$22 for a lesson. Top cat catamarans cost US$18 an hour and US$30 for a lesson.

Gasfinolhu (☎ 442078), a high-range resort 18 km from the airport, is operated by Dhirham Travels & Chandling (☎ 323371), Faamudheyri Magu, Malé. Gasfinolhu, which means 'tree on a sandbank' is an exclusive resort with 38 cabanas. The resort caters exclusively to Italians and charges US$100/200 for singles/doubles all year round.

Lhohifushi (☎ 441909), in the low to medium range (seasonal variation), is 17.5 km from the airport. It's operated by Altaf Enterprises (☎ 323378), 8 Ibrahim Hassan Didi Magu, Malé. It has 84 units and singles/doubles cost US$50/65 in low season and US$60/80 in high season. The rooms are more basic than most, with ceiling fans and unheated island water. A few rooms have air-con but this costs an extra US$30 a night. The resort generally has a fairly international mix of visitors, mostly from Germany, Japan, Switzerland and the UK. There are often French and Australian guests as well. Transfer to the island by dhoni costs US$30 return.

Kanifinolhu (☎ 443152), 16 km from the

airport, has been upgraded to a high to medium-range resort, but it doesn't have a great reputation. It's operated by Cyprea (☎ 322451), 25 Marine Drive, Malé. Singles/doubles cost US$94/140 in the low season and US$109/180 in the high season. Air-con costs an extra US$15 in the low season and US$19 in the high season. Transfer from the airport is by dhoni (US$30, 90 minutes) or by speedboat (US$60, 30 minutes). It's a popular resort for the younger crowd and has 113 rooms, some with air-con and all with desalinated water.

Eurodivers is in charge of Sub-Aqua on Kani. A one-week scuba package of 10 dives costs US$253. The PADI Open Water Certificate course, which includes nine dives, costs US$290. An extra US$9 should be added for each boat dive. A single resort dive costs US$29. Snorkelling is good at the southern tip of the island.

Little Hura (☎ 445934), a low to medium-range resort (depending on the resort) 16 km from the airport, is operated by the Hotel Alia (☎ 322197) in Malé. The name comes from the Huraa dynasty of sultans founded in 1759 by Sultan Al-Ghaazi Hassan Izzaddeen who built a mosque there. The resort's 43 cottages (singles/doubles US$42/72 in low season

and US$77/118 in high season) are built across the centre of the island so guests have a choice of two beaches. You can also walk across to the local island known as Hura. At low tide you can walk (or wade) across to Tari Village resort in about 45 minutes . Look out for stingrays. Transfer to the resort is either by speedboat (30 minutes, US$150 return) or by dhoni (90 minutes, US$25 return). Most of the guests are Germans; there are also fair-sized Dutch and British contingents.

Tari Village (☎ 442881), a medium-range resort 15 km from the airport, is operated by Treasure Island Enterprises (☎ 322165), 8 Marine Drive, Malé (although this may soon change). It is also known as *Kanuhura* or less commonly *Leisure Island*. It has 24 exceptionally spacious double-storey cottages, and singles/doubles cost US$90/110 in low season and US$120/160 in the high season. There's not much beach but the resort does a pretty good job of making up for that with excellent food, discos and other evening entertainment, tennis courts, and an intimate atmosphere.

Tari Village is the only resort where guests are able to use the kitchen themselves without there being a fuss. It's an up-market

Green Turtle

place mostly visited by Italians and Germans as well as a few Australians who are brought in by Foster Travel Service in Australia or Atoll Adventures in Malé. See Tour Operators section in the Maldives Getting Around chapter for more information.

Diving is run by the Happy Octopus Diving Center. SSI certification costs US$380 (all-inclusive). Speciality diver courses are available, including Deep Diver, Night Diver, Wreck Diver, Computer Diving, Advanced Open Water Diver, Rescue Diver and Dive Master. An introductory course of theory and three dives costs US$150. Each single dive costs US$40, a night dive costs US$60, a package of five dives goes for US$180, 10 dives for US$360 (including one night dive) and 20 dives for US$680 (including two night dives). These packages include boat trips, tank, weight belt, guide and, where necessary, an underwater light. Octopus and BCD can be rented if you do not have your own. Underwater cameras can be rented for US$25 per dive of US$40 for two dives.

Thulhaagiri (☎ 445929) is 11 km from the airport. It is a totally French resort. It is operated in Malé by Deens Orchid Agency (☎ 328435), 15 Marine Drive, Malé. Singles/doubles in low season are US$92/122. In the high season they cost US$112/130. Transfer to the island by dhoni costs around US$30 (return) and takes close to one hour.

The dive school runs under the original name of Tropical Gangsters Incorporated. The cost of the PADI Open Water Certificate course is US$380, all inclusive. A number of other courses and packages are available on request including Dive Master training which takes around three to four weeks.

Club Med/Farukolufushi (☎ 444552) is the second largest resort in the Maldives, with a capacity for 304 visitors, but it doesn't offer water-skiing or tennis. You can recognise the island by the restaurant's huge and sweeping thatched roof which looks like a traditional Sulawesian house. Club Med does not allow day visitors or overnight stays. The FIT rate of US$130/260 per night

for singles/doubles is theoretical only, as you cannot generally book directly with the resort or with their operator in Malé (at No 1 Ibrahim Hassan Didi Magu (☎ 322976)). Contact your travel agent at home for information on a Club Med/Farukolufushi package.

Club Med's big advantage is just how all-inclusive the packages are. The price that you finally end up paying includes full board, all beach sports, sailing and windsurfing including lessons if you need them. It also includes one dive per day for certified divers (in the morning). Afternoon dives cost an extra US$30 and night dives cost US$35. Nondivers have the option of doing a single resort dive free of charge or doing a Padi Open Water Certificate for only US$180 – the unchallenged cheapest course in the Maldives. There is a decompression chamber on the island, however, there does not always seem to be anyone on the island who knows how to operate it. If you are not staying at Club Med and are unfortunate enough to need the chamber, it will cost you US$600 per hour.

Ihuru (☎ 443502) is the most photographed resort in the Maldives. It has 40 thatch-roofed bungalows with singles/doubles for US$100/160 in both low and high seasons. The house reef, known as 'The Wall' is a handy diving spot. Also ask at the dive school about stingray feeding. The Sea Explorer Diving School has equipment for 30 divers. The Open Water Certificate course costs US$390 and takes one week to complete. A single dive costs US$38, while packages of six and 12 dives cost US$210 and US$375. Six days' unlimited diving costs US$300. Every boat trip to a dive site costs US$12.

Vabinfaru (☎ 443147), a medium to high-range (depending on the season) resort 16 km from the airport next to Ihuru, is operated by Dhirham Travels & Chandling (☎ 323369), Faamudheyri Magu, Malé. Singles/doubles cost US$130/160 in the low season and US$150/250 in the high season. This 31-bungalow resort is under French management and the guests are mostly

Italian, French and Australian. The accommodation is in thatch-roofed round bungalows which have bore water. The food is good and some of the sports and entertainment are free.

You can take excursions to the neighbouring islands of Himafushi, Thulhaagiri, Boduhithi and Giravaru for US$10 per person. Windsurfing, catamaran and water-skiing lessons range from US$22 to US$35. One scuba dive costs US$35, not including the boat trip, or US$360 for a certificate course.

Hudhuveli (☎ 443396) is a low to medium-range resort 9.5 km (50 minutes by boat, US$30 return) from the airport. It's operated by Deens Orchid Agency (☎ 328435), 15 Marine Drive, Malé and singles/doubles cost US$57/87 in low season and US$90/120 in high season. Hudhuveli means 'white sand'. There are 44 bungalows built along the centre of the island each with freshwater showers. You can make arrangements to visit a local fishing village on Himafushi. If you're visiting the resort a 'plain' meal will cost about US$15.

Lankanfinolhu was closed for 'major redevelopment' at the time of writing. It is expected to reopen some time in '94 as a five-star luxury resort, with 138 bungalows, under the name *Paradise Island*. For more information contact the operators, Villa Shipping & Trading Company (☎ 324478),

Villa Building Ibrahim Hassan Didi Magu, Malé.

Baros (☎ 442672), a low to medium-range resort 15 km (one hour by boat) from the airport, is operated by Universal Enterprises Ltd (☎ 322971), 38 Orchid Magu, Malé. Singles/doubles cost US$45/55 in the low season and US$110/120 in the high season. Baros, which is popular with UK visitors, is one of the oldest resorts and has been operating since 1973. It is half-moon shaped and has 55 bungalows, of which about half have air-con. Sub-Aqua Reisen of Munich runs the diving school. The *Turtle Restaurant* is named after the little turtles found in the stream which flows around it.

The Baros International Diving School offers the PADI Open Water Certificate for US$330. A single dive with all equipment costs US$30, while a package of six dives without equipment costs US$105. Six days' unlimited diving without equipment is US$185.

Bandos (☎ 440088), in the medium range, is eight km from the airport and is operated by Deens Orchid Agency (☎ 328435), 15 Marine Drive, Malé. Singles/doubles cost US$95/129 in the low season and US$110/140 in the high season. Transfer to the resort by dhoni takes around 45 minutes and costs US$20 return. It was the divers on Bandos, which is the diving capital of the islands, who started feeding the sharks

mouth-to-mouth giving rise to the tourism industry motto: 'where even the sharks are friendly'.

The resort has an incredible 203 bungalows. There's a 24-hour coffee shop (meals cost around US$12), an aquarium and, nearby, the uninhabited, unspoiled island of Kuda Bandos, which has been turned into a public reserve. A fully fledged, permanently staffed, medical clinic is due to open on Bandos in the near future, and it is expected that the resort will take over Club Med's unwanted role of recompressing bent divers from the surrounding resorts (ie putting divers with decompression sickness through the chamber).

Furanafushi is undergoing a multi-million dollar redevelopment and is expected to reopen as a top-end resort in late '93 or sometime in '94.

In the mean time, for divers from nearby resorts, Furanafushi is fringed by a number of interesting dive spots including Banana Reef (one of the most dived reefs in the Maldives) and South Furana. Also ask your dive school about the wreck of the *Maldives Victory*, a government cargo ship which sank off Hulhule Airport on 13 February 1981. There are other good reefs and caves nearby and the channel separating Furanafushi from Lankan Finolhu is the haunt of whale sharks.

Giravaru (☎ 440440), a medium to upper range resort 11 km from the airport, is operated by Phoenix Hotels & Resorts (☎ 323181), Fasmeeru, Marine Drive, Malé. Singles/doubles cost US$90/120 in low season and US$110/180 in high season.

Transfer to the resort by dhoni costs US$30 return. The facilities and 50 bungalows have been upgraded over the past few years. All the bungalows now have hot water and there is a freshwater swimming pool.

Giravaru's dive school is run by Eurodivers. A single dive costs US$26 and a package of 10 dives costs US$230. The PADI Open Water course costs US$300 and a resort course of four dives with no certificate costs US$150 (for beginners only). Each boat trip costs an extra US$8.

Kurumba Village (☎ 443081), a high-medium to high-range international resort three km from the airport, is operated by Universal Enterprises Ltd (☎ 322971), 38 Orchid Magu, Malé. Singles/doubles cost US$130/140 in low season and US$190/200 in high season. As there is a choice of restaurants on the island most people take bed and breakfast only, which is the price quoted. Full board can also be arranged directly with the resort. Transfer to the island is generally by dhoni, it takes 30 minutes and costs US$12 per person (one way).

Kurumba, which means 'young coconut', was the first resort in the Maldives. It has been continually expanded since it was built in 1972, including extensive renovations in 1987. It is the first of the Maldives' resorts to be classed as an international hotel, which means the rooms now have all the mod cons (except TV). You can keep up with world events by tuning into CNN in the room above the reception area. There are 169 rooms in thatched or tiled bungalows around the perimeter of the island, as well as a 24-hour

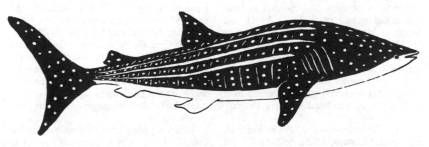

Whale shark

coffee shop, a nightclub, two bars, two restaurants, a freshwater swimming pool, a conference and banquet hall (for up to 500 people), and a games centre which has a gymnasium and another pool.

Because it is close to Malé there is more live entertainment than on other resorts, more day trippers, and more visits by government and business people.

Diving on Kurumba is run by Eurodivers. They charge US$375 for 15 dives with tanks and weights supplied; or US$270 for six days' unlimited diving. A single dive costs US$32, while a beginners resort dive is a bargain at US$25. The PADI Open Water course costs US$195, making it one of the best deals around. None of these prices include the cost of boat trips, which cost an additional US$12 each.

South Malé Resorts

Vaadu (☎ 443976) is a medium to high-range resort eight km from the airport. It's operated by H Henveyruge (☎ 325844), Meduziyaaraiy Magu, Malé. Singles/doubles cost US$94/122 in low season and US$105/155 in high season.

It is dubbed 'Vaadoo Diving Paradise' because the island is on the edge of the deep channel which separates North and South Malé atolls. It offers a great range of marine life and is surrounded by some of the best diving locations in the Maldives. Most of the guests are German, Italian and Japanese. The 31 cabanas have fresh water.

Laguna Beach or *Velassaru* (☎ 443042), a medium to high-range 104 bungalow resort 10 km from the airport, is operated by Universal Enterprises (☎ 322971), 38 Orchid Magu, Malé. Singles/doubles are US$95/105 in low season and US$165/175 in high season. Built in 1974, Laguna Beach officially became one of the top 300 hotels in the world until it went downhill. It's only now starting to pick up again. There are coral walls built as windbreaks among the cottages.

The German-owned dive school, Divecenter Laguna, offers both PADI and CMAS certificate courses. The Open Water

Certificate costs US$395, and takes one week to complete. You can also do a resort course which is a three-dive programme for beginners at a cost of US$120. Packages of six, 12 or six-day unlimited dives, which cost US$174/324/264 respectively, are also available.

Emboodhu Finolhu (☎ 444776) is a low to high-range resort (depending on the season and the standard of accommodation booked) eight km from the airport. It's operated by G Makhumaage (☎ 326483), Malé, and is leased and managed by Australians. Also ask Naseer at Paradise Tours & Travel (☎ 321501), Lonuziyaarai Magu, Malé, about the prices he can offer on Emboodhu Finolhu. There are two classes of accommodation, basic and deluxe. Deluxe singles/doubles are US$78/101 in the low season, US$123/146 in the high season and US$134/168 over Christmas. The basic bungalow rates are about 25% to 30% lower, but be forewarned that the basic bungalows are just that, while the deluxe bungalows are truly beautiful. Transfer from the airport by dhoni costs US$25 per person (round trip).

The resort has freshwater showers and there are 40 bungalows in all. The 24 deluxe bungalows, which are built over the water, all have air-con. One of the more natural resorts, it often has a good international mix of visitors, and the added advantage over other resorts in being very close to the airport (eight km).

An introductory course of three dives costs US$120 with tanks and weight belts provided. A single dive costs US$35 with all equipment supplied. There is an extra charge of US$6 for the boat trip and there is a range of diving courses, including the PADI Open Water Certificate course, which costs US$428 all-inclusive (boat trips excepted). Ask the dive school about Embudu Canyon and Shark Point, two of the hottest local dive spots (the school takes divers to one of around 40 sites all within about an hour's trip by dhoni).

Island hopping from Emboodhu Finolhu costs US$20 per person for a full day; while a half-day trip to Malé costs US$15.

Windsurfing costs US$4 an hour or US$20 a day and catamaran hire is US$10 per hour.

Embudu Village (☎ 444776), a medium-range resort eight km from the airport, is operated by Kaimoo Hotels & Travel Services Pty Ltd (☎ 322212), Roanuge, Malé. Singles/doubles are US$60/80 in the low season and US$85/110 in the high season, and they have hot water. Air-con will set you back an extra US$20 per night. Transfer from the airport by dhoni takes one to 1½ hours and costs US$25 return. It's a much bigger resort than nearby Emboodhu Finolhu with 106 bungalows and has an excellent house reef for snorkelling. There is a disco on the island once a week (usually Monday evenings), and either a magic or a limbo show on another evening. There is a TV room where you can pick up CNN 24 hours a day as well as some French stations. Most of the guests on the island are German, French and Scandinavian. There are also a few Dutch and British visitors. In the low season there are a few Australians.

The Diverland Embudu dive school offers a number of courses. PADI Open Water certification costs US$350 and takes eight days to complete. The Advanced Open Water course takes only two days at a cost of US$275. They also offer a number of speciality courses including Nightdiver, Underwater Naturalist, Wreckdiver, Deepdiver and Driftdiver with costs ranging from US$140 to US$250. For beginners there is a resort course which includes basic theory and two dives for US$85. A single dive for a certified diver costs US$33. Packages of eight and 12 dives are available for US$180 and US$338. Six consecutive days' of unlimited diving costs US$250 with all equipment supplied. Any dive which requires boat transport costs an extra US$9 plus a service charge for carrying the tanks.

Bolifushi (☎ 443517) is a low to medium-range resort 13 km from the airport. It's operated by Phoenix Hotels & Resorts (☎ 325309), Fasmeeru, Marine Drive, Malé. Singles/doubles cost US$55/75 in low season and US$65/90 in high season. All of the 32 chalets have fresh water and air-con.

Transfer to the island by dhoni costs US$30 per person (return).

Dhigufinolhu (☎ 443611), a medium to high-range resort 19 km from the airport, is operated by Dhigufinolhu & Veligandu Huraa Malé Office (☎ 327058), Orchid Higun, Malé. Singles/doubles cost US$100/130 in the low season and US$120/160 in the high season. There are 60 rooms all with air-con and hot and cold desalinated water.

Diving at both Dhigufinolhu and neighbouring Veligandu Huraa is run by the German based Aquanaut, a five-star PADI centre. The Open Water course costs US$359 all-inclusive. One week's unlimited diving goes for US$370.

Veligandu Huraa (☎ 443882), also called *Palm Tree Island*, is connected to Dhigufinolhu by a walkway over the shallow lagoon. The walkway also leads to a third, smaller island where the desalination plant, the generators, the dive school, the boats and the staff quarters are. What this means is that there is absolutely no machinery noise on either of the resorts. There is a bar in the middle of the walkway where it branches off to the three islands. Veligandu Huraa is a relatively new high-range resort 53 km from the airport. Singles/doubles cost US$145/170 in low season and US$150/190 in high season. There are only 16 rooms, all of them with thatched roofs and beach frontage. There is a very pleasant open-air restaurant surrounded by palm trees in the middle of the island. Transfer to either resort is generally by dhoni and costs US$50 per person (return).

Bi Ya Doo (☎ 447171) is a medium-range resort 28 km (2½ hours by boat) from the airport. It's operated by the Taj group through Prabalaji Enterprises (☎ 327014), H Maarandhooge, Malé. Singles/doubles cost US$80/90 in low season and US$115/125 in the high season with a US$15 supplement over Christmas. If you book a week on the resort for May, June, July, September or October, you should enquire about the free 2nd-week offer (you only pay the bed tax plus US$20 per day for food), however, you must enquire at the time of booking. There is a 10% discount for repeat guests who book directly with the resort. Transfer to the island by speedboat costs US$35 return. Speedboat or helicopter transfers can be arranged.

Bi Ya Doo is one of the few two-storey resorts in the Maldives. The 96 air-con rooms also have hot and cold water which, one brochure assures, is 'usually fresh'. Fresh vegetables are said to be supplied from a hydroponic garden. There is much coming and going between here and Bi Ya Doo's next door neighbour, Villi Varu resort, which is linked to Bi Ya Doo by ferry three times a day.

There are excellent snorkelling and diving sites around the island and facilities include a Dräger decompression chamber. The Nautico water-sports centre serves both Bi Ya Doo and Villi Varu. One dive, with full equipment, costs US$40 and a 10-dive package costs US$196 for shore dives and US$277 for boat dives. The PADI basic open-water course is US$380 and there is a range of advanced and specialised courses. The school uses 38 different dive sites, all within an hour's trip by dhoni from the islands.

At Bi Ya Doo and Villi Varu you can also water-ski for US$14.50 per three-minute round or windsurf for S$13.50 an hour. A catamaran will set you back US$19.50 an hour. You can also parasail or join a group and ride a giant banana behind a speedboat.

Villi Varu (Villivaru) (☎ 447070), also operated by the Taj Group, is 29 km from the airport. Room rates, special offers and transfer rates are the same as on Bi Ya Doo. Villi Varu is the smaller sister resort of Bi Ya Doo with 60 bungalows. The management of both Villi Varu and Bi Ya Doo has linked the operation of the two islands as closely as possible, even to the extent that one chef oversees the catering on both islands. This turns out to be a real bonus, as the food is said to be the best in the country, having had this honour bestowed upon it in an inter-resort catering competition in 1992 in which over 80% of the resorts in the Maldives took part.

Cocoa Island (☎ 443713) is a very high-range resort 28 km from the airport. It's owned by an ex-*Playboy* photographer and is operated from M Gulisthaanuge (☎ 322326), Fiyaathoshi Magu, Malé. Doubles (no singles), in two-storey chalets with thatched roofs, cost US$280/390 in the low/high season. The rates include full board, water-skiing, windsurfing, catamaran sailing, table tennis, volleyball, snorkelling gear and an excursion to a nearby fishing village. Transfer to the island from the airport or Malé is generally by speedboat. The 35-minute trip costs US$200 per person (round trip). Another option is to fly to the nearby island of Guraidu with Hummingbird Helicopters.

Maakunufushi is the traditional name of Cocoa Island which, with only eight chalets, is one of the exclusive retreats. Often the whole resort is rented out by one group. It's a real hedonist's hideaway, frequented mainly by Italians and German-speaking guests.

Kandooma (☎ 444452) is a low-range resort 31 km from the airport. It's operated by M Zebey (☎ 323360), Orchid Magu, Malé. Singles/doubles cost US$45/55 in the low season and US$55/65 in the high season. Kandooma opened in 1985 and has 65 rooms. Visits to the nearby island of Guraidu can be arranged. Most of the resort is allocated to the German travel agent, Jet Reisen, and there are a few Dutch and Japanese guests. Transfer to the island by dhoni takes two hours and costs US$35 return. By speedboat it takes 30 minutes and costs US$200 return. Helicopter transfers are becoming more popular and cost US$69 one way including pickup by dhoni from Guraidu helipad.

Bodufinolhu, or *Fun Island Resort*, (☎ 444558) is an upgraded medium-range resort 38 km from the airport. It is operated by Villa Shipping & Trading Company (☎ 324478), Villa Building Ibrahim Hassan Didi Magu, Malé. There are 100 rooms squeezed onto this tiny island which measures only 30 by 800 metres. If it feels a little crowded there are two smaller, uninhabited islands nearby that you can walk to at low tide.

There is a nice wooden terrace bar over the lagoon and the rooms all have air-con and hot and cold desalinated water. Singles/ doubles range from US$88/98 to US$122/132 throughout the year. Transfer from the airport is usually by speedboat (45 minutes) at a rate of US$70 per person (one way). If the weather is very rough, transfers are done by dhoni, which takes around three hours and costs US$20 per person (one way). Most of the guests on the island are German, English, French, Italian and Swiss, with an increasing number of Japanese. Two of the bungalows are allocated to Australians all year round.

The resort's scuba centre charges US$32 for one dive, however, note that beginners can take a single introductory dive free of charge before they decide whether or not to do a course. A package of 10 dives will set you back US$230, while a second package of 10 dives costs US$200. These prices do not include equipment hire or boat trips. The Padi Open Water course costs US$460 which includes all costs except for the boat trips. There is an extra US$8 charge for each boat trip. Equipment rental (if needed) costs US$6 per dive.

Other water-sports rates are: water-skiing – US$55 for 15 minutes; catamaran hire – US$30 per hour or US$250 per day; and windsurfing – US$14 an hour or US$145 a week. Parasailing is also on offer, while fishing, including boat and tackle, for a minimum of eight people costs US$12 per person. Island hopping costs US$30 per person for a full day including a barbecue lunch. An excursion to Malé costs US$80 per person for a full day.

Rannalhi is among the resorts being redeveloped. It should open again some time in '93 or '94. Contact the operators, Jetan Travel Services (☎ 323323), 55 Marine Drive, Malé, for more information.

Fihalhohi (☎ 442903), 42 km south from the airport, is operated by Dhirham Travels & Chandling (☎ 323369), Faamudheyri Magu, Malé. There are 92 rooms and singles/doubles range from US$56/66 to US$89/93 depending on the kind of room and the season. All the guests on Fihalhohi are Germans. Transfer by dhoni from the airport costs US$30 per person (return) and takes around three hours.

Subex International Diving Schools Switzerland is in charge of diving on Fihalhohi. Six days' of unlimited diving costs US$225. CMAS certification costs US$265 and takes six days to complete.

Olhuveli (☎ 442788), 39 km from the airport, is operated by Hunter Maldives (☎ 324952), Chandani Magu, Malé. Singles/doubles/triples in any of the 125 rooms are US$225/250/315 in the low season and US$275/300/365 in the high season. You can only swim on one side of this island as there is a bad current on the other. When the tide is low you can walk or swim over to an adjoining island. Olhuveli is a Japanese-run resort, and most of the visitors are Japanese with a smaller number of Italians. There is a swimming pool and a mini-golf course. The resort has a good reputation for big-game fishing (US$330 per half-day).

Diving is run by Ocean Paradise Pty Ltd. Depending on the instructor assigned, PADI or CMAS certification is available for US$380. Single dives cost between US$25 and US$30, excluding boat charges. You can go out in a dhoni at a cost of US$8 per dive or in a custom-built dive boat, which travels at up to 30 knots and is supposedly the only dive boat in the Maldives with a depth sounder. Olhuveli also has a dive chamber to allow guests to go much deeper than the 30 metres allowed in normal scuba gear. They also use a satellite navigation system to allow them to power through the atoll in their speed launches at night.

In late 1992 Olhuveli was still the undisputed ugliest resort in the Maldives, a pink concrete jungle, with almost no trees on the entire island. The management was instructed by the relevant government authorities to plant something like 400 palm trees. Apparently the management intends to import them from South-East Asia.

Rihiveli (☎ 443731) is a high-range resort 40 km from the airport. It's operated from Imad's Agency (☎ 323441), Jawahiriyya, Chandani Magu, Malé. It is French-managed and is popular with Australians. Singles/doubles cost US$155/186 in the low season and rise as high as US$290/390 in the peak season around Christmas. If you are looking for an island which has been left as natural as possible and has a good atmosphere, an international crowd and you don't mind the price, Rihiveli is bound to please you. Rihiveli, which means 'silver sand', is the southernmost resort in Kaafu. It has 46 bungalows and an open-air dining room built out over the lagoon. You can wade across to the uninhabited Rising Sun island and the Island of Birds. Free snorkelling, windsurfing, water-skiing, and catamaran and dhoni sailing are part of the package. There are also free two-day cruises around the atoll on yacht-style *shada* boats, which carry four people. Eurodivers run the diving school.

ALIF
Ari Atoll (I)
64 km from Malé, 18 inhabited islands, 46 uninhabited islands, 22 resorts (on 20 islands), population 9793

Alif includes **Rasdu** and **Toddu**, the two small atolls to the north of Ari Atoll. You may think that Toddu has something to do with toddy, but in fact the atoll grows watermelons. The capital and fishing centre of Alif is **Mahibadu**, and the islands of **Mammigili** and **Fenfushi** are the coral-stone quarries of the country. Fenfushi supplies much of the sand for building in Malé and is noted for its coral carvings.

More and more uninhabited islands have been allowed resort leases as the government opens up Alif for tourism. Transfer journeys from the airport to these resorts are rougher since you have to cross 40 km of open sea, but the craft are high-speed ferries, not motorised dhonis.

Diving
Ari Atoll is the Maldives's fastest growing

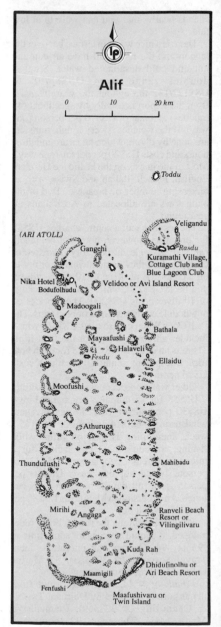

tourism destination. As is the case in Malé Atoll, all of the resort diving schools have a number of sites on which they dive. Most schools have sites which are known exclusively by them, however, there are also numerous sites which are known by one and all. Following is a brief description of a few of the more popular spots in the northern half of Ari Atoll.

Fesdu Top – 20 metres
hard and soft corals, turtles, schools of snapper, lobsters; caves with cracks and openings which allow sunlight to enter
Fesdu Faru – 25 to 30 metres
vast soft-coral reef dropping steeply in places to 30 metres; hard corals nearer the surface; occasional mantas and eagle rays; schools of snapper and yellow fin fusiliers; lobsters in a few small caves
Gathafushi Faru – 15 to 20 metres
another extensive soft-coral reef topped with hard corals; a few lobsters around
Sven Faru – 25 metres
two very beautiful caves with stingrays and lobsters; wonderful soft-coral formations; tremendous variety of small fish
Villingili Faru – 20 metres
lots of small caves with fissures and holes where sunlight can get through; schools of soldierfish; a favourite spot for underwater photographers
Hoholla Faru
similar cave formations to Villingili Faru; turtles, lobsters; large, intact hard-coral reef
Hoholla Tilla – 30 metres
very interesting hard and soft-coral covered cliff formations; batfish, red snapper, lots of moray eels, sleeping baby sharks
Kandolludu Tilla – 25 metres
gradually sloping ocean floor covered in soft corals; eagle rays, stingrays and mantas can often be seen
Maaya Tilla – 30 metres
steeply sloping ocean floor; considerable variety of fish; frequent sightings of medium-sized white tip and grey reef sharks; batfish, soldierfish, doctorfish, members of the Sepia family (squid, etc); interesting cliff formations; large cave
Malos Tilla – 30 metres
popular site on the outer edge of the reef; excellent visibility; fascinating caves with blue soft corals; grey reef sharks; large barracudas; frequent strong currents making for a fantastic drift dive
Fish Head – 30 metres
perhaps the most famous dive site in Ari Atoll, people spend up to two hours in a dhoni to get here; numerous white tip and grey reef sharks, often over two metres in length; more fish than you could count in a lifetime; strong currents; lots of boats and lots more divers – try to convince your diving guide to do it as an early morning dive

Resorts (from north to south)

Veligandu (☎ 450594) is a medium-range resort on Rasdu Atoll 57 km from the airport. It is operated by Crown Company Pty Ltd (☎ 322432), Orchid Magu, PO Box 2034, Malé. Singles/doubles are US$80/110 in low season and US$100/140 in high season. Transfer from Malé by speedboat costs US$80 per person (return) and takes around 90 minutes each way. Opened in 1985, Veligandu has 63 air-con rooms, some with open-air toilets. Guests on the island are mainly German, Austrian, Italian and Taiwanese.

Kuramathi (☎ 450527), is actually three resorts in one, *Kuramathi Village, Cottage Club* and *Blue Lagoon Club*. In all there are 190 bungalows and apartments. Blue Lagoon Club has all its 50 bungalows built over the lagoon, while the other two resorts all have beach fronts. Kuramathi is in Rasdu Atoll which is a part of the administrative atoll or Ari. Situated 55 km from the airport, all three resorts are operated by Universal Enterprises (☎ 322971), 38 Orchid Magu, Malé. Singles/doubles cost US$70/80 in low season and US$100/110 in high season. The island was 'inhabited' up until 1970, but Kuramathi is now one of the largest resorts in the Maldives.

Kuramathi's coral reef is close to the island on one side, making it good for snorkelling, and distant on the other to allow for windsurfing and swimming. In 1868 the *Reindeer*, sailing from Mauritius, was wrecked on the reef here.

Velidoo (Velidu) (☎ 450595) is a medium-range resort some 64 km from the airport. Although it is a relatively new resort, it is quickly gaining a reputation for the quality of the nearby dive sites. It has 30 fairly spacious bungalows, although considering the size of the island, it is highly likely that this figure will increase quite substantially over the next few years. For the time being singles/doubles cost US$80/90 in the low season and US$100/150 in the high season. Transfer from Malé by speedboat takes around two hours and costs anywhere from US$200 to US$500 per person (return) depending on the number of people. Helicopter transfer including dhoni pickup from the helipad costs US$300 per person (return). The operators address is c/o Shoanary, Henveiru, Malé (☎ 322149). Pretty much all the guests are brought in by Ventana in Italy and ESCO Reisen in Switzerland. Velidoo is also known as *Avi Island Resort.*

Gangehi (☎ 450505) is an exclusive 25-room resort, 73 km from the airport. It is operated by Holiday Club Maldives (☎ 323364), H Sea Coast, Marine Drive, Malé. Singles/doubles cost US$115/165 in the low season and US$130/190 in the high season.

Nika Hotel (☎ 344616), an 'ultimate'-range resort 69 km from the airport, is operated by the Nika Hotel Office (☎ 325091), Faridi Magu, Malé. Singles/doubles/triples cost US$175/260/370 in the low season and rise to US$285/440/600 in the high season.

Nika has 26 luxurious bungalows, undoubtedly the most beautiful in the Maldives, and the island is surrounded by jetties where you can park your yacht. The Italians conceived the place, manage it and patronise it as well. There are also a few Germans and other Europeans and the very occasional Japanese visitor.

Madoogali (☎ 450581) is another high-range resort, 78 km from the airport. It is operated from the Madoogali Malé Office

(☎ 323222), Marine Drive, Malé, and singles/doubles cost US$120/240 in the low season and US$150/300 in the high season. The transfer from the airport will cost you anywhere from US$160 to US$290. Madugali has 50 bungalows with air-con and the water is desalinated. The island was home to 43 Maldivians until 1943 when they were transferred to Mandu Island.

Maayafushi (☎ 450588) is a low to medium-range resort 61 km from the airport. It's operated from H Morning Sun (☎ 326658), Malé. Singles/doubles cost US$55/65 in the low season and US$75/80 in the high season. Until recently this was an Australian-run resort. It is now under Swiss management and has 60 newly renovated thatched rooms. You can go for a picnic on uninhabited Magala.

Bathala (☎ 450587), is operated from 55 Marine Drive, Malé (☎ 323323). It's a low to medium-range resort 58 km (3½ hours by boat) from the airport. Singles/doubles are US$60/65 in low season and US$80/85 in high season. Transfer from Malé by speedboat takes 90 minutes and costs US$120 return. From Kandoludhu helipad it takes 35 minutes by dhoni and costs US$20 return.

Bathala has 37 round-thatched bungalows. Like nearby Halaveli, it is clear that the developers put a little thought into the place, although the food is not quite of the same standard as Halaveli's. Bathala is considered to be a hardcore divers' island, which is great for nondivers, as this means that the island is often deserted during the day when the dive groups are out. Note that the dive school follows the CMAS standard of one regulator per diver as opposed to the double-regulator octopus required by PADI. Most people bring their own equipment (octopus/regulator and BCD) and wet suit. There are no wet suits for hire through the dive school. If you are on the resort in late October or early December, ask at the dive school about whalesharks. There are plenty of mantas around from January to August. Gray reef sharks and white tip sharks can be found all year.

Halaveli (☎ 450559), a medium-range resort 55 km from the airport, is operated by Eastinvest Ltd (☎ 322719), Akiri, Marine Drive, Malé. There are 50 thatched bungalows in this Italian-style resort and singles/doubles are US$65/90 in the low season and US$110/150 in the high season. It's an extremely beautiful, well-thought-out resort, only 700 metres in diameter and surrounded by white beach. If it weren't for the catamarans on the beach, you could be excused for thinking it was a fishing village as you sail by. Although Halaveli was not cited in the 1992 inter-resort culinary competition, the food is superb. Basically all the guests are Italians brought in by Grandi Viaggi, although FIT's of any nationality are welcome, if there is room. If you speak Italian and want to at least pretend you're roughing it, this is definitely the resort to choose. Note that unannounced visitors are not welcome.

The dive school is operated by Tropical Gangsters Incorporated. They offer a number of courses and packages including Dive Master training. The Padi Open Water Certificate course costs US$380.

Ellaidu (☎ 450586), a medium-range resort 57 km from the airport, is operated by Safari Tours (☎ 323524), Chandani Magu, Malé. There are 50 bungalows and singles/doubles cost US$70/90 in low season and US$70/100 in high season. Transfers to Ellaidu are either by helicopter or by speedboat. The speedboat transfer, which takes around 90 minutes, costs US$80 return (per person).

The dive school is run by Sub-Aqua of Munich. A package of six days' unlimited diving costs US$245. A diving course with certification by PADI, NAUI, VIT or CMAS takes from four to six days and costs US$430 all-inclusive. The kind of certificate you receive depends on the qualifications of the instructor.

Fesdu Fun Island (☎ 450541) is a low-range resort, 64 km from the airport, operated by Universal Enterprises Ltd (☎ 322971), 38 Orchid Magu, Malé. Fesdu has 50 bungalows, most of them round thatched houses. Singles/doubles cost

US$55/70 in the low season and US$65/75 in the high season. All beds are allocated to the German travel agent TUI and all guests are German. Transfers from the airport are generally done by speedboat via Kuramathi. The trip takes 2½ hours and costs US$75 one way per person. The other option, which is becoming more popular, is to fly to Kandoludhu by helicopter and take a dhoni from there.

Moofushi (☎ 450517) is a medium to high-range resort (depending on the standard of accommodation booked) 88 km from the airport. The resort, which has 60 beachfront rooms, caters exclusively to Italians. The operator is WDI Private (☎ 326433), 1/7 Marine Drive, Malé. Singles/doubles range in price from US$100/120 to US$190/210 throughout the year, except over Christmas when prices jump to an incredible US$330/350. Transfer to the island is most commonly with Hummingbird Helicopters to Embudu, then by dhoni from there at a cost of US$350 return per person. The other option is to come in by speedboat (a two-hour trip) for US$150 per person (return).

Athuruga (☎ 450508) is an all-Italian resort 67 km from the airport. All of the 42 bungalows are allocated to the Italian agent Franco Rosso, and the resort especially aims to attract clients interested in big-game fishing. Singles/doubles cost US$80/150 in the low season and US$150/200 in the high season.

Thundufushi (☎ 450515) is another Franco Rosso resort 75 km from the airport. It also has 42 bungalows and caters for much the same market as Athuruga. Both resorts are operated from the Athuruga & Thundufushi Malé Office (☎ 324435), Faridi Magu, Malé. Prices are the same as on Athuruga. Thundufushi has a hairdressing salon, which is apparently busy all week.

Diving on both Athuruga and Thundufushi is run by Franco Rosso's The Crab Diving Center. A single dive costs US$30 and a 10 dive package goes for US$250. These prices include all equipment except BCD and octopus/regulator. The PADI Open Water course costs US$380 with all necessary equipment included in the price.

Mirihi (☎ 450500) is a luxury resort some 88 km from the airport. All the guests are German speaking. There are 26 bungalows, most of them built over the water. Singles/doubles cost US$80/110 in low season and US$115/150 in high season. Return transfer from the airport by speedboat costs US$110 per person. The operator is Velangali (☎ 324910), 2 Muiveyo Magu, Malé. Rasja Travel (☎ 321488), Husnuheena Magu, Malé, can organise a good deal for this island.

Angaga (☎ 450520) is one of the better resorts to choose if you are looking for a good international mix. The resort, which is 69 km from the airport, is popular with Australians, British, Swiss, Scandinavians, Germans and other Europeans, as well as the occasional Japanese. Singles/doubles in the 51 thatch-roofed bungalows cost US$90/100 in the low season and US$120/140 in the high season. There are also various interim rates. The operator is Angaga Malé Office (☎ 323076), Malé. Transfer from Malé takes around 2½ hours by speedboat, however, most Angaga guests fly to Maafushivaru helipad with Hummingbird Helicopters and are met by one of the resort's dhonis. The round trip from the helipad costs US$20. See the Maldives Getting Around chapter for information on helicopter rates to Maafushivaru.

Angaga's dive school, which is run by Sub-Aqua, and the resort management have come up with a novel way of preserving the house reef and other surrounding dive sites. Any diver who brings a crown-of-thorns starfish back to the island with them from a dive, can cash it in for a free beer. An all-inclusive dive course with certification by either PADI or CMAS costs US$430.

Maafushivaru or *Twin Island* (☎ 450524) is a very compact and rather crowded modern luxury resort 80 km from the airport. It caters only to Italians, and then only to those who booked from home through Turisanda in Milan (☎ (02) 75201). There are 40 bungalows (10 built on a jetty over the water). There is no FIT rate and the rates given by Turisanda include transfer from Malé by helicopter to the nearby helipad of the same name (three minutes away by dhoni). For what it is worth, the operator is Universal Enterprises (☎ 322971), 38 Orchid Magu, Malé.

The dive school is run by Projetto Atlantide, a Bologna based organisation. A single dive costs US$30, while a PADI or CMAS certification course costs US$400. This price includes insurance, which is not generally mentioned by other dive schools in the Maldives.

Kuda Rah (☎ 450550) is a luxury resort 96 km from the airport. It is operated from 2/F, H Merry Side (☎ 322335), Marine Drive, Malé. The resort has a decompression chamber, although at the time of writing, there was nobody on the island who could operate it. There are 30 rooms with singles/doubles costing US$140/175 all year round. Transfer is by speedboat or by helicopter to Maafushivaru or Ari Beach, and dhoni from the helipad. Kuda Rah is said by some to be the most exclusive resort in the Maldives, but if you are not coming through an Italian travel agent you'll probably never find out.

Among the facilities on the island is possibly the only full-sized pool tables in the country, and a floodlit grass tennis court. There is also a decompression chamber and there will soon be a trained European doctor permanently on staff. It is also the only resort using solar panels to supply a 24-hour-a-day hot water service.

Dhidufinolhu (☎ 450513), also called *Ari Beach Resort*, is a low to medium-range resort 100 km from the airport. It's operated from 52 Marine Drive (☎ 321930), Malé, and costs US$48/76 for singles/doubles in the low season and US$98/134 in the high season. Transfer from Malé is generally by helicopter. There are 76 rooms, most with air-con and desalinated water.

The dive school is run by Eurodivers. A single 'discovery' dive for beginners costs US$15, otherwise a single dive costs US$25. There are various dive packages available

including five dives for US$116, 10 dives for US$220 and six days' unlimited diving for US$224. These prices include all equipment, but do not include any boat trips out to the dive sites. PADI Open Water certification costs US$308 all-inclusive (boat trips excepted). Boat trips cost US$8 or US$84 for 12 people. You can also rent an underwater camera for US$20. Film is available in the resort shop.

Ranveli Beach Resort or *Vilingilivaru* (☎ 450570) is a medium-range resort 77 km from the airport. It is operated by Nexus Trade & Travel (☎ 313121), 57 Marine Drive, Malé. There are 56 bungalows with singles/doubles costing US$61/122 all year round.

In addition to the resorts outlined here, there are a number of forthcoming developments in Ari Atoll. It is likely that resorts will be opened on the following islands Rangali Finolhu, Nalaguraidhoo, Dhiffushi, Vakarufalhi, Machafushi, Vilamendhoo and Huvahendhoo, during the life of this edition.

VAAVU

Felidu Atoll (J)
67 km from Malé, five inhabited islands, 19 uninhabited islands, two resorts, population 1697

Vaavu, which also includes **Vattaru Atoll**, is sparsely populated and undistinguished. The people of **Felidu**, the capital island, eke out a living from fishing, boatbuilding and selling T-shirts to the tourists who arrive regularly on outings from **Dhiggiri** and Alimatha resorts. **Keyodu**, the neighbouring island, and **Rakeedu**, to the south, are the other main islands.

Resorts

Alimatha (☎ 450544), a medium-range resort 61 km from the airport, is operated by Safari Tours (☎ 323524), Chandani Magu, Malé. The resort has 70 rooms and singles/doubles cost US$80/100 in the low season and US$95/145 in the high season. Large numbers of Italian underwater enthu-

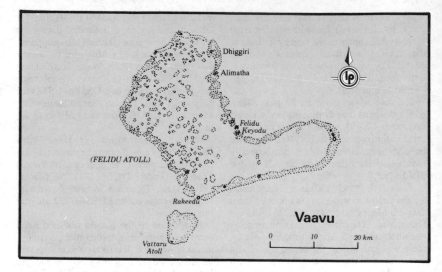

siasts, attracted by excellent diving prospects, visit Alimatha and nearby Dhiggiri during the high season, under the Club Vacanze flag. The resort has a decompression chamber.

Dhiggiri (☎ 450592), also operated by Safari Tours, is a medium-range resort 59 km from the airport. There are 30 bungalows with singles/doubles costing US$70/90 in the low season and US$70/105 in the high season. Transfer to both Alimatha and Dhiggiri is generally by speedboat. The trip takes around 90 minutes and costs US$80 return (per person).

The Swiss-run Manta Diving Base has instructors who speak English, German and French. They offer PADI Open Water certification for US$395. Advanced, Rescue and Dive Master courses can also be arranged on request. Dive packages available include five dives for US$160, 10 dives for US$225 and six days' unlimited diving for US$250. A single dive costs US$35. These prices include all equipment, so if you have your own equipment with you, the prices come down.

MEEMU
Mulaku Atoll (K)
120 km from Malé, nine inhabited islands, 25 uninhabited islands, 0 resorts, population 4186

Muli is the capital island but **Dhiggaru**, in the north of the atoll, is the most populated. **Kolhufushi** and **Mula** islands grow lots of yams.

FAAFU
North Nilandu Atoll (L)
120 km from Malé, five inhabited islands, 10 uninhabited islands, 0 resorts, population 2614

Thor Heyerdahl's book *Maldive Mystery* devotes an entire chapter to Faafu's central island and capital **Nilandu**. His expedition there unearthed five phallic lingams, and the ruins of a pre-Islamic gate which he believed to have been one of seven surrounding a great pagan temple complex. Of Nilandu, Heyerdahl wrote:

Five teams of archaeologists could dig here for five years and still make new discoveries...the magnitude

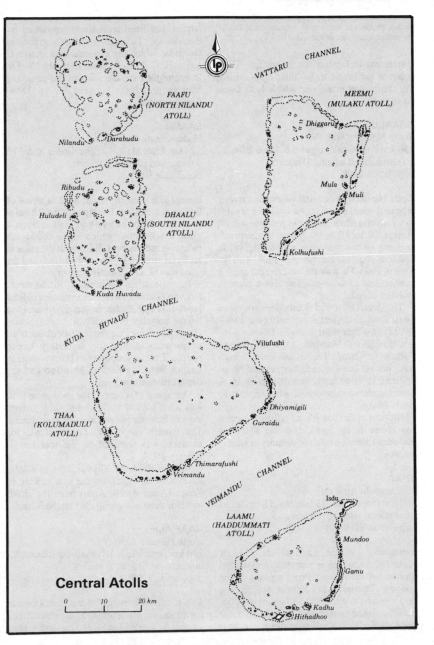

Central Atolls

0   10   20 km

of this prehistoric cult centre seemed quite out of proportion to the size of the island.

Darabudu is famous for its turtles. They come to the island to lay their eggs during the south-west monsoon, which lasts from April to October.

DHAALU
South Nilandu Atoll (M)
150 km from Malé, eight inhabited islands, 50 uninhabited islands, 0 resorts, population 4199

Kuda Huvadu, the capital island, is another archaeological paradise. As well as a mysterious mound, there is an old mosque which Heyerdahl said has the finest 'fingerprint' masonry he has ever seen; surpassing, in his opinion, that of the famous Inca wall in Cuzco, Peru. He was amazed to find such a masterpiece of stone-shaping art on such an isolated island.

The waters around Kuda Huvadu also boast some shipwrecks, including the 1340-ton *Liffey* which went down in 1879.

Uninhabited **Maadeli**, also known as Salazar or Temple Island, has ruins which have not yet been investigated, including an ancient mosque and, according to H A Maniku, the foundations of what appears to be dwellings.

Ribudu is famous for its goldsmiths and *ras roanu* (king rope), and the island of Huludeli rivals it with a community of silversmiths.

THAA
Kolumadulu Atoll (N)
192 km from Malé, 13 inhabited islands, 54 uninhabited islands, 0 resorts, population 8189

Veimandu is the capital island of Kolumadulu, which is a great circular atoll and one of the major fishing regions of the country. **Thimarafushi Island**, which was destroyed by fire in 1902 and again in 1905, has flourished to become the atoll's most populated island. **Vilufushi Island**, the next

largest, has been completely overtaken by the village. There is a sultan's grave on **Guraidu**, which the historian and archaeologist H C P Bell visited in 1922. On **Dhiyamigili** there are ruins of the palace of Mohammed Imaaduddeen II, an 18th-century sultan.

LAAMU
Haddummati Atoll (O)
224 km from Malé, 12 inhabited islands, 75 uninhabited islands, 0 resorts, population 9101

Laamu is a very important atoll in terms of fishing and history. The signs of pre-Muslim civilisations are everywhere and include a giant black dome which rises above the palms on **Isdu Island**. Who built the ancient artificial mound, known as a *hawitta*, and for what reason, is not really known.

Because of his research of similar structures on **Gamu Island**, on the eastern side of Laamu, H C P Bell believed the mounds to be the remains of Buddhist stupas, while Heyerdahl thinks maybe the Buddhists built on mounds left by the legendary Redin people. There are mounds on other islands in Laamu including **Kadhu**, **Mundoo** and the capital **Hithadhoo**.

One thing's for sure, if the mound on Isdu was some kind of navigational aid it proved to be of little use to several modern seafarers. The British cargo ship *Lagan Bank*, for instance, was wrecked on the reef on 13 January 1938.

An Air Maldives' Skyvan flies to Kadhu twice a week – once on the way to Gan in Seenu (Addu Atoll). Apart from the small airfield, there is nothing else on the island.

GAAF ALIF
North Huvadu Atoll (P)
330 km from Malé, 10 inhabited islands, 83 uninhabited islands, 0 resorts, population 7295

This is the northern half of the giant Huvadu (or Suvadiva) Atoll which is separated from Laamu by the 90 km wide One and a Half

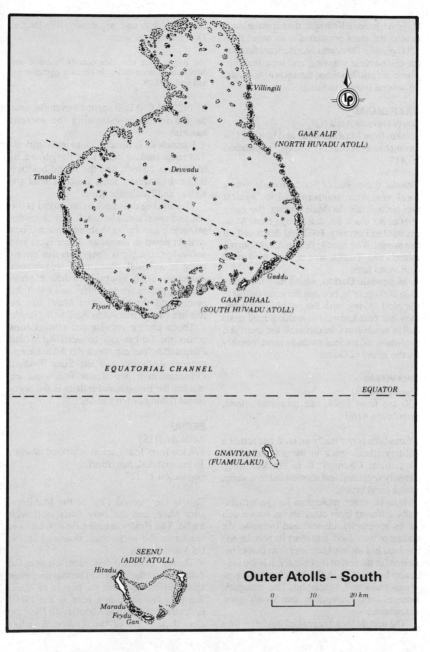

Villingili

GAAF ALIF
(NORTH HUVADU ATOLL)

Tinadu

• Devvadu

Gaddu

Fiyori

GAAF DHAAL
(SOUTH HUVADU ATOLL)

EQUATORIAL CHANNEL

EQUATOR

GNAVIYANI
(FUAMULAKU)

SEENU
(ADDU ATOLL)

Hitadu

Maradu
Feydu
Gan

Outer Atolls – South

0   10   20 km

Degree Channel. **Villingili**, the capital island, is also the most populated with more than 1200 people. **Devvadu** islanders are famous for their textile weaving and rope making. There are also hawittas, the ancient mounds, on several islands in this atoll.

GAAF DHAAL
South Huvadu Atoll (Q)
360 km from Malé, 10 inhabited islands, 154 uninhabited islands, 0 resorts, population 10,417

Tinadu, the capital of South Huvadu, was a focal point in the 'southern rebellion' against the central rule in Malé during the early 1960s. So much so, that troops from Malé invaded in February 1962 and destroyed all the homes. The people fled to neighbouring islands and Tinadu was not resettled until four years later.

Meanwhile **Gaddu**, which now has more than 2000 people, became the main island in the atoll. Along with the people on **Fiyori**, they are best known for making reed mats called *tundu kuna*. In this atoll too there is a profusion of ancient mounds most notably on the island of Gamu.

GNAVIYANI
Fuamulaku (R)
430 km from Malé, one inhabited island, population 6160

Fuamulaku is not really an atoll but rather a solitary island stuck in the middle of the Equatorial Channel. It is six km long, densely vegetated and surrounded by a steep, rough coral beach.

It is, however, more than just geographically different from other atolls. As a result of its geography, climate and isolation the nature of the island, and even its people, has evolved in a more exotic way than that experienced in the rest of the country. It is the only really lush island in the Maldives and produces fruits and vegetables, like mangoes, oranges and pineapples, that won't grow elsewhere.

The people look bigger and healthier than

other islanders and, apparently, live longer. Thor Heyerdahl wrote:

The people were also exceptionally beautiful and displayed far more variety in physical type than we had seen in Malé.

In 1922, H C P Bell spent an eventful time on the island investigating the ancient hawittas.

Fuamulaku is divided into eight districts. The main landing point is at Rasgefanu, in Malégamu district, and the island has two inland freshwater lakes, Bandara Kuli (or Kelhe) and Dadimage Kuli.

The one big drawback to the island is the sea and coastline. The small reef is hardly protective and the coral-shingle beach drops straight down to the water. There is no safe anchorage, fishing is dangerous and swimming is suicidal because of treacherous currents. Still, Fuamulaku has a great drawing power for travellers and (with the permit and the plane from Malé) can be reached easily from Addu Atoll to the south.

There are no regular sea connections across the 50-km gap between Addu and Fuamulaku. You can check the Addu Development Authority and the State Trading Organisation to see if any fast boats are making the trip, otherwise there is the occasional fishing or ferry dhoni.

SEENU
Addu Atoll (S)
478 km from Malé, seven inhabited islands, 36 uninhabited, one resort,
population 15,177

This is the 'second city' of the Maldives, after Malé, and the only other atoll with traffic. The rivalry between the two cities is similar to the north-south divisions in the USA and the UK.

There is a fierce independent streak in the Addu folk, reflected in the fact that they even speak differently from the people of Malé. Tensions last came to a head in the 1960s under the leadership of Abdulla Afif Didi, the elected president of the 'United Suvadiva

Islands'. The shortlived southern uprising was quashed, however, by an armed fleet sent south by Prime Minister Ibrahim Nasir. Afif fled the country, but is still talked about on his home island of **Hitadu**.

Where isolation had a big influence on Fuamulaku's character, it was the Royal Air Force which shaped the personality of Addu Atoll. The British had an air base on the island of Gan during WW II and again from 1956 to 1976.

They built a causeway connecting Feydu, Maradu and Hitadu islands, paved the roads and employed most of the population on or around the base. They left an airport, an industrial estate, a 'holiday village' and a lot of unemployed people who spoke better English than anyone in the rest of the country. When the tourist industry took off in the 1970s, many of the men of Addu went to Malé to work on resorts or in stores and continued to serve the *don miha* (tourists or expats).

The only registered places to stay and eat in the Maldives, apart from the resorts, are here on Seenu – the southernmost atoll. If you are looking for someone to 'sponsor' a visit to the islands and get you a permit, chances are you'll find someone from Addu Atoll although, technically, a permit is not needed if you are staying at Gan's Ocean Reef Club.

Gan

The remains of several mosques and other earlier ruins in this region were all flattened by the RAF. The British took over the whole of Gan and installed all the comforts of home. Now, apart from the resort, it's like a ghost town – quiet and eerie.

However, with the help of Australian aid, the airport is being slowly modernised with the intention of one day being able to accommodate large numbers of tourists. At present only the 18-seater Skyvan arrives three times a week.

Hangars and other maintenance buildings have been taken over by two Hong Kong garment factories. These businesses bus in 500 local women, but also employ about 500 Sri Lankan girls, who live for a year or two in the former barracks and work nightshift without any leave.

The cinema is still operational and there is a post office and a Bank of Maldives. Sadly, the swimming pool is now more like a cesspool and the golf course is closed and so overgrown it's hard to spot the clubhouse, let alone the fairway. Pakistanis employed by the RAF, for cooking and other domestic chores, built a mosque which is still standing and, though no longer used, is more elaborate than the Maldivian one.

The *Ocean Reef Club*, run by Phoenix Hotels & Resorts (☎ 323181), Fasmeeru, Marine Drive, Malé, is quite different to all the other resorts in the Maldives. The rate of development has picked up considerably since Phoenix took over. At the time of writing, the finishing touches to the Club were being completed, and the first 30 double rooms were open to visitors. By the end of '93 there are expected to be 250 rooms, however, seeing is believing. Perhaps the most unexpected aspect of the resort is its 18-hole international-standard golf course. At the time of researching this book, 13 fairways and two greens were complete, and work was definitely ongoing. The first 'international tournament with some of the top players in the world' was apparently scheduled barely six weeks later (at the same time as the Johnny Walker Classic in Jamaica where the top 28 players in the world were all expected to play).

Other facilities in the resort include a swimming pool (half built at the time of research), a dive school, tennis and squash courts and big-game fishing boats.

Perhaps the best reason to come to Gan, however, is the fact that you can visit the nearby islands of Feydu, Maradu and Hitadu (see the following for more information). It is quite impossible to foresee what will happen to these islands and their population if tourism takes off, however, the management of the Ocean Reef Club insists that they will do everything in their power to ensure that their island culture is preserved as much as possible.

Hitadu

After driving straight through Feydu and Maradu you come to Hitadu, the big capital of the atoll. A taxi from Gan airport or the Holiday Village costs between Rf 50 and Rf 60.

Hitadu is clustered around Aazee Magu, the long central avenue. Electricity is available on the island from 6 to 11 pm. There is a VSO nurse in charge of the hospital when there is no doctor posted to the island.

The best place to swim is Cortez (pronounced 'kottey') Beach at the northern point of the island where there is a break in the reef. Elsewhere the coast is too rocky or shallow for bathing. Near Cortez are the ruins of a sultan's fort.

Across the lagoon from Hitadu, on the other side of the heart-shaped atoll, are the 'Siamese' islands of Huludu and Meedu. On the latter there is a revered cemetery, called Koagannu, where several important chiefs are buried.

Down by the fishing harbour there are four local cafés or tearooms, including the *Marine*. The only place to go for a European meal is *Target Point* on Aazee Magu. Otherwise there are a few other places scattered around the village serving Maldivian food, however, in general the food does not seem to be as good as in Malé.

My personal experience of Gan and the surrounding islands was, without question, the terrestrial highlight of my visit to the Maldives. The reception I was given by the local population on Feydu, Maradu and Hitadu was overwhelming. Since 1976, when the British left Gan, there have been very few foreign visitors to the region. In general the people seem to be very excited about the long awaited influx of tourists, as they tend to have fond memories of the British.

Before you decide to take your holiday in Gan, however, you should carefully think about what you want from your holiday. If you are looking for lazy days on the beach, pick another resort. There are beaches down here, and the diving is said to be reasonable, but this alone is not enough to justify the cost. If, however, you are interested in seeing the real, unspoiled Maldives, Gan is the place for you.

Before visiting Gan and the surrounding islands, it is important that you understand the problems that Western culture has caused in the more frequently visited island villages in Malé and Ari Atoll. Whenever tourists from nearby resorts arrive for the standard 30-minute visit, there is a flurry of activity as people open up their tourist shops to sell imported Balinese and Sri Lankan goods; low quality, mass produced T-shirts from Malé; red coral jewellery from the Mediterranean; and shells, turtle shell and coral products from Maldivian waters. Worse still, children approach tourists asking for 'one dollar'. On an island with a population of only 400 or so, these activities cannot have a positive effect on the culture, and tourists end up gaining no insight whatsoever into the realities of the Maldivian island lifestyle.

The island villages of Feydu, Maradu and Hitadu in Addu Atoll are considerably larger than most of those in Malé and Ari Atoll, so they have a much better chance of absorbing these kinds of problems, however, tourists have a responsibility to ensure that the indigenous population remains proud of its own culture. There is nothing wrong with enterprising villagers making money out of the tourists, but we should let them know that we don't want shells, coral, turtle shell or Balinese batik. If visitors make this attitude clear from the start, perhaps local artisans will seize the opportunity to show that they too have something to offer.

Top: Looking towards Maafushivaru Resort (MB)
Upper Middle: Deserted beach (MB)
Lower Middle: Rihiveli Resort (MB)
Bottom: Tari Village (MB)

A (MB), B (PM)
C (PM), D (PM)

ISLANDS
OF THE
EAST INDIAN
OCEAN

Andaman & Nicobar Islands

These two island groups are part of the Republic of India. The Andaman and Nicobar islands together form a union territory, and lie in the Bay of Bengal 1000 km south of Calcutta.

Of the two groups, only the Andamans can accommodate individual travellers. The Nicobar Islands are closed to foreigners altogether, although Indian nationals can visit freely.

Facts for the Visitor

VISAS & EMBASSIES
These days virtually everybody needs a visa to visit India, and if you intend to stay longer than 90 days you will also have to go through the paperwork and red tape involved in extending a visa.

Indian visas are available from Indian consular offices and usually cost around US$5 or the equivalent in another currency. Make sure you know what the price is, though. We've had several complaints from people who sent in the visa fee requested on the form, only to discover much later that the fee had been changed and their visa request was on hold until they sent the correct amount.

For political reasons UK citizens have to pay a much higher visa fee (£23), and many British residents of Australia have been tripped up by this, as there is no indication on the visa form that different fees apply to them.

We've also had a couple of letters from people who, when they enquired why their visa was taking so long to issue, were told it could be rushed through for an additional fee. Corruption in high places?

Where you apply for a visa also seems to make a difference. Numerous travellers have written to complain that in Athens it's absolutely terrible getting an Indian visa, but in Ankara, capital of neighbouring Turkey, it's no problem at all. In South-East Asia some people say Bangkok is fine for getting this visa, others say that it's chaotic; while in Chiang Mai, in the north of Thailand, it's a breeze.

In some countries (Malaysia and Nepal for example) the Indian Consular Office insisted that British passport holders supply a letter from the British Consular Office confirming that they really were British. This costs the unfortunate Brits another US$5 or so.

Make sure your visa is a multiple-entry one if you intend to depart and return. Some people unwittingly end up with single-entry visas which do not permit you to return to India. Another headache is that some offices will not allow you to renew your visa until it is less than 14 days away from expiry. The visa renewal hassles are not due to reluctance to let people stay longer, but to the usual Indian red tape and bureaucracy.

Note
Even if you have a visa, you are not allowed to visit the Andamans without a special permit. See the Andaman Islands section for details.

Indian Embassies
Some of the major Indian consular offices overseas include:

Australia
   3-5 Moonah Place, Yarralumla, ACT 2600 (☎ (06) 273-3999)
   153 Walker St, North Sydney, NSW 2060 (☎ (02) 955-7055)
   238 Bell St, Coburg, Vic 3058 (☎ (03) 350-4684)
Bangladesh
   120 Rd 2, Dhanmodi Residential Area H, Dhaka (☎ (2) 50-3606)
Myanmar (Burma)
   545-547 Merchant St, Yangon (Rangoon) (☎ (1) 82-550)
Canada
   10 Springfield Rd, Ottawa K1M 1C9 (☎ (613) 744-3751)

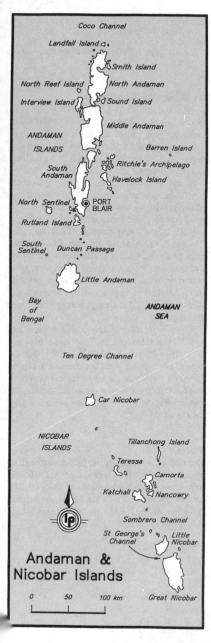

Denmark
Vangehusvej 15, 2100 Copenhagen (☎ (1) 3118-2888)

Egypt
5 Aziz Ababa St, Zamalek, Cairo (☎ (2) 341-3051)

France
15 Rue Alfred Dehodencq, 75016 Paris (☎ (1) 45 20 39 30)

Germany
Adenaverallee 262, 5300 Bonn (☎ (228) 54-050)

Italy
Via XX Settembre 5, 00187 Rome (☎ (6) 46-4642)

Japan
2-11 Kudan Minami 2-Chome, Chiyoda-ku, Tokyo (☎ (3) 262-2391)

Jordan
1st Circle, Jebel Amman, Amman (☎ (6) 62-2098)

Kenya
Jeevan Bharati Building, Harambee Ave, Nairobi (☎ (2) 22-566)

Malaysia
20th floor, West Block, Wisma Selangor Dredging, 142-C Jalan Ampang, Kuala Lumpur (☎ (3) 261-7000)

Nepal
Lainchaur, GPO Box 292, Kathmandu (☎ 41-0900)

Netherlands
Buitenrustweg 2, The Hague (☎ (70) 346-9771)

New Zealand
180 Molesworth St, Princess Towers, Wellington (☎ (4) 73-6390)

Pakistan
G-5 Diplomatic Enclave, Islamabad (☎ (51) 81-4371)
India House, 3 Fatima Jinnah Rd, Karachi (☎ (21) 52-2275)

Singapore
India House, 31 Grange Rd (☎ 737-6777)

Sri Lanka
36-38 Galla Rd, Colombo 3 (☎ (1) 21-605)

Switzerland
Effingerstrasse 45, CH-3008 Berne (☎ (31) 26-3111)

Syria
40/46 Adnan Malki St, Yassin Nouwelati Building, Damascus (☎ (11) 71-9580)

Tanzania
11th floor, NIC Investment House, Samora Ave, Dar es Salaam (☎ (51) 20-295)

Thailand
46 Soi 23 (Prasarnmitr), Sukhumvit Rd, Bangkok (☎ (2) 258-0300)
113 Bumruangrat Rd, Chiang Mai 50000 (☎ (53) 24-3066)

UK
> India House, Aldwych, London WC2B 4NA
> (☎ (071) 836-0990)
> 82 New St, Birmingham B2 4BA
> (☎ (21) 643-0366)

USA
> 2107 Massachusetts Ave NW, Washington DC
> 20008 (☎ (202) 939-7000)
> 3 East 64th St, New York, NY 10021-7097
> (☎ (212) 879-7800)
> 540 Arguello Blvd, San Francisco, CA 9418
> (☎ (415) 668-0662)

Visa Extensions

If your stay in India is going to be for more than 90 days and you have to extend your visa, then you'll need to have a few days to spare while you wait for it to come through. The time taken can vary from one hour (Bangalore) to 10 days (Cochin), and many people have reported that no extensions *at all* are being issued in Goa. Officially there is no charge for visa extensions, although public servants fishing for baksheesh are not unheard of. Four identical passport photos are needed.

If you leave the country and pop across the border to Nepal after 60 days, for example, when you return you will only have until the original 90 days run out. In other words, you do not have 30 days left, nor do you start the 90 days again. A 90-day visa is just that; it lasts for 90 days from the date of the first entry into India, regardless of the number of days you actually spend in India.

If you stay more than 90 days you are also supposed to get an income tax clearance before you leave. See the section on Tax Clearance Certificates for details.

Foreigners' Registration Offices

Visa renewals and also permits for the Andaman Islands are issued by the Foreigners' Registration offices. The main offices include:

Bombay
> Special Branch II, Annexe 2, Office of the Commissioner of Police (Greater Bombay), Dadabhoy Naoroji Rd (☎ 26-8111)

Calcutta
> 237 Acharya J C Bose Rd (☎ 47-3301)

Madras
> 9 Village Rd (☎ 47-8210)

New Delhi
> 1st floor, Hans Bhavan, Tilak Bridge (☎ 331-9489)

Tax Clearance Certificates

If you stay in India for more than 90 days you need a 'tax clearance certificate' to leave the country. This supposedly guarantees that your time in India was financed by your own money, not by working in India or by selling things or playing the black market.

A few years ago getting a tax clearance certificate was a major operation requiring all sorts of forms and lots of time. Today it is much simpler and more straightforward.

Basically all you have to do is find the Foreign Section of the Income Tax Department in Delhi, Calcutta, Madras or Bombay and turn up there with your passport, visa extension form, any other similar paperwork and a handful of bank exchange receipts (to show you really did change foreign currency into rupees).

You fill in a form and wait for between 'only 10 minutes' (for the 'best-case' people) to 'only a couple of hours' (for the worst). You're then given your tax clearance certificate and away you go. Most travellers report that the only time they were asked to produce this certificate was when they were leaving the country.

MONEY

The unit of currency is the Indian rupee (Rs) which is divided into 100 paise (p). There are paise coins in denominations of five, 10, 20, 25 and 50, as well as a Rs 1 coin; and there are notes of Rs 1, 2, 5, 10, 20, 50 and 100.

US$1	=	Rs 31
A$1	=	Rs 22
UK£1	=	Rs 46
C$1	=	Rs 25
DM1	=	Rs 19
1FF	=	Rs 5.5
Y100	=	Rs 26

Currency Exchange Forms

You are not allowed to bring Indian currency into the country or take it out. You are allowed to bring in unlimited amounts of foreign currency or travellers' cheques, but you are supposed to declare anything over US$1000 on arrival. All money is supposed to be changed at official banks or moneychangers, and you are supposed to be given a currency exchange form for each transaction.

In actual practice you can secretly bring rupees into the country with you. They can be bought at a useful discount price in places like Singapore or Bangkok and can be brought in fairly openly from Nepal, where you'll also get a slightly better rate.

Banks will usually give you a currency exchange form but occasionally they don't bother. It is, however, worth getting this form for several reasons. Firstly, you will need one for any re-exchange when you leave India. Secondly, certain official purchases, such as airline tickets, must be paid for either with foreign currency or with rupees accompanied by sufficient exchange forms to account for the ticket price. Thirdly, if you stay more than 90 days and have to get an income tax clearance, this requires production of a handful of exchange forms to prove you've been changing money all along and not earning money locally.

Travellers' Cheques

Due to problems of fraudulent use some banks, principally State Bank of India branches, will not accept American Express travellers' cheques. Although most of the time these cheques are OK, it's probably wise to bring a few other travellers' cheques just in case.

Credit Cards

Although credit cards are widely accepted in India, their use in the Andamans is restricted to the resort hotels.

Tipping

In tourist restaurants or hotels, where service s usually tacked on in any case, the normal 10% tipping figure generally applies. In smaller places, where tipping is optional, you need only tip a couple of rupees, not a percentage of the bill. Hotel porters usually get about Rs 1 per bag, while Rs 1 to Rs 2 is a good level for bike watching and Rs 5 to Rs 15 is the norm for extra services from hotel staff.

TOURIST OFFICES
Representatives Abroad

The Government of India Tourist Office maintains a string of tourist offices overseas where you can get brochures, leaflets and some information about India and the Andamans. The quality of information in the tourist office leaflets and brochures is often very high and they are worth getting hold of. On the other hand, some of the overseas offices are not always as useful for obtaining information as those within India.

The overseas offices are given in the following list; there are also smaller 'promotion offices' in Osaka (Japan) and in Dallas, Miami, San Francisco and Washington DC (all in the USA).

Australia
   Level 1, 17 Castlereagh St, Sydney NSW 2000 (☎ (02) 232-1600)
Canada
   60 Bloor St West, Suite No 1003, Toronto, Ontario M4W 3B8 (☎ (416) 962-6279)
France
   8 Blvd de la Madeleine, 75009 Paris (☎ 42 65 83 86)
Germany
   Kaiserstrasse 77-III, D-6000 Frankfurt-am-Main-1 (☎ 23-5423)
Italy
   Via Albricci 9, 20122 Milan (☎ 80-4952)
Japan
   Pearl Building, 9-18 Ginza, 7-Chome, Chuo ku, Tokyo 104 (☎ 571-5062)
Malaysia
   Wisma HLA, Lot 203 Jalan Raja Chulan, 50200 Kuala Lumpur (☎ 242-5285)
Netherlands
   Rokin 9-15, 1012 KK Amsterdam (☎ 20-8991)
Sweden
   Sveavagen 9-11, S-III 57, Stockholm 11157 (☎ (08) 21-5081)

Switzerland
   1-3 Rue de Chantepoulet, 1201 Geneva (☎ (022) 732-1813)
Thailand
   Kentucky Fried Chicken Building, 3rd floor, 62/5 Thaniya Rd, Bangkok 10500 (☎ 235-2585)
UK
   7 Cork St, London W1X 2AB (☎ (081) 734-6613)
USA
   30 Rockefeller Plaza, 15 North Mezzanine, New York NY 10112 (☎ (212) 586-4901)
   3550 Wilshire Blvd, Suite 204, Los Angeles CA 90010 (☎ (213) 380-8855)

Andaman Islands

Named after the monkey god, Hanuman, these islands were originally inhabited by six Negrito tribes. In recent times, however, large numbers of Indians have arrived from the mainland to settle here. Despite this the islands are still very much a backwater.

Although patience, persistence and time are all needed in large quantities, the Andamans offer some spectacular diving and snorkelling and the chance to explore rarely visited islands.

HISTORY

As the Andamans lie on the ancient trade routes between India and the Far East, they were known to mariners from as early as the 7th century, and probably long before that. Marco Polo wrote of them in the 13th century, warning of the fiercely hostile people who would kill and eat any outsider who ventured onto the islands. These reports were 'substantiated' in later centuries and the islands became synonymous with murder and brutality, although it was subsequently shown that the islanders did not practise cannibalism.

The Andaman Islands were first settled by the British in the late 18th century when Captain Archibald Blair, sailing on behalf of the British East India Company in Calcutta, founded a naval station on Chatham Island, now known as Port Blair. Attempts were then made to settle areas in the north of Great Andaman, but the hostility of the local inhabitants forced the British to abandon those plans.

In 1858 a penal colony was established in Port Blair, mainly as a solution to dealing with the large numbers of Indians held by the British following the so-called 'Indian Mutiny' of 1857. The first batch of 200 'mutineers', two doctors and 60 British naval troops arrived aboard the *Semiramis* on 10 March 1858.

These first convicts were put to work clearing extensive areas of jungle and reclaiming swampy areas. Despite the huge number of casualties from sickness and disease in the early years, the settlement gradually took shape. Because of the high mortality rate, however, the prisoners nicknamed the settlement *Kalapani* – 'water of death'.

A letter from the superintendent of the penal colony, J P Walker, to the Secretary of India in June 1858 gives the following statistics on the number of convicts that arrived on prison ships that year and their survival rate.

Received per *Semiramis* from Calcutta, 10 March	200
Received per *Roman Emperor* from Kurachee, 6 April	171
Received per *Edward*, from Kurachee, 13 April	130
Received per *Dalhousie* from Calcutta, 15 April	140
Received per *Sesostris* from Singapore, 12 June	132
Total	773
Died in hospital	64
Escaped uncaptured	140
Suicide	1
Executed	87
Living	481

The islands really gained notoriety in 1872 when a visiting viceroy, Lord Mayo, was assassinated by a Muslim convict, Sher Ali.

In 1876 the British introduced the *Andaman & Nicobar Manual*, which included the following definition:

Transportation entails hard labour with strict discipline, with only such food as is necessary. Any mitigation of the above is an indulgence which may at any time be withdrawn in part or whole.

By 1881 the population had grown to 14,628, mostly convicts. A vast majority of the convicts, who were released after they had served their time, actually stayed and settled in the Andamans.

Following a visit by the Lyall & Lethbridge Commission, sent to the Andamans by the British to investigate the penal system, a decision was taken to build a jail as it was thought the conditions were too good compared with other jails on mainland India. Also there was nowhere to keep prisoners in solitary confinement, which was one of the favourite forms of incarceration at the time. Construction of Port Blair's Cellular Jail began in 1891.

During WW II the Japanese occupied the islands after the British beat a hasty retreat, taking their most prized prisoners with them to Calcutta. The Japanese established a major defence base and evidence of their presence, such as huge concrete bunkers, can still be seen today.

During the period of Japanese occupation, many Indians were arrested and tortured on suspicion of being British spies. Most were in fact members of the Andaman Branch of the Indian Independence League, an anti-British force formed on the mainland. Other men, women and children were said to have been taken out to sea and dumped in the water to drown.

After the war the British decided to close down the penal settlement. The decision was reported in the *Amrita Bazaar Patrika* newspaper:

New Delhi, Sept 1, 1945. The Government of India has decided to abolish the penal settlement in the Andaman Islands as a major step towards their reoccupation. The reasons for its abolition are, it is pointed out, firstly political bitterness which the dispatch of prisoners to those islands created, secondly jails being a provincial subject, the centre has no needs to run the penal settlement, and thirdly communication difficulty.

When India gained independence from Britain, the islands became part of the Indian Union. The main activity since then has been the logging of the forests. The government goes to great lengths to make it known that this is all in the best interest of the tribal people, and that they are bringing civilisation to these stone-age tribes. The fact is that the tribes have been decimated by imported diseases and their cultures have been severely undermined.

In an effort to develop the islands economically, the government has completely disregarded the needs and land rights of the tribes and has encouraged massive transmigration from the mainland – mainly of Tamils who were expelled from Sri Lanka – which has pushed the combined Andaman and Nicobar population from 50,000 to 278,000 in just 18 years. The original islanders' culture is being swamped. However, it's not only the people who have been squashed in the path of 'development'. Vast tracts of forest were felled in the '60s and '70s. There has been some replanting of the land with 'economic' timber like teak. The government has also adopted a somewhat more responsible attitude toward settlement and the protection of the indigenous peoples. The tribal settlements are off limits to unauthorised visitors, so it is hoped that their culture, and indeed the tribes themselves, will survive.

GEOGRAPHY
Together with the Nicobar Islands, the Andamans are a part of a mostly submarine mountain range joining normally Myanmar (Burma) and the Indonesian island of Sumatra. The 204 islands of the group cover a total of 6340 sq km.

The three main islands in the group are North, Middle and South Andaman, which are known collectively as Great Andaman. Other important islands include Landfall, Interview, Ritchie's Archipelago, Baratang and Rutland. Little Andaman Island lies some 80 km south of South Andaman, and is separated from the main group by Duncan Passage.

There is a large number of small islands dotted in and around the passages which separate the islands of Great Andaman. Port Blair is the administrative capital and is situated on a sheltered harbour on the south-west coast of South Andaman. Islands in the vicinity which can be visited include Ross, Grub, Jolly Buoy, Red Skin, Snob and Boat.

The main islands are extremely hilly and are covered in dense forest (where it hasn't been cleared). The hills rise steeply, the highest being Saddle Peak (750 metres) in North Andaman. There are no permanent rivers and only a very few perennial streams.

CLIMATE

The climate of the Andamans is warm all year round, with generally high humidity, although the afternoon sea breezes temper this. Daytime temperatures average around 30°C and rarely fall below 22°C.

Most of the islands' annual rainfall of 3161 mm occurs during the south-west monsoon season from June to September, with lighter falls in May and throughout the months of October and November during the north-east monsoon. The wettest month is usually June with an average rainfall of 590 mm, while from January to April the averages range from three mm (in March) to 71 mm.

Despite being affected by cyclones in the Bay of Bengal, the Andamans rarely suffer any severe damage, although transport and communications links may be cut for a few days at a time. The best time for a visit is from mid-November to April.

FLORA & FAUNA

The native Andaman redwood (*pterocarpus dalbergioides*) is exported to Europe and is used locally for building boats, houses and furniture. The tree is found throughout the islands, although large tracts in South Andaman have been felled for export.

There is really not much in the way of wildlife. There exist only 20 species of mammal, including the dugong. Turtles are fished from the surrounding waters.

GOVERNMENT

The Andaman & Nicobar islands, forming a union territory of India, come under the jurisdiction of the president of India. They are administered locally by a lieutenant governor and a local council of five members.

ECONOMY

The economy of the islands is based around the timber industry, although fishing plays an important role on a local scale.

The major crops grown include rice, coconuts and areca nuts (betel nut).

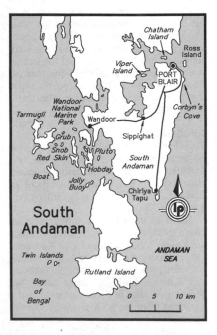

POPULATION & PEOPLE

The combined population of the Andaman & Nicobar islands is currently around 278,000, most of whom are immigrants from the Indian mainland and Sri Lanka. These days the tribal people of the Andamans numbe only about 600, down from well over 5000 before the arrival of the British in the mid-19th century.

In the past the government's policy towards the tribal people of the Andamans leaned more heavily towards assimilation rather than protection. Former prime minister Jawaharlal Nehru, however, had the right idea:

There is no point in trying to make of them a second-rate copy of ourselves. They are a people who sing and dance and try to enjoy life; not people who sit in stock exchanges, shout at each other, and think themselves civilised. We do not mean to interfere with their way of life, but want to help them live it according to their own genius and tradition.

The tribes are of Negrito stock and inhabit only small pockets throughout the islands.

The Great Andamanese tribe once numbered 5000 but today is reduced to 19, and these people are all of mixed blood. They live in huts constructed by the government on tiny Strait Island off the east coast of Middle Andaman. In the early days of British settlement diseases such as malaria, syphilis, diphtheria and measles rapidly halved the tribe's numbers. The Europeans also brought with them opium, tobacco and alcohol, and these were given as reward when the tribespeople caught and turned in escaped convicts from the penal settlement.

Unlike the Andamanese it is not disease that is wiping out the Onge. An anthropological study that was made in the 1970s suggested that they had become severely demoralised by loss of territory. Two-thirds of the Onges' island of Little Andaman has been taken over by the Forest Department and 'settled'. The 100 or so remaining members of the Onge tribe are confined to a 100 sq km reserve at Dugong Creek. In spite of the study, the government allowed further development including the building of roads, jetties and a match factory. They've even built a number of tin huts for these nomadic hunter-gathers to live in.

The Onge are small, dark-complexioned hunters and gatherers, who wear no clothes other than tasseled genital decorations and have striking facial decorations made from an ochre paste which also gives protection from flies and mosquitoes.

The Onges still live largely off the forest, although they do barter coconuts and honey for manufactured produce, such as flour, tobacco, tea and wheat, from the government store. Dogs were introduced early this century and the Onges have domesticated them and use them for hunting the wild pigs which inhabit the islands. Dugong and turtle are also part of the Onges' diet, although these creatures are becoming quite rare.

The Jarawa are suffering from similar encroachment of territory, but are at least putting up a fight, killing one or two Indian settlers each year. The 250 remaining Jarawa occupy the 750-sq-km reserve on South and Middle Andaman islands. Around them forest clearance continues at a horrific rate and the Andamans Grand Trunk Rd, now under construction, runs through part of their designated territory.

The Sentinelese, unlike the other tribes in either the Andamans or Nicobar, have consistently repulsed any attempts by outsiders to make friendly contact with them. Every few years, contact parties arrive on the beaches of North Sentinel Island, with gifts of coconuts, bananas, pigs and red plastic buckets, only to be showered with arrows. It's as if the Sentinelese know that the only way they will be able to preserve their cultural identity and their physical and mental health is by having nothing to do with the 'civilised' world outside. About 100 Sentinelese remain and North Sentinel Island is their exclusive territory.

RELIGION
The religion of the Andamanese is not well documented. It is known that one tribe has a supreme god called Puluga, whose appearance is firelike but is actually invisible. He is immortal and is angered by certain sins. The people also believe in other spirits which reside in either the forest or the sea. The sun is the wife of the moon, and the stars are their children.

LANGUAGE

The local language is Andamanese, although it is spoken by very few people these days. As is the case in mainland India, English and Hindi are the languages of popular communication. Andamanese is unusual in that, as far as can be established, it is not related to any other language.

PERMITS

Foreigners need a permit to visit the Andaman Islands. The permit allows you to visit only the Port Blair area and the islands of Red Skin, Jolly Buoy, Cinque, Neil and Havelock. Certain other islands can be visited with an additional permit, obtainable from the District Commissioner of Police in Port Blair. Overnight stays are permitted only at Port Blair and on Havelock Island. The permit is valid for just 15 days. If you have a very good excuse you might be able to get a two or three-day extension, but nothing longer than that.

Permits are issued to visitors, without fuss, on arrival in Port Blair by air. Those arriving by ship are usually required to get their permit in advance (taking a few hours from the Foreigners' Registration Office in either Madras or Calcutta) before the Shipping Corporation will issue tickets. Immediately on arrival by ship, visit the deputy superintendent of police (near the Annapurna Cafe in Aberdeen Bazaar) to register your arrival, or when you leave you could have problems proving you've not been here longer than 15 days.

Having gone through the rigmarole of getting the permit, you have to be stamped out of the place when you leave as well. Indian red tape is alive and well in the Andamans.

TOURIST OFFICES

There are two local tourist offices in the Andamans, both in Port Blair. One is run by the local municipality, the other by the government of India.

For more information within India, contact either the Public Relations Officer, Andaman & Nicobar Administration

(☎ 387015), F 105 Kasturba Gandhi Marg, New Delhi; or the Public Relations Office, Andaman & Nicobar Administration (☎ 442604), 3-A Auckland Place, Calcutta.

POST & TELECOMMUNICATIONS

The Indian postal service is fairly efficient, although letters posted in the Andamans can take a while to arrive at their destination.

Telephone links with the mainland are tenuous at best. It is not at all uncommon for the line to be inexplicably 'out' for hours on end. Don't come here if you need to communicate with the outside world.

TIME

As part of the central government's attempts to make the islanders feel as though they belong, the Andaman Islands run on Indian mainland time. This is despite that fact the islands are much closer to Myanmar (Burma) than they are to India. The result is that it gets light at about 4 am, and darkness starts to set in at around 5 pm – a crazy situation.

ELECTRICITY
The electricity supply is 240 volts, 50 cycles. Unlike elsewhere in the country, there is plenty of power in Port Blair. The huge generators down near the port pump out power 24 hours a day. As it is all subsidised, hotels and restaurants here are probably the best lit in the country.

BOOKS
Leaving aside the usual histories and anthropological studies, there is a ripping colonial yarn titled *Murder in the Andamans* by M M Kaye (Penguin, London, reprinted 1986). It's a whodunit set during WW II. Ms Kaye is perhaps better known for penning *The Far Pavilions*.

FILM & PHOTOGRAPHY
Film should definitely be brought with you from the mainland or, preferably, from outside India. It is available locally but the quality is suspect.

ACCOMMODATION
The only hotels in the Andamans are in Port Blair. There are both private and government-run places, and these range all the way from filthy flophouses to resorts with star ratings.

GETTING THERE & AWAY
Air
Indian Airlines (☎ 21-108) has flights between Port Blair and Calcutta (US$134) on Monday, Tuesday, Thursday and Saturday. There are flights between Port Blair and Madras (US$136) on Tuesday, Wednesday, Friday and Sunday. The 25% youth discount is applicable on these fares. The flights can also be included on the US$400, three-week flight pass. They take two hours, leaving the mainland very early in the morning and returning the same day.

The Indian Airlines office is in the orange wooden shack round the corner from the post office. The staff are very friendly and the office has a computer link. Flights can be heavily booked and you need to have a confirmed ticket to be sure of a seat. Wait-listed passengers usually miss out. The office is open from 9 am to 4 pm every day.

Boat
The schedules are rather erratic. There used to be more than four sailings a month between Port Blair and Madras or Calcutta on the vessels operated by the Shipping Corporation of India (SCI). There was even once a route between Visakhapatnam and Port Blair. By 1992 most of them had been withdrawn for repairs and only one boat was operating on the Port Blair to Calcutta run, going twice a month. Contact SCI for the latest information and schedules since the Madras route may be restarted. For tickets out of Port Blair, given the uncertain schedules, it's probably better to arrange these in Calcutta or Madras (if possible).

The trip takes three to four days and is never particularly comfortable as the sea can be rough. Foreigners usually have to travel deluxe (two-berth), 1st (two or four-berth) or 2nd class (four or six-berth) for Rs 1256/1154/874 per berth. If you can get a ticket for bunk class it'll cost just Rs 188. Prices are the same for both the Calcutta and Madras routes. Food costs Rs 88 per day and is usually nonstop thalis (rice, lentil vegetable curry) for breakfast, lunch and dinner, so you need to bring something to supplement this boring diet.

The SCI may insist that you have a permit before selling you a ticket. If they don't, you can get one in Port Blair. However, if you get your permit in advance, you must still register with the deputy superintendent of police on arrival in Port Blair or there may be problems when you leave, since they won't know how long you've been on the island.

The Port Blair SCI office (☎ 21-347) is in Aberdeen Bazaar. In Calcutta the SCI office (☎ 28-2354) is on the 1st floor at 13 Strand Rd. In Madras, the SCI (☎ 52-4964) is at Jawahar Building, Rajaji Salai (opposite the Customs House). In Visakhapatnam, the office where you can find out if this route is operating is Garuda Pattabhiramayya (☎ 65-584) opposite the main gate at the port. Two photos and a whole lot of form-filling are required, and bookings close four days before sailing.

GETTING AROUND
Air
The Monday flight from Calcutta goes on to Car Nicobar. Indian Airlines also operates a helicopter service between Port Blair and a few of the outlying islands, and to Car Nicobar. This route is not generally open to foreigners.

Road
There is a small road network around South Andaman, although to travel outside the Port Blair area a permit is required from the District Commissioner. (See the previous Permits section.)

Buses operate from the bus station in Port Blair, although they serve a limited number of destinations. It's also possible to hire taxis or bicycles for exploring. See the Port Blair Getting Around section for more details.

Boat
There are boat services to other islands, but foreigners need special permission to travel on them. As most of the islands are not open to foreigners anyway, these boats are of limited use. See the Getting Around section under Port Blair for more details.

PORT BLAIR
Port Blair is the administrative capital and only town of any size in the islands. It has the lively air of any Indian market town, but lacks the crush of people, bullock carts and vehicles that usually crowd the scene. It is pleasantly situated on the main harbour and, as it's a hilly town, there are good views from quite a few vantage points.

Orientation
The town is spread out over a few hills, but the main concentration of hotels, the bus station, passenger dock and Shipping Corporation of India office are in the main bazaar area, known as Aberdeen Bazaar. The airport is a few km south of town over at least one steep hill.

Information
Tourist Offices There is a regional tourist counter (☎ 20380) at the Tourist Home at Middle Point. This is where you need to enquire about boats to other islands, and what permits are needed. It is about 20 minutes walk from the centre.

The helpful Andaman & Nicobar Tourist Office (☎ 20933) is at the gate to the Secretariat, which is at the top of the hill overlooking the town. There is also a railways out-station booking office, and a Shipping Corporation of India (SCI) office there.

The Government of India Tourist Office (☎ 21006) is in a crazy location, half-way between the airport and the Secretariat building, at least 20 minutes' walk from the centre. It has nothing of interest anyway, so don't waste your time.

For more information about the tribal people of these islands an interesting series of paperbacks, published for the Anthropological Survey of India, is available from Living Literature Bookshop. The library, on the same road as the post office, is also a good place to find information about the islands.

At 5.30 pm on Monday, Wednesday and Friday the Tourist Home has a free screening of a couple of documentary films about the islands. One is dreadful but the other is well worth seeing. The library on the same road as the post office is also a good place for information about the islands.

Money Although Port Blair boasts no less than seven banks, foreign exchange facilities are available only at the State Bank of India and at the larger hotels.

Post Office The post office is not far from the centre, and the telegraph office is in a wooden shack next door. It is open from 7 am to 10 pm on weekdays, and from 8 am to 6 pm on weekends. International calls can be

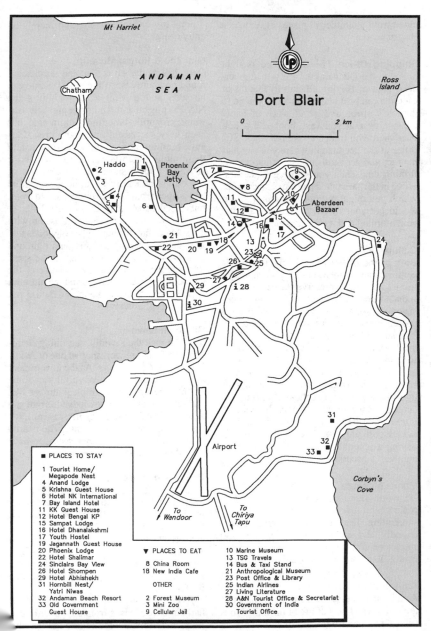

Mt Harriet

Chatham

ANDAMAN
SEA

Ross
Island

Port Blair

0   1   2 km

Haddo

Phoenix
Bay
Jetty

Aberdeen
Bazaar

Airport

Corbyn's
Cove

To
Wandoor

To
Chiriya
Tapu

■ PLACES TO STAY

1 Tourist Home/
   Megapode Nest
4 Anand Lodge
5 Krishna Guest House
6 Hotel NK International
7 Bay Island Hotel
11 KK Guest House
12 Hotel Bengal KP
15 Sampat Lodge
16 Hotel Dhanalakshmi
17 Youth Hostel
19 Jagannath Guest House
20 Phoenix Lodge
22 Hotel Shalimar
24 Sinclairs Bay View
26 Hotel Shompen
29 Hotel Abhishekh
31 Hornbill Nest/
   Yatri Niwas
32 Andaman Beach Resort
33 Old Government
   Guest House

▼ PLACES TO EAT

8 China Room
18 New India Cafe

OTHER

2 Forest Museum
3 Mini Zoo
9 Cellular Jail

10 Marine Museum
13 TSG Travels
14 Bus & Taxi Stand
21 Anthropological Museum
23 Post Office & Library
25 Indian Airlines
27 Living Literature
28 A&N Tourist Office & Secretariat
30 Government of India
   Tourist Office

made from a number of places in Aberdeen Bazaar.

Shipping Office The SCI office is right opposite the Dhanalakshmi Hotel in Aberdeen Bazaar. Buying a ticket to Madras or Calcutta can be a real circus. First you go to this SCI office and get a piece of paper confirming that you have booked a ticket; from there you trudge up the hill to the SCI office at the Secretariat, where you pay half the fare and get another piece of paper confirming this. Then you go back to the first office in the bazaar and pay the balance, after which you might reasonably think that you would get your ticket. No, come back the next morning and it will be issued.

Cellular Jail
Built by the British at the beginning of this century, the cellular jail is now a major tourist attraction, preserved as a shrine to India's freedom fighters. It originally consisted of six wings radiating out from a central tower, but only three remain today. The jail still gives a fair impression of the terrible conditions under which the detainees were incarcerated. It's open daily from 8 am to noon and from 2 to 5 pm, and there's no entry charge. Don't miss the sound-and-light show which is excellent. The English-language show is at 7 pm each night. A minimum of 10 people is required, but since tickets cost only Rs 3 it would be worth buying a few extra tickets to make up the numbers if necessary.

Marine Museum
It's worth visiting this museum to identify some of the fish you may have seen while snorkelling. The Nicobarese curator is very friendly and informative about the 350 species on display here. It's open every day from 8.30 am to 12.30 pm and 1.30 to 5 pm.

Anthropological Museum
At this small museum there are displays of tools, dress and way of life of the indigenous tribes. It's open from 9 am to noon and 1 to

4 pm daily except Sunday, and there's no entry charge.

Mini Zoo & Forest Museum
Over 200 Andaman & Nicobar species are found nowhere else in the world. Some can be seen at the Mini Zoo, including the Nicobar pigeon and Andaman pig. The saltwater crocodile-breeding programme has been very successful and many crocodiles have been returned to the wild. Fortunately their natural habitat is dense mangrove swamps – there have been no reports of crocodiles attacking swimmers here. The zoo is open from 7 am to noon and 2 to 5 pm, but closed on Monday. Entry is Rs 0.50.

Nearby is the small Forest Museum with a display of the different types of woods that grow here including padauk, with light and dark-coloured wood occurring in the same tree. Elephants are still used at some of the lumber camps. Entry is free and the museum is open from 9 am to noon and 3 to 5 pm (daily except Sunday).

Chatham Sawmill
You can visit the sawmill, seasoning chambers and furniture workshop in one of Asia's largest wood processors. As the government tourist literature enthuses, you'll see 'some of the rare species of tropical timber like padauk'. If they're acknowledged as rare you wonder what they're doing in a sawmill. It's open from 6.30 am to 2.30 pm. The nearby Wimco match-splint factory seems to have closed, one hopes permanently.

Organised Tours
A range of tours combining most sights or visits to islands are offered by the A&N tourist office (☎ 20-380), Shompen Travels (☎ 20-425) in the Hotel Shompen, Island Travels (☎ 21-358) in Aberdeen Bazaar, and Andaman Beach Resort (☎ 20-599). Shompen Travels runs a trip (daily except Monday) to either Jolly Buoy or Red Skin for Rs 300.

Every afternoon at 3 pm, a 1½-hour harbour cruise leaves from the Phoenix Bay Jetty. To get there walk in through the blu steel gates with the sign 'Pass Holders Only'. The trip costs Rs 20 and the main point of 'interest' is the huge, floating dry-dock facility. The tour stops briefly at tiny Viper Island where the remains of the gallows tower built by the British still stand. This was the original penal settlement before the Cellular Jail was built.

Diving

Although facilities are limited, diving is possible. One recent traveller to the islands wrote:

We stayed at the *Andaman Beach Resort* as we wanted to do some diving around there. The manager of the resort is in charge of the Indian School of Under Water Welfare. He and his wife know just about everyone on the island and can organise visa extension, expeditions to islands and deep-sea fishing. They can also conjure up plane tickets from nowhere.

The hotel runs boat trips to Wandoor National Marine Park virtually every day, although you need a minimum of four people. The trips cost about Rs 150 a shot, but give you five or six hours on an island. It's pricey but better value than trips arranged by the tourist office.

The fish and coral life are incredible. There are lots of sea snakes, turtles and dolphins to see. Anyone visiting the Andamans for diving should be aware that the best coral and visibility is at the outlying islands. Visibility is not too good off the main island. You can hire diving gear, snorkels, masks and fins. You can even organise an underwater camera for the day.
Debbie Martyr – England

Places to Stay

Accommodation is geared to tourists who are the main visitors although, even in the high season, it is possible to bargain prices down quite a bit.

If you want to be near a beach, the only place to go is Corbyn's Cove, where there's one expensive resort hotel and two cheap government places. Since all the accommodation is quite spread out, it's worth hiring a bicycle or moped to get around.

Places to Stay – bottom end

Best value at Corbyn's Cove is the old *Government Guest House*, just above the beach. However, there are only four rooms here, all with attached bathrooms and balconies, at Rs 25/50. Reservations must be made at the A&N tourist office. Most travellers stay at the friendly *Hornbill Nest* (Yatri Niwas) which is about one km north of Corbyn's Cove, with views across the sea. It's a fairly new place with dorm beds at Rs 35 in four and six-bedded rooms and doubles for Rs 70, all with attached bathrooms. Mosquito nets are provided. There's a good restaurant but some dishes need to be ordered in advance.

The *Youth Hostel* in Aberdeen Bazaar is a reasonable place with dorm beds for Rs 10 (Rs 20 for nonmembers) and a few double rooms. There's a restaurant for residents with set lunches and dinners at Rs 8 for non-vegetarian, Rs 6.50 for vegetarian.

Also in Aberdeen Bazaar, the *Sampat Lodge* is basic, but friendly with rooms for Rs 35/50. The *KK Guest House* is run down with tiny rooms for Rs 25/45. The nearby *Hotel Bengal KP* is much better with clean singles/doubles for Rs 40/60 with attached baths. Also in Aberdeen Bazaar is *Ram Nivas Lodge* with singles with common bath at Rs 25, doubles with attached bath for Rs 65.

Along the road to Haddo there's the excellent *Jagannath Guest House* with spotless singles/doubles/triples for Rs 50/100/150, all with attached baths. Further along the same road the *Phoenix Lodge* is not so good with rooms for Rs 40/50 with common bath.

In Haddo there's the basic *Krishna Guest House*, a small friendly place with dorm beds for Rs 15, and singles/doubles for 25/40 with common bath. *Anand Lodge* nearby is better value with rooms for Rs 20/30 or Rs 30/50 with attached bathroom.

The *Central Lodge*, out past the Hotel Shompen at Middle Point, is a wooden lodge with a verandah, friendly management and rooms from Rs 25/50.

Places to Stay – middle

The *Tourist Home/Megapode Nest* (☎ 20-207), at Haddo on the hill above the bay, is a good place with a range of rooms, although your own transport would be useful here. There are doubles for Rs 100 or Rs 250 with air-con, all with attached baths. For up-market air-con accommodation, the

Nicobari Cottages represent excellent value at Rs 350 for a double and are part of this complex. There's a good restaurant and great views over the harbour.

The *Hotel Abhishekh* (☎ 21-565) is good value with clean single/doubles/triples for Rs 80/120/160 or Rs 160/190/230 with air-con. All rooms have attached bathrooms and the hotel has its own restaurant. Only a few years old, it's well run by a friendly manager. Equally good value is the spotless *Hotel Shalimar* (☎ 21-963), which is on the road to Haddo. Rooms are Rs 80/125/180 with attached bath and air-con doubles are Rs 260.

The *Hotel Dhanalakshmi* (☎ 21-953) in Aberdeen Bazaar has good rooms for Rs 115/150 or Rs 205/240 with air-con. All rooms have attached baths and there's a restaurant.

Rooms at the *Hotel Shompen* (☎ 20-360) are overpriced at their quoted rate of Rs 240/310 or Rs 320/390 with air-con. However, outside the peak of the high season you should be able to get discounts of 50% to 75%. There's a restaurant here and a travel agency that runs tours to some of the islands.

Near the Phoenix Bay jetty, the *Hotel NK International* (☎ 20-113) is nothing special with double rooms for Rs 200, or Rs 300 with air-con.

Places to Stay – top end

On the road to Corbyn's Cove is the *Sinclairs Bay View* (☎ 21-159). Only recently taken over by the Sinclairs group, rooms are still a bit tatty, although renovations are under way. They cost Rs 365/550 or Rs 399/690 with air-con. There are good views over the sea but no beach. Tours can be organised from here.

Out at Corbyn's Cove, the *Andaman Beach Resort* (☎ 21-462) is excellently located in a very quiet part of the island, just across the road from the beach. Rooms in the main block are Rs 650/800, and in the very pleasant air-con cottages, rooms cost Rs 830/1000. As with everywhere else discounts are negotiable outside the peak season. There's a bar, restaurant, foreign exchange facilities and a boat for hire.

With views over the sea, the *Welcomgroup Bay Island Hotel* (☎ 20-881) is the top hotel here. Beautifully designed by the well-known Indian architect Charles Correa, it's made almost entirely from local padauk wood. The staff are very friendly, but rooms are rather overpriced, ranging from US$45/55 right up to US$120. Only the more expensive rooms have air-con. The hotel has a good restaurant and open-air bar – good for a quiet beer (Rs 66), although the wind usually gets up in the late afternoon. There's no beach nearby but the hotel has a sea-water swimming pool. Below the hill, a private pier extends into the bay with a 'human aquarium'. You climb down into a glass-windowed chamber to view the multi-coloured fish that congregate here to be fed.

Places to Eat

Most of the hotels have restaurants, but if you want fish, prawns or lobster, you may have to order in advance.

There are a number of cheap places in Aberdeen Bazaar. The *Annapurna Cafe* is a recommended restaurant for vegetarian and non-vegetarian dishes. The *Manila Cafe* and *Anand Hotel* are also good for a snack. In the hotel of the same name, the *Dhanalakshmi* stays open late and main dishes are Rs 20 to Rs 25. Nearby is the tiny *Kattappamman Hotel* where masala dosas are Rs 4 and banana-leaf thalis cost Rs 8. You pay extra for meat (Rs 4) and have to clear your own leaf away.

Along the road to Haddo, the *New India Cafe* is a very popular place serving mainly south Indian dishes. Masala dosas are Rs 5, fried fish Rs 4 and chicken biryani Rs 15. Further along this road, near Hotel Shalimar is the *Royal Restaurant* with tandoori dishes for Rs 20 and fish for Rs 12.

At Corbyn's Cove *The Waves* has snacks and sandwiches and fish dishes can be ordered in advance. It's said to be run by the police which might account for the good supplies of cheap beer (Rs 25) available here.

The *China Room*, run by a delightful Burmese couple, is the best place to eat in Port Blair. It's really just the front room of their house, but the quality of the seafood they serve is nonetheless superb. Prices range from Rs 20 for basic dishes like vegetarian noodles to Rs 95 for Szechuan-style lobster or Peking duck, though these require 24 hours notice. Their garlic prawns (Rs 35) are excellent, and it's worth going there for lunch to discuss the menu for a slap up dinner the following night.

Getting There & Away
See the Andamans Islands Getting There & Away section for details of transport to/from Port Blair.

Getting Around
Road There are no cycle-rickshaws or auto-rickshaws, just taxis buzzing around Port Blair. They have meters (and charts since the meters need recalibrating) but drivers need a bit of persuasion to use them. From the airport, the trip to Aberdeen Bazaar should cost Rs 20, a little less to Corbyn's Cove. A taxi trip between Corbyn's Cove and Aberdeen Bazaar would cost around Rs 25.

There's a tourist bus which runs between the airport and the Andaman Beach Resort at Corbyn's Cove. It is free if you stay at the hotel. From the bus stand in Port Blair, there are regular departures to Wandoor (Rs 3, 1½ hours).

It's best to have your own transport to explore parts of the island. You can hire bicycles in Aberdeen Bazaar for Rs 15 per day. An even better way to get to around is by moped or motorbike. Roads are not bad and very quiet. TSG Travels (☎ 20-894) rent motorbikes (Suzuki 100s), mopeds or scooters all for Rs 120 per day. Moped rental includes fuel.

Boat Private boats can be hired from the tour operators but charges are high, around Rs 9000 to Rs 10,000 per day. Boats are restricted in the Wandoor National Park, but from Chiriya Tapu you may be able to rent a boat from local people for a day trip to Cinque Island for Rs 800 to Rs 1000. This would need to be arranged in advance.

AROUND PORT BLAIR
Mt Harriet
Permission is required from the Forest Department at the Secretariat for visits to this area, across the water from Port Blair. There's a nature trail up to the top and if regulations are relaxed it may be possible to stay in the *Forest Department Guest House.*

Ross Island
Twenty minutes across the water from Port Blair is Ross Island, chosen by the British for their administrative headquarters. In the early part of this century, there would have been manicured lawns leading up to the ballroom, umbrellas round the swimming pool and daily services in the church. Deserted since the British left during WW II, the jungle has taken over and peacocks and spotted deer forage amongst the ruined buildings. On the top of the hill stand the remains of the church, its tower strangled by roots and vines.

Ross Island is a distinctly eerie and rather sad place but well worth a visit. There are ferries from Phoenix Bay jetty at 8.30 and 10.30 am, 12.15 and 2 pm daily, except on Wednesday. From Ross Island there are departures at 9.15 and 11 am, and 12.30 and 4 pm. No permits are required but you must sign in on arrival, since the island is in the hands of the navy.

Corbyn's Cove
Corbyn's Cove is the nearest beach to Port Blair, 10 km from the town and four km beyond the airport. Out in the bay there is a small island surrounded by coral and you can sometimes get people to take you over in their fishing boats. Some people swim out to it but this is inadvisable as the current can be strong. There are a number of places to stay here and a snack bar by the beach.

It's a long, though pleasant, walk along the cliffs from Port Blair. Taxis cost about Rs 25 each way.

Sippighat
The government-run Sippighat Water Sports Complex is 11 km from Port Blair on the

road to Wandoor National Park. Open daily (except Monday) from 8 am to 5 pm, it's more a boating rather than a swimming complex as it's inland on a river and there's no beach. However, you can rent kayaks for Rs 20 per hour or 10 horsepower motorboats for Rs 60 per hour.

On the same road, 15 km from Port Blair, is the government experimental farm, where tour groups often stop. New types of spices, such as cinnamon, pepper, nutmeg and cloves are being tested here.

Wandoor National Park

This 280-sq-km park comprises 15 islands and diverse scenery including mangrove creeks, tropical rainforest and reefs supporting 50 types of coral. Boats leave from Wandoor village, which is 29 km from Port Blair, at around 10 am (daily except Monday) for visits to Jolly Buoy or Red Skin islands. Although it's worth going along to see the coral (there are usually a few snorkels for hire), only just over an hour is spent at the islands. It is very frustrating to get to such a stunningly beautiful place only to have to leave so soon. The trip costs Rs 100 for foreigners (Rs 35 for Indians). An entry permit (Rs 2) for the park must first be purchased at the kiosk by the jetty.

You can reach Wandoor by bus from Port Blair (Rs 3, 1½ hours) or by joining a tour. There are a number of good sandy beaches at Wandoor and a *Forest Guest House* with great views over the sea, but it's supposedly for VIPs only.

Chiriya Tapu

Thirty km south of Port Blair is this small fishing village with beaches beside the mangroves. It's possible to arrange to take boats from here to Cinque Island.

Other Islands

Although the following islands are open for foreign visitors, it may still be necessary to get your permit endorsed at the Secretariat. Apart from the red tape, most of the islands require quite a lot of travelling time to reach

them, leaving little time for being on the islands themselves.

Cinque Island The coral and beaches here are reputedly even more impressive than at Red Skin and Jolly Buoy. It's two hours by boat from Chiriya Tapu or three hours from Phoenix Bay. This island has been targeted for future tourist development.

Neil Island Forty km east of Port Blair, this forested island is now inhabited by what the government euphemistically calls Bengali 'settlers'.

Havelock Island Fifty-four km east of Port Blair, Havelock covers 100 sq km and is also 'settled'. There are good beaches, coral reefs and basic government accommodation: a *Yatri Niwas* should now be open. At present this is the only other place in the Andamans where you're allowed to stay apart from Port Blair. Ferries depart from Phoenix Bay jetty.

Nicobar Islands

Part of the union territory of the Andaman & Nicobar Islands, this group of 19 islands lies between the Andamans and the Indonesian island of Sumatra. It is separated from the Andamans by the 150-km-wide Ten Degree Channel.

The largest inhabited islands are Camorta and Nancowry, and the main island of the group is Car Nicobar. Seven of the islands are uninhabited.

Unfortunately the Nicobar Islands are off limits to foreigners, mainly, it seems, so that the tribal people remain undisturbed. One wonders, therefore, why Indian nationals can visit at will.

HISTORY

Like the Andamans, the Nicobar Islands were known to mariners from very early on. More recently the islands became the object of interest for missionaries keen to find new converts.

From the 17th century various European countries occupied the islands, but it was the British who made the most serious attempt, taking formal control in 1869. A penal colony was also established here by the British for 20-odd years in the late 19th century.

The islands were occupied by the Japanese during WW II, but after the war were reoccupied by the Brits. In 1948 they became part of independent India.

GEOGRAPHY
With a total land area of 1953 sq km the islands are generally much flatter than the Andamans, although Great Nicobar peaks at 642 metres.

CLIMATE
The climate of the Nicobar Islands is much the same as the Andamans, with rainfall of around 3000 mm annually. The rainfall is spread throughout the year, the driest months being February, March, April and October.

The year-round temperatures vary from 18°C to 30°C.

POPULATION & PEOPLE
The 29,000 Nicobarese are the only indigenous people in either Nicobar or the Andamans whose numbers are not decreasing. They are fair-complexioned horticulturalists who have been partly assimilated into contemporary Indian society. Living in village units led by a headman, they cultivate coconuts, yams, bananas and farm pigs.

Inhabiting a number of islands in the Nicobar group, centred on Car Nicobar, the majority of the Nicobarese are Christians.

The Shompen are another, much smaller, tribal group found on Great Nicobar. So far they have resisted integration into Indian society and tend to shy away from areas occupied by immigrants from the mainland, preferring to lead their lives according to their own traditions.

RELIGION
Although originally animists, the majority of Nicobarese these days have converted to Christianity and belong to the Church of India. The religion was introduced by south Indian missionaries.

GETTING THERE & AWAY
Indian Airlines operates a weekly flight from Calcutta to Car Nicobar, via Port Blair in the Andaman Islands.

There is also a helicopter service connecting Car Nicobar with Port Blair.

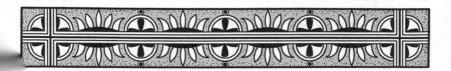

Cocos (Keeling) Islands

The Cocos Islands include 27 flat coral islands in a horseshoe-shaped atoll south of Indonesia and west of Australia. Like its nearest neighbour, Christmas Island, the atoll is an Australian territory.

It is a popular stopping point for yachts sailing the Africa/Indonesia/Australia routes, but all other visitors must fly in from Perth, Australia or Christmas Island.

Facts about the Islands

HISTORY
Uninhabited North Keeling Island, 24 km north of the main group, was discovered in 1609 by Captain William Keeling of the East India Company. The islands in the main atoll were also uninhabited and remained so until they were settled in 1826 by an English adventurer named Alexander Hare who brought with him his Malay harem and slaves.

A year later John Clunies-Ross, a Scottish seaman, started a second settlement with his family. He began improving the natural coconut groves and brought in more Malays to help harvest the coconuts for copra. When Hare left in 1831, Clunies-Ross became the sole overlord of the islands.

The Cocos were declared a British possession in 1857 and became the responsibility of the British government in Ceylon in 1878. They were attached to the Straits Settlements in 1886 and, in the same year, Queen Victoria granted all land to the Clunies-Ross family. In 1903 the islands became part of the British crown colony of Singapore.

During WW I the German cruiser *Emden* put a raiding party on Direction Island in the north of the atoll. Soon after, in 1914, the *Emden* was destroyed by HMAS *Sydney* on the shore of North Keeling. During WW II the Japanese bombed the islands but did not occupy them.

After WW II a civil administration was appointed to the atoll, which remained part of British Singapore until it was passed to Australia.

In 1955 the Cocos Islands were accepted as a territory by Australia, although a strict Whites-only immigration policy by the Australian government almost stopped the transfer.

The Clunies-Ross family continued to own and run the islands until 1978 when the Australian government bought out the present John Clunies-Ross for $6.25 million. Australian currency was introduced but the new overlords began taking steps towards establishing Cocos-Malay self-government.

In 1984 the islanders were allowed to vote on 'self-determination'. Against the wishes of John Clunies-Ross, who wanted independence with Australian protectorate status, the islanders voted to remain part of Australia.

John Clunies-Ross, the fifth generation descendant of the Scottish sea captain who settled the islands, lost his millions in a failed shipping company. He moved to Perth where he was declared bankrupt, although he won a court battle with the government to keep his Great House on Home Island.

The 100 year old Great House (sometimes called Oceania House) is a large two-storey manor. Inside are teak-panelled walls and a spiral staircase leading up to the five bedrooms. Bronze busts of the Clunies-Ross generations stood guard in the hallways. Until recently the son of the elder Clunies-Ross, known as Young Johnny by the islanders, lived on Home Island and leased out the family's Great House to tourists. The house was sold in 1992 and is now a private residence.

The atoll is now governed by an administrator who is also in charge of police, courts and immigration. The Cocos Islands Council is the local government body.

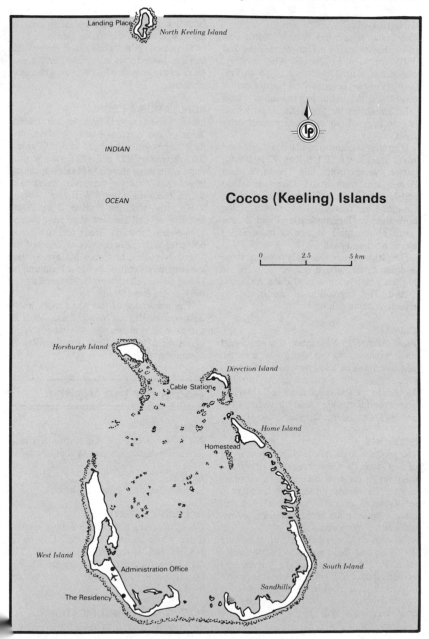

Cocos (Keeling) Islands

GEOGRAPHY

The Cocos Islands are 2946 km north-west of Perth, 985 km from Christmas Island and 3685 km west of Darwin. The territory, which has a total land area of 14 sq km, consists of two coral atolls – North Keeling Island and the main, larger southern atoll (also known as the South Keelings) which has 26 islets. Both atolls are protected by reefs.

The largest island around the lagoon of the south atoll is the 10-km-long West Island, where the aerodrome lies. The other main islands are South Island, Direction Island and Home Island, which is the base of the Clunies-Ross family. At the mouth of the horseshoe is Horsburgh Island and 24 km north of the main lagoon is uninhabited North Keeling Island.

The larger islands are only between three and six metres above sea level, with the highest point being a sand dune on South Island. The vegetation of the islands is mainly coconut palms.

CLIMATE

From March to November the south-east trade winds sweep the islands. Most of the annual rainfall of 2300 mm comes between December and February, during the 'doldrums' period when there is little wind. Temperatures remain steady between 24°C and 30°C throughout the year.

ECONOMY

The production of copra is the main activity of the Cocos, the Co-operative Society is the main employer and there is no unemployment in the islands. Enough fish is caught to satisfy local demand, but most food and other supplies must be imported from Australia and Singapore.

No-one on Cocos pays tax, all goods are duty free and there are no power or water rates. In 1984 the Australian government embarked on a A$10 million housing project to provide more and better accommodation for the islanders. In 1981 it opened an off-shore quarantine station.

Meteorological data gathered in the Cocos Islands is important for forecasting weather for a large area of the Indian Ocean.

The Cocos Islands have their own postal service, but education, medical and dental services are provided by the Australian government.

POPULATION & PEOPLE

Most of the Cocos inhabitants are descendants of the original Malay workers, and their dependents, brought in by Clunies-Ross between 1827 and 1831. At one time there were more than 2000 Malay-speaking islanders, but most of these were resettled in Sabah, Malaysia, after WW II.

Recently, with the decline of the copra industry, several hundred more have moved to Western Australia. There are now about 650 people living in the Cocos. Most of the Cocos Islanders, or Cocos-Malays as they are sometimes called, live in a kampung on Home Island, along with the descendants of the Clunies-Ross family.

The remainder of the population, about 230 people, live on West Island. Most of these are Australians on two-year contracts, about 40 of whom work for the island's administration.

Facts for the Visitor

VISAS

All visitors except Australian citizens require an Australian visa to visit Cocos.

MONEY

See the Christmas Island chapter.

HOLIDAYS & FESTIVALS

Cocos observes the same holidays as Australia, which includes Australia Day on 26 January and Anzac Day on 25 April. The Hari Raya, the period following the Muslim fasting month of Ramadan, is also observed by the Malays.

POST & TELECOMMUNICATIONS

The islands have their own postal servic

including a philatelic bureau. Outside communication is done through the administration by radio telephone to Perth. There are no TVs or newspapers, only an island radio station.

BOOKS
Books covering the history of the Cocos Islands and the Clunies-Ross dynasty include *Kings of the Cocos* by John Scott Hughes (Methuen, London, 1950) and *Cocos Keeling: The Islands Time Forgot* by Ken Mullen (Angus & Robertson, Sydney, 1974). For a very readable, detailed historical introduction to the Cocos Islands, look for *The Cocos (Keeling) Islands: Australian Atolls in the Indian Ocean* by Pauline Bunce (Jacaranda, Perth, 1988). It also contains informative articles on the geology and the economy of the group as well as a good selection of colour prints. *Cocos (Keeling) Islands: Cocos Malay Culture*, by the same author and publisher, has interesting articles on various aspects of the local culture including weddings, basket weaving, and the environment among others.

HEALTH
See the Health section in the Facts for the Visitor chapter at the start of the book. The water supply on the islands is poor – but there's plenty of (dehydrating) beer. Bring mosquito repellent.

ACTIVITIES
Diving, snorkelling, fishing, windsurfing, surfing and swimming are your lot on the Cocos Islands.

Direction Island (or 'DI' as it is referred to) is the prime site for diving. It is particularly known for an excellent drift dive where you ride a strong rip current over beautiful coral gardens teeming with schools of exotic fish.

On Direction Island itself is a monument to the German cruiser *Emden*, destroyed by the Australian cruiser *Sydney* during WW I. After the sinking ship was forced to run aground on the reefs off North Keeling Island, some of the crew members who were not killed or taken prisoner commandeered an island boat and sailed it all the way back to Germany.

Dieter Gerhard at Cocos Dive & Tackle (☎ 6515) operates a boat for fishing and diving trips, and apparently knows all the best spots for both.

Rumours of surfers standing awestruck on the beach as they are confronted by a six-metre (18-foot) swell attract a number of hardened surfies to the islands every year. Six foot is said by some to be standard, but then surfing stories are always difficult to substantiate. The season for consistent waves is from April to September.

There are also tennis courts on the islands and an unusual golf course with its fairways surrounding the airfield. The Cocos Olympics are held each October.

ACCOMMODATION
At present the only official place to stay is the administration's *West Island Lodge* (☎ 6674). Double or twin rooms with breakfast cost US$69 per day. Most visitors, however, have the accommodation included in the cost of a package as it works out cheaper.

While it was previously possible to stay at the 100-year-old *Great House* (one-time Clunies-Ross family residence), the house was sold in 1992. While packages including accommodation in the Great House were still available at the time of writing, it seems likely that by the end of 1993, it will no longer be available to tourists. Check with Indian Ocean Holidays in Perth to find out whether it is still possible (see Getting There & Away later in this section for more information on packages).

For some time the Cocos Island Co-operative (☎ 6672) has been planning a resort in the islands. There is some hope that the *Plantation Village Resort* may open in the second half of 1993. It is envisaged that the resort will be similar to some of the more basic resorts in the Maldives.

The only public bar in the Cocos Islands is the *Cocos Club* on West Island.

Getting There & Away

At the time of writing, the Australian Government through the Department of Territories Island Liaison Office (☎ 09 481-1705) in Perth, was operating an ad hoc charter service out to both the Cocos Islands and Christmas Island. Prior to writing, the route had been flown by Australian Airlines, Indian Ocean Airlines and again by Australian Airlines before finally being passed on to Ansett WA.

The easiest way to get to the Cocos Islands is to book through Indian Ocean Holidays (☎ (09) 388-2777, fax (09) 381-2030), 368 Hay St, Subiaco, Western Australia. Most people buy a package, and until it is finally decided which airline will permanently fly the route, the only fixed prices available are packaged. One of the most popular arrangements is for eight days and seven nights with five days fishing, accommodation, breakfast and dinner. The price varies according to the number of people in the group, and all prices quoted are ex Perth. The costs are A$1395/1446/1516 per person for groups of six/five/four. So long as the Clunies-Ross Great House is available, a one-week package including full board costs A$1644 per person twin-share. Two weeks costs A$2460 per person twin-share.

The cheapest package available includes eight days and seven nights accommodation at the *West Island Lodge* for A$1130/979 for singles/per person twin-share. With breakfast included the prices increase to A$1088/1038. Accommodation and all meals costs A$1282/1231. It works out considerably cheaper if you take a two-week package. Diving packages can also be arranged.

The Cocos aerodrome, on West Island, is also used by Australian air force and US air force or US navy planes – the latter usually from Diego Garcia.

Getting Around

There are cars and trucks on West Island. You can hire bicycles, mopeds or cars from the West Island Store (☎ 6674). The going rates are A$10/20 for mopeds/cars per day and 'minimal' for bicycles. Small boats provide inter-island ferry services.

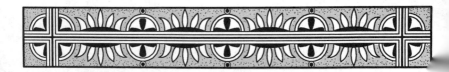

Christmas Island

A journalist who visited Christmas Island at the end of 1987, described the place an 'an amazing hybrid of an Australian mining town and a rural South-East Asian community'.

The smells of the Taoist temples and the atmosphere of Asia mix with the Holden cars, supermarket checkouts, and the beer cans littering the beauty spots. Although it's not in quite the same 'tropical paradise' league as the neighbouring Cocos Islands, Christmas Island does have some spectacular cliff scenery and, instead of being flat and coral, is high and forested.

This remote tropical territory of Australia is currently experiencing a huge cultural and economic upheaval as it endeavours to make the transition from a giant phosphate mine to an international casino resort.

The European, Chinese and Malay population is at sixes and sevens. Only the island's wildlife remains constantly rich, endearing and safe.

Christmas Island is 360 km south-west of Java, 2300 km north-west of Perth and around 850 km east of Cocos.

Facts about the Island

HISTORY
A British East India Company captain, William Mynors, gave the island its name when he spotted it on Christmas Day in 1643. The first recorded landing was made by the English navigator and part-time pirate William Dampier in March 1688.

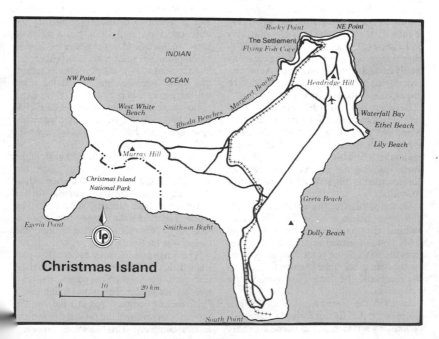

Christmas Island

It wasn't until near the end of the 19th century, however, that the island was found to be rich in lime phosphate, which is used as fertiliser. In June 1888 the island was declared British and later the same year George Clunies-Ross, from the Cocos Islands, established the first settlement in Flying Fish Cove with a party of Malays. Three years later he and Sir John Murray were granted a lease to begin mining phosphate.

In 1897 about 200 Chinese labourers, eight Europeans and five Sikh police officers arrived and the lease was taken over by the Christmas Island Phosphate Company Ltd. During WW II the island was occupied by the Japanese who, if nothing else, laid out a golf course on the terrace at Waterfall Bay in the north-east part of the island.

In 1946 Christmas Island also became part of the British colony of Singapore. Two years later the island's phosphate industry was bought jointly by Australia and New Zealand, who employed British Phosphate Commissioners (BPC) as the managing agents. The island became a crown colony on 1 January 1958 and an Australian territory nine months later, with the mining company totally owned by the government. An administrator was put in charge of the island to be responsible to the Minister for Territories.

Between 1970 and 1980 there were 3000 people on the island. The Union of Christmas Island Workers (UCIW) was formed in 1976, almost with foresight of the crisis which began the following year when the government, knowing the phosphate was running out, resettled about 1800 Asian residents in Australia.

On top of this, freight charges and production costs began to soar. The Phosphate Mining Company of Christmas Island (PMCI) was founded in 1981 to take over from the BPC. Three years later the government began to bring the island into line with the mainland, beginning by introducing income tax.

In 1985 the Christmas Island Services Corporation (CISC) was formed to take over community services, and an island assembly was elected to take over local government. The move was made in order to get away from a 'paternalistic structure to a more democratic system'. More recently the Corporation was renamed Christmas Island Shire Council, but it retained the CISC acronym.

But the lifeblood of the island was still draining away. After a series of cutbacks in the workforce, more than 450 workers left in 1984 under a voluntary redundancy scheme. The government started looking for alternatives. The only real one was tourism, although the use of the island as a forward-defence base to replace RAAF Butterworth in Malaysia was mooted.

In 1986 the government gave the go-ahead for a A\$35 million casino-resort development, work on which was due to start in late 1989. There have been numerous hitches during the development, however, at this stage it looks like the complex will open in late 1993.

The Australian Government had said it was prepared to continue subsidising the mine operation until 1989, but a series of bans and limitations by the powerful miners' union prompted authorities to act earlier.

At the end of 1987 the government sacked the island assembly and closed the mine amidst much outcry. At one stage, extra police were sent to the island in case civil unrest broke out. Rents, electricity, water and sewerage costs had been increased, which added to the workers' ire.

The island workers continued to fight the closure, claiming mining was still viable, but at the same time pushed for higher redundancy payments, which many of their former colleagues had already received. The workers supported the casino-resort, but saw it as only a 'life raft'. Even the future of the casino was far from certain.

The government was eventually persuaded that the phosphate mines could be reworked, but insisted on putting the contract up for tender. The island union and a Perth mining company put in a bid, but the government awarded the project to the giant Elders company. This decision, howeve was overturned in court on appeal by the workers.

Indeed 1987 on Christmas Island was some year. Not only did the phosphate industry close down, but there was the first murder trial ever held on the island. Two Chinese men were charged with the murder of another over a gambling win. The judge ordered that the trial be abandoned after five days, because he felt it was impossible to get an impartial jury from the island community. The men were eventually convicted in Perth in 1988.

The murder case, though, had already caused problems as it was realised that Christmas Island was still being run under British colonial laws, which had operated in Singapore before WW II. Because of the absence of any serious crime, no-one had bothered to introduce modern Australian criminal legislation. With the murder trial as the strongest catalyst, Christmas Island was brought into judicial line with the mainland in 1992.

GEOGRAPHY

The triangular island is about 17 km long, 10 km across at its widest point and covers an area of 135 sq km. The coastline is mostly sheer rock cliffs, and coral reefs surround the island. Within five km of the shore, the ocean floor falls away to a depth of 200 metres.

Christmas Island is the remnant of an extinct, submarine volcano which formed about 60 million years ago. As the island emerged, coral reefs formed and limestone was deposited. The island then subsided, only to re-emerge 10 million years ago in a series of uplifts which have resulted in the terraced limestone cliffs that give it a stepped appearance.

The island has risen to a height of 260 metres above sea level. Hills at the north, south and west ends surround an inland basin plateau which, millions of years ago, was a lagoon. About 14% of the island is now taken up by the open-cut phosphate mines.

Water drains quickly through the porous limestone to the harder base rock, creating many caves and sink holes. The largest cave is the one-km-long Lost Lake Cave, which is only accessible from the sea.

Surface water is rare, and water for domestic use is drawn from the caves and from bores into the interface between the limestone and volcanic rock.

CLIMATE

The wet season occurs between December and April when north-west monsoons bring occasional gales, heavy rain and high swells. From May to November the climate is 'dry'.

The gentle south-east trade winds blow across the island while the north coast is sheltered and calm. Temperatures range between 22°C and 28°C throughout the year, and humidity ranges from 80% to 90%.

FLORA & FAUNA

The Christmas Island National Park takes up 12% of the island's rainforest and is set around Egeria Point in the south-west. It was set up in 1980 and is managed by the Australian National Parks & Wildlife Service. The ANPWS has a resident conservation official on the island (originally posted to ensure protection from mining operations), and there are usually visiting scientists doing research. It is proposed to extend the park to cover 65% of the island.

Flora

The island's lush rainforest has a 40-metre-high canopy and little undergrowth. Crabs eat all the leaves at their level, while elsewhere great swathes have been cut through the rainforest by the phosphate operations.

Coconut Crab

Although there are 21 plants endemic to the island, including native orchids and trailing hoyas, none are spectacular. There is no commercial agriculture on the island, but pawpaw and guava trees grow abundantly. The coastal vegetation is sparse; it's been reduced to saltbush and some pandanus trees.

Fauna

Christmas Island is home to thousands of birds – and 120 million crabs. The giant 'robber' or 'coconut' crab, the largest terrestrial crustacean in the world with a crushing power in its claw that is almost four times as powerful as the human jaw, is not as plentiful as the prolific red crab.

During the breeding season at the beginning of the monsoon in November, the shores are awash with swarms of red crabs heading for the sea. They descend in their millions from burrows in the rainforest. A zoologist from a Melbourne university said:

The dramatic annual mass migration of the red crabs is one of the great sights of the natural world.

The baby crabs emerge on the shore about a month after spawning and make their way back up to the forest. If you see a blue crab, it's a freshwater one and is protected.

Of the sea birds which congregate on Christmas Island, three are endemic to the island: the Christmas Island frigate, the beautiful golden bosun and the very rare Abbot's booby, which nests in the central-west part of the island. Of the land birds, seven species are found only on Christmas Island. They include the imperial pigeon, the emerald dove and the Christmas Island hawk-owl, the only endangered species.

There are few other animals or mammals save for the large fruit bats, some feral cats and rats.

ECONOMY

The island's economy was solely based on phosphate mining until the end of 1987. The Phosphate Mining Corporation of Christmas Island employed 700 workers, members of the all-powerful Union of Christmas Island Workers led by their English general secretary Gordon Bennett. In 1979 the members staged a hunger strike to achieve parity wages with other mainland unions.

Income tax was introduced only in 1985, and is now equivalent to the full mainland rate.

The resort, with its casino, is hoping to attract business people from Singapore, Malaysia and Indonesia as an alternative destination to the ever-popular Bali.

POPULATION & PEOPLE

Of the 1100 people on the island, 66% are of Chinese descent, 12% are Malay and 22% are European. About 30% of the population are Australian citizens while the rest hold resident status.

English is the official language of the island and is taught in the schools, but most of the Chinese stick to their various dialects and the Malays use their own language.

Buddhist temples and shrines are dotted about the island and there is a mosque in the main settlement at Flying Fish Cove.

Facts for the Visitor

VISAS

All visitors, except Australian citizens and residents, require an Australian visa to visit Christmas Island.

MONEY

The currency used on Christmas Island, and in the Cocos, is the Australian dollar, which is divided into 100 cents. There are coins of five, 10, 20 and 50 cents, and $1 and $2. There are notes of $5, $10, $20, $50 and $100.

US$1	=	A$1.49
UK£1	=	A$2.30
C$1	=	A$1.15
DM1	=	A$0.90
1FF	=	A$0.26
Y100	=	A$1.18

There is a Westpac bank next to the Administration building.

HOLIDAYS
The island's holidays and festivals are governed by Christian, Muslim and Buddhist events. Other holidays include:

Australia Day
    26 January
Anzac Day
    25 April
Queen's Birthday
    June
Territory Day
    5 October

POST & TELECOMMUNICATIONS
Like the Cocos Islands, Christmas Island has an autonomous postal service and issues its own stamps. The island is linked to the international telecommunications network via satellite. Telex and fax facilities are also available. Christmas Island has its own international telephone code. Following your country's international access code, dial 6724 followed by the number you are calling.

ELECTRICITY
The domestic power supply is 240 volts.

MEDIA
There is a television service which is on the air from 3 to 11 pm during the week and longer on weekends, broadcasting taped Australian Broadcasting Corporation (ABC) programmes from Perth.

The Christmas Island Shire Council owns and runs a radio station which broadcasts in English, Malay and Mandarin. There is also a weekly newspaper, the *Christmas Island News*.

ACTIVITIES
Settlement and Kampung in the Cove have swimming pools. There are several sporting clubs, including ones for go-karting, boating, cricket, soccer, table tennis and golf. Opportunities also arise for deep-sea fishing and diving.

Walking
The island offers plenty of scope for the explorer with scenic walks along the clifftops, through the bird colonies on the terraces and through the rainforest (see map for route).

There is also an abandoned settlement at South Point.

Beaches
Only Margaret, Rhoda and West White beaches on the north coast along from the Cove are worth visiting for the usual hedonistic pursuits, although they are hard to get to. More accessible are Greta, Dolly, Lily and Ethel beaches on the east coast. Greta Beach is the best for seeing the millions of red crabs scuttling to the seashore in November and December.

There are blowholes on the coast at Smithson Bight.

Flying Fish Cove
Flying Fish Cove, popularly called just 'the Cove', is the main settlement on the island and the only port.

Although enclosed by steep cliffs, it is not a particularly attractive place. It comprises a collection of differently styled housing settlements on separate levels for each ethnic community. There is a Malay kampung, a Chinese residential area known as Poon Saan, and a European area called the Settlement. Other housing areas are Silver City and Drumsite. Taman Sweetland, the former PMCI settlement, is now deserted.

The port and administration area is grouped around the cove at the lowest level, and the airport and playing fields are up on the plateau. The administrator's house is at Smith Point, south of the Cove.

Waterfall Bay
This bay on the north-east coast is the site for the hotel and casino development. The golf course, not too far from Ethel and Lily beaches, is along the road to Waterfall Bay.

ACCOMMODATION
There are no hotels or guesthouses on the

land. The 220-bed, five-star *Christmas Island Resort* hotel and casino at Waterfall Bay should be open in mid-to-late 1993. Until then, basic accommodation can be found at *Temple Court* (☎ 8189 or 8752). Bathroom facilities are shared and the kitchen can be used by guests.

The only other viable option is at *VQ3 Lodge* (☎ 8383) which has refurbished Chinese quarters for rent. Both places charge around A$70 per night for a room.

If you have trouble getting through to either of these two places on the phone, contact the Administration for the Territory of Christmas Island (☎ 8501 or 8519 to reach the housing officer directly), Government Offices, Christmas Island 6798, Indian Ocean.

FOOD

Chinese and Malay restaurants of the formica-canteen style in the Settlement and at Poon Saan offer a variety of Asian meals. The *Chinese Noodle Shop* is a local favourite, while *Rumah Tinngi* serves basic European-style food.

ENTERTAINMENT

The two main social clubs are the Poon Saan Club, which is a Chinese gaming room, and the Christmas Island Club. There's a free open-air cinema at Poon Saan.

Contact the Christmas Island Shire Council Community Service for details of what's on.

Getting There & Away

Christmas Island is serviced by the same flights that go to the Cocos Islands from Perth. Until the Casino opens in mid to late 1993, the same difficulties associated with getting to the Cocos Islands will apply to Christmas Island. For the time being,

however, Indian Ocean Holidays (☎ 09 388-2777, fax 09 381-2030), 368 Hay St, Subiaco, Western Australia, offers a couple of packages (ex-Perth). Eight days and seven nights including return airfares, accommodation with shared facilities, and airport transfers costs A$1097 per person twin-share. If you want to include a hire car in the deal it costs A$1170 per person for a minimum of two people.

At one time there was also a fortnightly charter flight from Singapore, but only at certain times of the year. It is hoped that once the casino opens, there will be more frequent charter flights, possibly from Jakarta and Singapore. The airport has been upgraded in preparation for the expected influx.

The only port is at Flying Fish Cove, the main settlement, although it is often closed to shipping because of large north-west swells running in the November-March season. Ships used to come in regularly to take away the phosphate; the giant outloading cantilever still hangs over the port. The Australian National Lines runs supply ships from Perth to the island.

Getting Around

There are five major roads, surfaced in crushed limestone, that run across the island, and there is a sealed road around the Flying Fish Cove Settlement. Many of the islanders have cars basically to save them the murderous walk up to Poon Saan and Drumsite, 200 metres higher up from the Settlement.

Visitors can hire 4WD vehicles from the Christmas Island Shire Council (CISC) (☎ 8300) for A$80 a day.

There is also a railway running from the cove down to the southern tip of the island but, with the closing of the mines, this is no longer used.

British Indian Ocean Territory

The remote Chagos Archipelago (724 km south of the Maldives) is all that remains of the British colonies in the Indian Ocean. The entire group is scattered over an area of 54,389 sq km of ocean, although the total land area is only around 60 sq km. The Chagos group used to be known as the Oil Islands because their only *raison d'être* was the copra industry which supplied oil to light the lamps of Port Louis, Mauritius. Now they

are known as the location of Diego Garcia, the US military base leased from the British.

Before going any further into the whys and wherefores of the Chagos, it is worth noting that as a 'tourist' you can only travel there by private yacht. There are no civilian flights or ships into the area and the southern atoll of Diego Garcia is strictly out of bounds. To the north of the 100-km wide Great Chagos Bank are the atolls of Peros

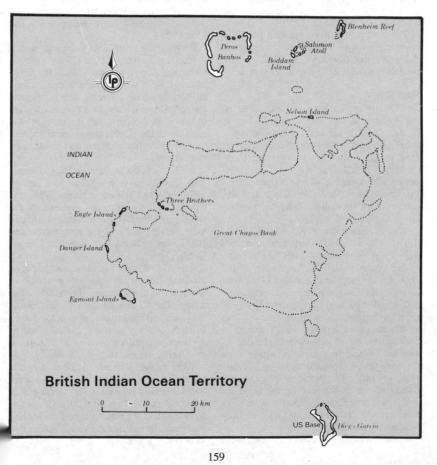

British Indian Ocean Territory

159

Banhos and Salomon. The other atoll, Blenheim, is more of a reef than an atoll and is uninhabitable.

Yachts and other private vessels are permitted by the British to moor and land on these atolls, but are checked over and kept under close surveillance lest they drift too close to Diego Garcia. The military personnel are reputed to be generous with their help, even to the extent of supplementing yachties' stores with the surplus of food they seem to have. If you are considering taking a little time to sail around the BIOT, you would be well advised to get hold of a copy of the British Admiralty's *South Indian Ocean Pilot 9th Edition* (1990).

The archipelago has a tropical maritime climate. Average temperatures throughout the year range from 25°C to 29°C. Annual rainfall is around 2250 mm to 2500 mm.

HISTORY

The Chagos archipelago was discovered by the Portuguese and settled in 1776 by the French. Two of the early settlers set up a fishing business, and were effectively given free reign over the islands and their resources, with the one snag that they had to put up with an influx of lepers from Isle de France (Mauritius). Before the end of the century there were over 300 lepers living on Diego Garcia.

The islands became British under the Treaty of Paris in 1814, with little change to the way of life which was devoted to cultivating coconuts. By the beginning of the 20th century there were almost 450 families living in the Chagos archipelago, with over 500 people on Diego Garcia, the majority of them having been born on the islands. Due to the nature of leprosy, which remained endemic in the islands, women tended to survive longer than men, resulting in a majority female population, and a matriarchal society. The women played the dominant role in bringing up the children, and it was accepted practice for women to have extramarital relations while their husbands were out fishing.

Until 1965 the Chagos Archipelago, or the

Oil Islands, together with Rodrigues Island, came under the control of the British governor in Mauritius whose Seychelles' counterpart looked after the Aldabra and Amirantes groups of islands.

That year, the British Labour government pledged the Mauritians independence and UK£3 million in compensation if they gave up their claim to the Chagos group. The deal was done.

Meanwhile, Farquhar, Desroches and Aldabra were taken away from Seychelles and, together with the Chagos group, became the British Indian Ocean Territory (BIOT). The islands came under British colonial law and used the currencies of Seychelles and Mauritius.

Behind the territorial juggling was a defence agreement with the US according to which the Americans would lease the BIOT islands (one of which would be chosen for a military base) for 50 years. The Americans wanted Aldabra, home to thousands of giant tortoises, as the base, but the thought of a run-in with the world conservationist movement over the likely effects on tortoise town put them off.

In 1970 the US decided on Diego Garcia, with its old war-time RAF airfield, and by 1976 they had settled in there. When the Seychelles were given independence in the same year Farquhar, Desroches and Aldabra were handed back to the new nation and BIOT was reduced to simply the Chagos archipelago.

The 2000 Chagos islanders, who had been on the islands for as long as five generations, were not as fortunate as the Aldabra tortoises. The Creole inhabitants, or Ilois as they had become known, who worked for a French copra company called Chagos Agalega, were all removed by the British and resettled in Mauritius.

After hunger strikes and pressure by the Mauritius government, the islanders were compensated by Britain. The leftist politicians still call for a return of the Chagos to Mauritius and the return of the Ilois to their homeland, but the islanders seem resigned to their fate.

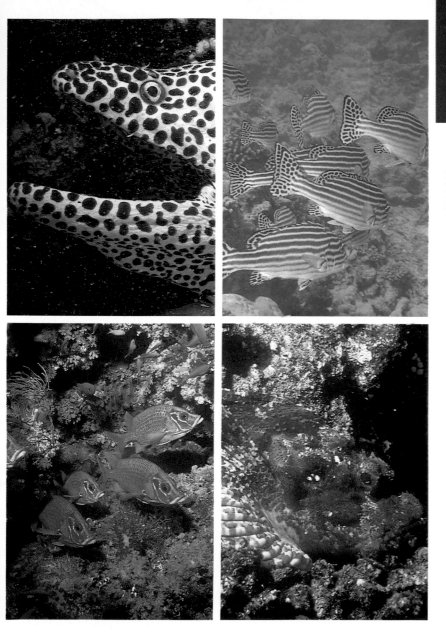

Top Left: White Morray (PM)   Top Right: Oriental Sweetlips (MB)
Bottom Left: Sqirrelfish (PM)   Bottom Right: Scorpion Fish (PM)

Top Left: Blackdotted Pufferfish (PS)   Top Right: Moorish Idols (PS)
Bottom Left: Hawksbill Turtle (PM)   Bottom Right: Spotted Sweetlips (PM)

The prime minister of Mauritius, Mr Aneerood Jugnauth, said the annexation of the Chagos was 'a fraud and illegal act, since it took place before our independence'. At the same time his country is gaining much through trade with the USA.

BIOT is run from London by the East Africa Department of the Foreign Office. There is an administrator resident on Diego and the other islands are uninhabited.

SALOMON ATOLL

The Salomon Atoll is a group of 11 islands with a total land area of just five sq km. Only Boddam Island, at the south end of the atoll, was inhabited before the British-US clearance.

The ruins of the pier and the former settlement are still evident as are those of old homes (including the manager's chateau and the administrator's house), shops, offices, a school and a church.

The fruit trees planted by the 300 or so islanders still bear fruit regularly and the rain tanks still collect water to replenish the stores of passing yachts. Boddam is the most popular 'port' in the group for yachties. The chickens have long since run wild.

PEROS BANHOS

This is a much larger atoll about 10 km west of Salomon. On it stand ruins similar to those on Salomon. There is a total of 29 islands in the atoll, with a total land area of just over 10 sq km.

DIEGO GARCIA

Between the northern atolls and Diego Garcia lies the Great Chagos Bank, a giant sandy and coral bank stretching 50 km from north to south and 90 km from east to west. Diego is the largest island in the archipelago with a land area of 44 sq km.

Diego Garcia atoll is shaped roughly like a footprint. The US forces call it the 'Footprint of Freedom', while the sailors who are posted there refer to it as 'The Rock'.

The atoll, as well as producing copra, was a coaling station for ships crossing the Indian Ocean. The *Lusitania* was one of its more famous customers. Now it is base to a classified number of US servicepeople (estimated at 3000) who are subject to British laws. An administrator is in charge of the atoll and is supported by a small Royal Navy detachment, a magistrate, doctor, some clerks and a few police officers.

The base, on the north-west end of the atoll, has cinemas, shops, bars, a Kentucky Fried Chicken outlet and all the trappings of hometown USA. It also has, in varying numbers and at varying times, battle cruisers, submarines, supply ships, tankers, bombers, fighters, reconnaissance aircraft and the full support facilities necessary for the use of the Rapid Deployment Joint Task.

At the other end of the atoll is the village of the former inhabitants, now a ghost town. In between stretches the base's runway, which is three km long.

Lakshadweep Islands

These palm-fringed coral islands with their beautiful lagoons are every bit as inviting as those in the Maldives. However, due to the almost total lack of infrastructure they have effectively been off limits to tourists until very recently. With the opening up of four of the inhabited islands to Indian tourists and the development of a resort for both foreigners and Indians on the uninhabited island of Bangaram, the restrictions are gradually being eased.

Known as the Laccadive Islands until 1973, the Lakshadweep Islands lie in the Arabian Sea some 200 km off the coast of Kerala, in south-west India, and are a northern extension of the Maldives. The name means '100,000 islands' – a slight misnomer as there are in fact only 36 of them, 12 of which are coral atolls.

Ten of the islands are inhabited. They are Andrott, Amini, Agatti, Bitra, Chetlat, Kamat, Kalpeni, Kavaratti (headquarters), Kiltan and Minicoy. The Lakshadweep Islands form the smallest of the Union Territories of India and are the country's only coral islands.

Facts about the Islands

HISTORY

Legend has it that the islands were first settled by sailors from Kodungallur (Cranganore) who were shipwrecked there after going in search of their king, Cheraman Perumal, who had secretly left on a pilgrimage to Mecca. The first historical records, however, date from the 7th century when a *marabout* (Muslim saint) was shipwrecked on the island of Amini. Despite initial opposition to his efforts to convert the inhabitants to Islam, he eventually succeeded and when he died he was buried in Andrott. His grave is revered to this day as a sacred site.

In the 11th century an Arab scholar split the archipelago into the Maldives and the Laccadives. In the 15th century the Portuguese moved in and built forts, although they were evicted by the local inhabitants only half a century later. The islands became a dependent state of the Raja of Cannanore (in Kerala) in the 16th century.

The islands were annexed by the East India company in 1799 after the British victory at the Battle of Srirangapatnam. In 1956 the Lakshadweep Islands became a union territory of the Republic of India.

CLIMATE

The average minimum daily temperature is 24°C, the maximum 31°C. The best time for a visit is from mid-September to mid-May.

POPULATION & PEOPLE

The people of the Lakshadweep, the Moplahs, are of mixed Arab and Indian descent and number about 51,000. Some 93% of the population are Muslims of the Shafi school of the Sunni sect. The majority

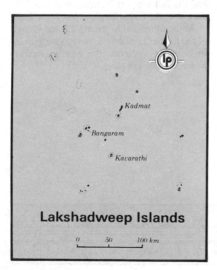

Lakshadweep Islands

Kadmat

Bangaram

Kavarathi

0   50   100 km

speak Malayalam, a Keralan (Indian) language, but use Arabic script for the written form of the language. However, the people on the largest island, Minicoy, speak Mahl, which is very similar to the Divehi language of the Maldives.

The main activities are the manufacture of copra coir from coconut husk fibre, fishing and boat building. Tourism is an emerging industry.

Facts for the Visitor

PERMITS

All foreign tourists need permits to visit Lakshadweep. These are generally only issued if you are joining a package tour, and are only valid for the uninhabited island of Bangaram.

You can obtain permits from the Administrator (☎ 69131), Union Territory of Lakshadweep, Indira Gandhi Rd, Willingdon Island, Kochi (Cochin), or the Liaison Officer Lakshadweep (☎ 38-6807), 202 Kasturba Gandhi Marg, New Delhi. Four passport photos are needed.

ACCOMMODATION

Except on Bangaram, where there is a purpose-built tourist resort with limited recreational facilities, no tourist accommodation exists on the islands other than government guesthouses and the private huts of the package-tour organisation SPORTS (see the tours section), on Kavaratti and Kadmat. Likewise, there are no restaurants or snack bars other than those at the tourist complexes, apart from the occasional 'meals' restaurants serving local food.

Package tourists are accommodated and fed on board ship except at Bangaram, Kavaratti and Kadmat.

On Bangaram Island there is the *Bangaram Island Resort* which offers full board for US$75/140/375 (twin-share per person/single/deluxe bungalow accommodating four people). In the high season the ʒ are US$125/240/625. Leisure activities

such as scuba diving, snorkelling, deep sea fishing and boat trips are extra. For reservations at the resort contact the Manager, Bangaram Island Resort, Casino Hotel (☎ 34-0221), Willingdon Island, Kochi.

Getting There & Away

AIR

Vayadoot flies to Agatti from Kochi (Cochin), Kozhikode (Calicut) and Madras for US$134/120/103 respectively. Transfer to Bangaram Island is by speedboat (US$30) or by helicopter (US$75) during the monsoon season (from May to September).

BOAT

The Shipping Corporation of India vessel, the MV *Bharat Seema*, makes the trip to and from the islands three to five times a month. In India the vessel departs from Cochin in Kerala and the trip takes about 18 hours. Passengers should be prepared for rough seas.

TOURS

Package tours by luxury ship are arranged through SPORTS (Society for the Promotion of Recreational Tourism & Sports) (☎ 34-0387), Lakshadweep Office, Indira Gandhi Rd, Willingdon Island, Kochi (Cochin).

These tours take place on the MV *Tipu Sultan*, which plies regularly between Kochi and Lakshadweep between September and April. Both two-berth and four-berth air-con cabins are available with common bathroom facilities as well as 1st-class cabins with own bathroom. Bed linen and towels are provided. Only Indian food is available on board.

The other vessel which plies the same route as the *Tipu Sultan* on a regular basis is the MV *Bharat Seema*.

Bookings for the tours should be made in advance as the ships' programmes are subject to change at short notice. Four different package tours are available, one of them lasts five days and the others, four.

Index

PLANET TALK
Lonely Planet's FREE quarterly newsletter

We love hearing from you and think you'd like to hear from us.

When...is the right time to see reindeer in Finland?
Where...can you hear the best palm-wine music in Ghana?
How...do you get from Asunción to Areguá by steam train?
What...is the best way to see India?

For the answer to these and many other questions read PLANET TALK.

Every issue is packed with up-to-date travel news and advice including:

- *a letter from Lonely Planet founders Tony and Maureen Wheeler*
- *travel diary from a Lonely Planet author - find out what it's really like out on the road*
- *feature article on an important and topical travel issue*
- *a selection of recent letters from our readers*
- *the latest travel news from all over the world*
- *details on Lonely Planet's new and forthcoming releases*

To join our mailing list contact any Lonely Planet office (address below).

LONELY PLANET PUBLICATIONS
Australia: PO Box 617, Hawthorn 3122, Victoria (tel: 03-819 1877)
USA: Embarcadero West, 155 Filbert St, Suite 251, Oakland, CA 94607 (tel: 510-893 8555)
TOLL FREE: (800) 275-8555
UK: 10 Barley Mow Passage, Chiswick, London W4 4PH (tel: 081-742 3161)
France: 71 bis rue du Cardinal Lemoine – 75005 Paris (tel: 1-46 34 00 58)

Also available: Lonely Planet T-shirts. 100% heavyweight cotton (S, M, L, XL)

Guides to the Indian Subcontinent

Bangladesh – a travel survival kit
This practical guide – the only English-language guide to Bangladesh – encourages travellers to take another look at this often-neglected but beautiful land.

India – a travel survival kit
Widely regarded as *the* guide to India, this award-winning book has all the information to help you make the most of the unforgettable experience that is India.

Karakoram Highway the high road to China – a travel survival kit
Travel in the footsteps of Alexander the Great and Marco Polo on the Karakoram Highway, following the ancient and fabled Silk Road. This comprehensive guide also covers villages and treks away from the highway.

Kashmir, Ladakh & Zanskar – a travel survival kit
Detailed information on three contrasting Himalayan regions in the Indian state of Jammu & Kashmir – the narrow valley of Zanskar, the isolated 'little Tibet' of Ladakh, and the stunningly beautiful Vale of Kashmir.

Nepal – a travel survival kit
Travel information on every road-accessible area in Nepal, including the Terai. This practical guidebook also includes introductions to trekking, white-water rafting and mountain biking.

Pakistan – a travel survival kit
Discover 'the unknown land of the Indus' with this informative guidebook – from bustling Karachi to ancient cities and tranquil mountain valleys.

Sri Lanka – a travel survival kit
Some parts of Sri Lanka are off limits to visitors, but this guidebook uses the restriction as an incentive to explore other areas more closely – making the most of friendly people, good food and pleasant places to stay – all at reasonable cost.

Tibet – a travel survival kit
The fabled mountain-land of Tibet was one of the last areas of the world to become accessible to travellers. This guide has full details on this remote and fascinating region, including the border crossing to Nepal.

Trekking in the Indian Himalaya
All the advice you'll need for planning and equipping a trek, including detailed route descriptions for some of the world's most exciting treks.

Trekking in the Nepal Himalaya
Complete trekking information for Nepal, including day-by-day route descriptions and detailed maps – a wealth of advice for both independent and group trekkers.

Also available:
Hindi/Urdu phrasebook, *Nepal* phrasebook and *Sri Lanka* phrasebook.

Lonely Planet Guidebooks

Lonely Planet guidebooks cover every accessible part of Asia as well as Australia, the Pacific, South America, Africa, the Middle East, Europe and parts of North America. There are five series: *travel survival kits*, covering a country for a range of budgets; *shoestring guides* with compact information for low-budget travel in a major region; *walking guides*; *city guides* and *phrasebooks*.

Australia & the Pacific
Australia
Australian phrasebook
Bushwalking in Australia
Islands of Australia's Great Barrier Reef
Outback Australia
Fiji
Fijian phrasebook
Melbourne city guide
Micronesia
New Caledonia
New South Wales
New Zealand
Tramping in New Zealand
Papua New Guinea
Bushwalking in Papua New Guinea
Papua New Guinea phrasebook
Rarotonga & the Cook Islands
Samoa
Solomon Islands
Sydney city guide
Tahiti & French Polynesia
Tonga
Vanuatu
Victoria

South-East Asia
Bali & Lombok
Bangkok city guide
Cambodia
Indonesia
Indonesia phrasebook
Laos
Malaysia, Singapore & Brunei
Myanmar (Burma)
Burmese phrasebook
Philippines
Pilipino phrasebook
Singapore city guide
South-East Asia on a shoestring
Thailand
Thai phrasebook
Vietnam
Vietnamese phrasebook

Middle East
Arab Gulf States
Egypt & the Sudan
Arabic (Egyptian) phrasebook
Iran
Israel
Jordan & Syria
Middle East
Turkish phrasebook
Trekking in Turkey
Yemen

North-East Asia
China
Beijing city guide
Cantonese phrasebook
Mandarin Chinese phrasebook
Hong Kong, Macau & Canton
Japan
Japanese phrasebook
Korea
Korean phrasebook
Mongolia
North-East Asia on a shoestring
Seoul city guide
Taiwan
Tibet
Tibet phrasebook
Tokyo city guide

Indian Ocean
Madagascar & Comoros
Maldives & Islands of the East Indian Ocean
Mauritius, Réunion & Seychelles

Mail Order

Lonely Planet guidebooks are distributed worldwide. They are also available by mail order from Lonely Planet, so if you have difficulty finding a title please write to us. US and Canadian residents should write to Embarcadero West, 155 Filbert St, Suite 251, Oakland CA 94607, USA; European residents should write to 10 Barley Mow Passage, Chiswick, London W4 4PH; and residents of other countries to PO Box 617, Hawthorn, Victoria 3122, Australia.

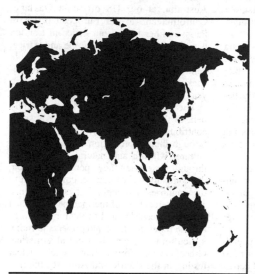

Indian Subcontinent
Bangladesh
India
Hindi/Urdu phrasebook
Trekking in the Indian Himalaya
Karakoram Highway
Kashmir, Ladakh & Zanskar
Nepal
Trekking in the Nepal Himalaya
Nepali phrasebook
Pakistan
Sri Lanka
Sri Lanka phrasebook

Africa
Africa on a shoestring
Central Africa
East Africa
Trekking in East Africa
Kenya
Swahili phrasebook
Morocco, Algeria & Tunisia
Arabic (Moroccan) phrasebook
South Africa, Lesotho & Swaziland
Zimbabwe, Botswana & Namibia
West Africa

Central America & the Caribbean
Baja California
Central America on a shoestring
Costa Rica
Eastern Caribbean
Guatemala, Belize & Yucatán: La Ruta Maya
Mexico

North America
Alaska
Canada
Hawaii

South America
Argentina, Uruguay & Paraguay
Bolivia
Brazil
Brazilian phrasebook
Chile & Easter Island
Colombia
Ecuador & the Galápagos Islands
Latin American Spanish phrasebook
Peru
Quechua phrasebook
South America on a shoestring
Trekking in the Patagonian Andes
Venezuela

Europe
Baltic States & Kaliningrad
Dublin city guide
Eastern Europe on a shoestring
Eastern Europe phrasebook
Finland
France
Greece
Hungary
Iceland, Greenland & the Faroe Islands
Ireland
Italy
Mediterranean Europe on a shoestring
Mediterranean Europe phrasebook
Poland
Scandinavian & Baltic Europe on a shoestring
Scandinavian Europe phrasebook
Switzerland
Trekking in Spain
Trekking in Greece
USSR
Russian phrasebook
Western Europe on a shoestring
Western Europe phrasebook

The Lonely Planet Story

Lonely Planet published its first book in 1973 in response to the numerous 'How did you do it?' questions Maureen and Tony Wheeler were asked after driving, bussing, hitching, sailing and railing their way from England to Australia.

Written at a kitchen table and hand collated, trimmed and stapled, *Across Asia on the Cheap* became an instant local bestseller, inspiring thoughts of another book.

Eighteen months in South-East Asia resulted in their second guide, *South-East Asia on a shoestring*, which they put together in a backstreet Chinese hotel in Singapore in 1975. The 'yellow bible' as it quickly became known to backpackers around the world, soon became *the* guide to the region. It has sold well over half a million copies and is now in its 8th edition, still retaining its familiar yellow cover.

Today there are over 140 Lonely Planet titles in print – books that have that same adventurous approach to travel as those early guides; books that 'assume you know how to get your luggage off the carousel' as one reviewer put it.

Although Lonely Planet initially specialised in guides to Asia, they now cover most regions of the world, including the Pacific, South America, Africa, the Middle East and Europe. The list of *walking guides* and *phrasebooks* (for 'unusual' languages such as Quechua, Swahili, Nepali and Egyptian Arabic) is also growing rapidly.

The emphasis continues to be on travel for independent travellers. Tony and Maureen still travel for several months of each year and play an active part in the writing, updating and quality control of Lonely Planet's guides.

They have been joined by over 50 authors, 90 staff – mainly editors, cartographers & designers – at our office in Melbourne, Australia, at our US office in Oakland, California and at our European office in Paris; another five at our office in London handle sales for Britain, Europe and Africa. Travellers themselves also make a valuable contribution to the guides through the feedback we receive in thousands of letters each year.

The people at Lonely Planet strongly believe that travellers can make a positive contribution to the countries they visit, both through their appreciation of the countries' culture, wildlife and natural features, and through the money they spend. In addition, the company makes a direct contribution to the countries and regions it covers. Since 1986 a percentage of the income from each book has been donated to ventures such as famine relief in Africa; aid projects in India; agricultural projects in Central America; Greenpeace's efforts to halt French nuclear testing in the Pacific and Amnesty International. In 1993 $100,000 was donated to such causes.

Lonely Planet's basic travel philosophy is summed up in Tony Wheeler's comment, 'Don't worry about whether your trip will work out. Just go!'.